IMAGES
of America

STONE HARBOR

For my grandparents, who gave us Stone Harbor.

IMAGES
of America

STONE HARBOR

T. Mark Cole and Cheryl Glasgow

ARCADIA
PUBLISHING

ISBN 978-0-7385-0522-0

Published by Arcadia Publishing
Charleston, South Carolina

Printed in the United States of America

Library of Congress Catalog Card Number: 2001088724

For all general information contact Arcadia Publishing at:
Telephone 843-853-2070
Fax 843-853-0044
E-mail sales@arcadiapublishing.com
For customer service and orders:
Toll-Free 1-888-313-2665

Visit us on the Internet at www.arcadiapublishing.com

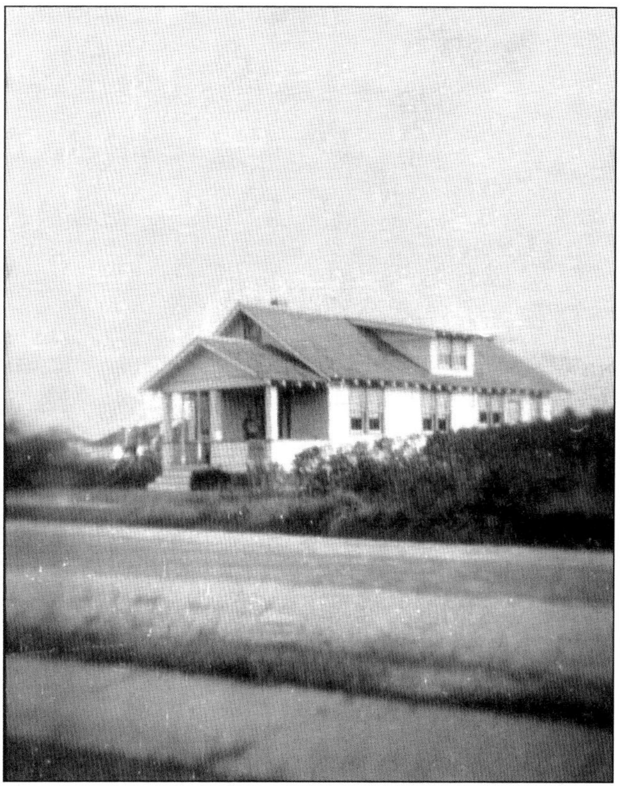

This is the earliest view of the "Colebin."

Contents

About the Photographs		6
Introduction		7
Acknowledgments		8
Bibliography		8
1.	From Dunes to Development: The Early Years	9
2.	The Golden Season: The 1930s	35
3.	Changing Times: The 1940s and 1950s	53
4.	A New Season: The 1960s and 1970s	97
5.	Timeless	117

About the Photographs

The photographs in this book are taken from two different collections. The first set, being the early years of Stone Harbor, is from a real estate brochure from the South Jersey Realty Company. This brochure, along with postcard images and early newspapers, were cherished Stone Harbor mementos of my grandmother.

The second set, which makes up the bulk of this book, is a small selection of the many photographs showing everyday life of summering in Stone Harbor. The photographs were taken by my grandfather, Percy J. Cole, between the 1930s and the 1970s. Raised in an artistic family, my grandfather pursued chemistry and glassblowing as a profession. He therefore found that photography spoke to his artistic and analytical sides. The earlier photographs were taken of very patient subjects with his Zeiss Ikon plate camera, resulting in high-quality images. After World War II, my grandfather purchased a 35-millimeter Contax camera, which made photography easier and produced more action shots. He was, however, still very particular in setting up each shot.

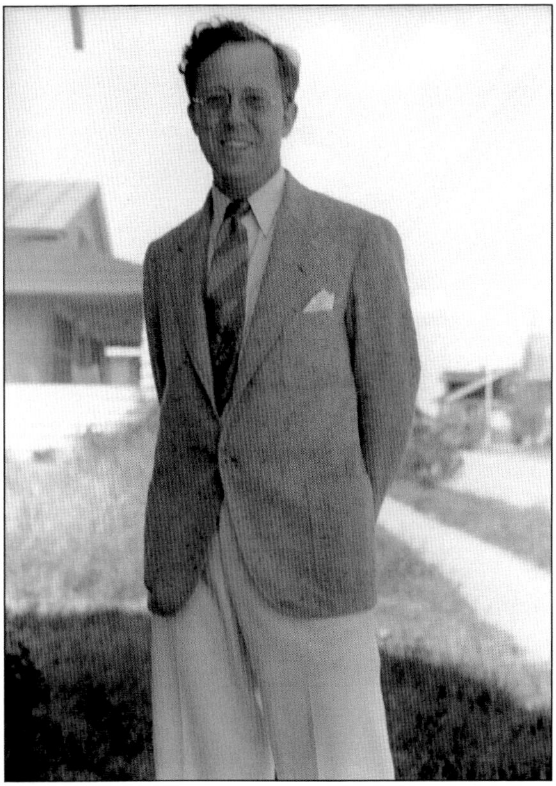

Percy J. Cole is shown here in the summer of 1933.

INTRODUCTION

We sailed along for days and days,
And had the very best of plays.

—Robert Louis Stevenson

For centuries, the barrier islands of southern New Jersey stood isolated by the ocean on one side and by salt marshes on the other. The beach met each wave, formed its dunes, and saw an occasional passerby. In the late 19th century, however, the area known as "Stoneharbor" began to change. By 1893, the Abbottsford Inn and six houses offered getaway retreat vacations via the Pennsylvania Railroad through Townsend's Inlet and Avalon. When Howard, David, and Reese Risley purchased the area in 1905, they laid a firm foundation for the growth of Stone Harbor throughout the 20th century.

The Risleys were men of vision, but their carefully detailed development plan was grounded in practicalities. As Reese Risley wrote of their effort in the *Stone Harbor Herald*, "nothing was left to chance." By 1911, the Risleys' South Jersey Realty Company was responsible for the dredging of three new basins, the graveling of wide streets, and the establishment of waterworks and sewage systems. The most essential element for future expansion, however, was up-to-date transportation from points in New Jersey and Philadelphia. In 1911, the Risleys dedicated a second railroad on the Reading line entering Stone Harbor, and the Stone Harbor Boulevard was open to a waiting public. The collection of homes, apartment houses, and early businesses took on the identity of a community. A school, a firehouse, a lifesaving station, a Roman Catholic church, and an Episcopal church were already part of town life. In 1914, the borough was incorporated. Howard Risley acted as the first council president.

The number of visitors increased steadily. The Risley brothers developed a system to encourage these potential owners to buy and build. Lots were offered "free" for the purchase of bonds. The bonds cost $80 apiece, with a par value of $100. The number of bonds varied with the location of the lot and the number of lots a purchaser desired. The lots were certainly worth the amount paid for the bonds, and subscribers also shared in the net proceeds from tolls, railway fares, and freight charges.

Stone Harbor was fast becoming the premier beach community on the Jersey shore in the 1920s, culminating with the reopening of the Stone Harbor Yacht Club in 1929. The club was the center of social life and became famous for the development of the Comet-class fleet. As the rest of the nation was hit hard by the Great Depression, so was Stone Harbor. The pace of life slowed down until the 1940s, when war was on most people's minds.

The 1940s are also remembered for a commitment to wildlife. The Stone Harbor Bird Club changed its name to the Witmer Stone Club in 1946. Witmer Stone, a longtime barrier resident, was a well-known author and naturalist. The famous bird sanctuary and heronry was established in 1947. It was later registered as a national landmark. The 1950s saw improvements such as the construction of a new municipal building and post office, the First National Bank, and (a sign of the time) the first motel.

During the 1960s—in the day of fast cars, motorboats, television, and an increasing summer population—Stone Harbor's beaches remained first choice as a place to relax. The Risley brothers knew this fact and considered beach preservation a top priority. After the first major storm hit Stone Harbor in the year of incorporation, 1914, the town council built a bulkhead, six jetties, and (as a luxury) a boardwalk. The second major storm, in 1944, destroyed that boardwalk and the piers. In 1962, the most severe storm to the area resulted in the construction of a new bulkhead, made of stone and timber.

The conservation of its wildlife and natural resources has added much to the unique atmosphere of this beach resort. Beach preservation was the goal of a 1970s campaign called Save the Point, designed to keep the southern tip of the island from development. A compromise was reached in which housing limits were set at 121st Street. In 1972, Stone Harbor dedicated the Wetlands Institute, a nonprofit organization that continues to foster education, research, and stewardship of wetlands and coastal ecosystems. The land for the wetlands was purchased by two caring residents, and the building itself was purchased with funds from the World Wildlife Fund International.

My family's connection with Stone Harbor began with my grandmother's aunt, who was an original bond holder in the free-lot plan. By the time my parents were born, both my maternal and paternal grandparents sought summer refuge by the sea. Stone Harbor was the natural choice, and the purchase of the house assured us a permanent summer home at the shore. The memories of my parents' summers were extended to the next generation through my sisters and me. The activities of my grandparents and parents became our activities. Summering at the shore offered a security—a sense that life remained the same. I hope that the history and memories presented in this book will serve as a reflection for the many other families who enjoy and love Stone Harbor.

—T. Mark Cole

Acknowledgments

Sincere thanks go to the following people, who offered their memories, technical skill, and support as we compiled this book: Timothy and Marzee Cole, John J. Noone, Linda Lease, Lisa Daly, and Lou Glasgow.

Bibliography

Advertisement brochure for Stone Harbor. 1911.

Boyer, George F. and J. Pearson Cunningham. *Cape May County Story*. Egg Harbor City, New Jersey: The Laureate Press, 1975.

Beitel, Herb and Vance Enck. *Cape May County: A Pictorial History*. Norfolk/Virginia Beach, Virginia: The Donning Company, 1998.

Dorwart, Jeffrey M. *Cape May County, New Jersey*. New Brunswick, New Jersey: Rutgers University Press, 1992.

Stevenson, Robert Louis. *A Child's Garden of Verses*. New York: Rand, McNally, and Company, 1902.

Stone Harbor Historical Book Committee. *History of Stone Harbor:1914–1964*. Stone Harbor, New Jersey: 1964.

Stone Harbor Herald, Vol. 7, No. 3, July 1914.

Wilson, Harold. *The Jersey Shore, Volume I*. New York: Lewis Historical Publishing Company, 1953.

Wilson, Harold. *The Jersey Shore, Volume II*. New York: Lewis Historical Publishing Company, 1953.

Woods, George B., Homer A. Watt, George K. Anderson, and Karl J. Holzknecht. *The Literature of England, Volume II*. Chicago: Scott, Foresman and Company, 1958.

One

From Dunes to Development: The Early Years

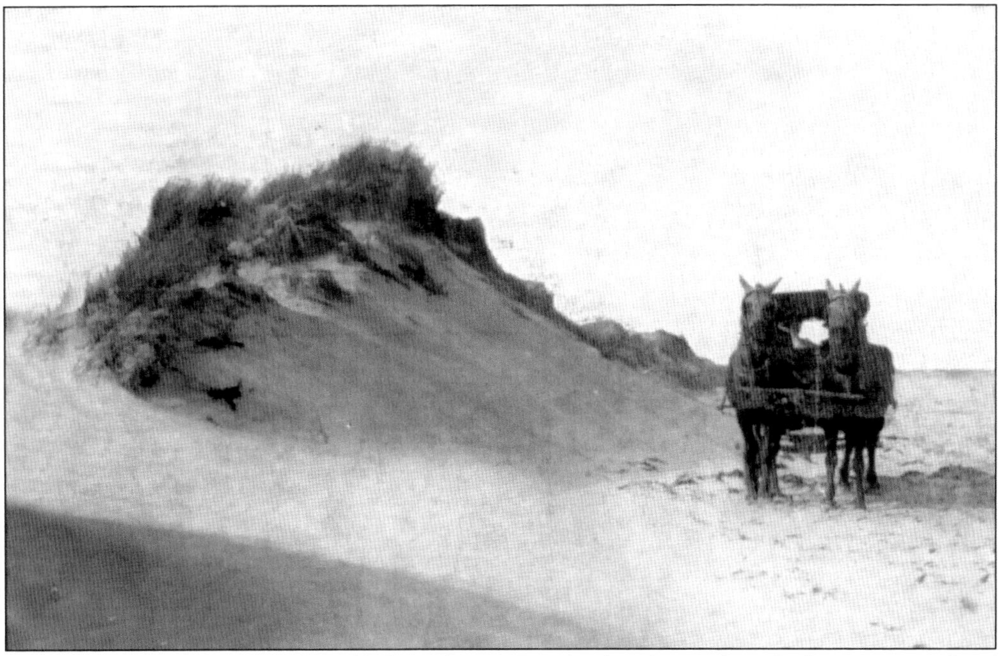

Seven Mile Beach, formerly called Tatham's Beach, has been described as "a stretch of sand dune, red cedars, and bayberry bushes, a barren waste with a life-saving station." In this early image, a pair is being driven along the beach past large dunes in what was to become Stone Harbor.

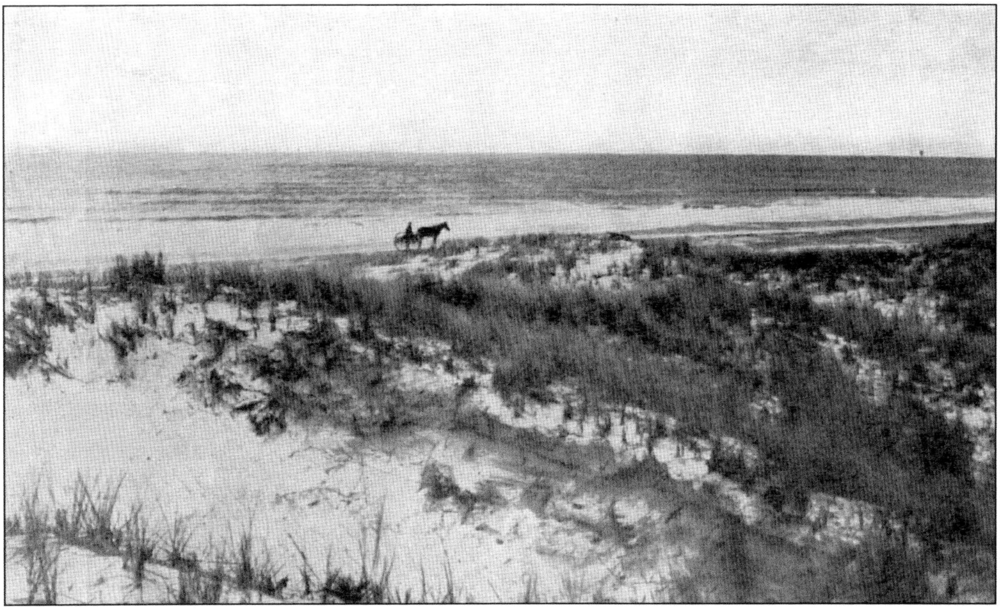

Named for an English sea captain who found refuge from a storm here, the area was first called Stoneharbor. In 1931, the name was changed to Stone Harbor. In its undeveloped state, as seen in this *c.* 1900 photograph, the beach area was often used by settlers for grazing livestock.

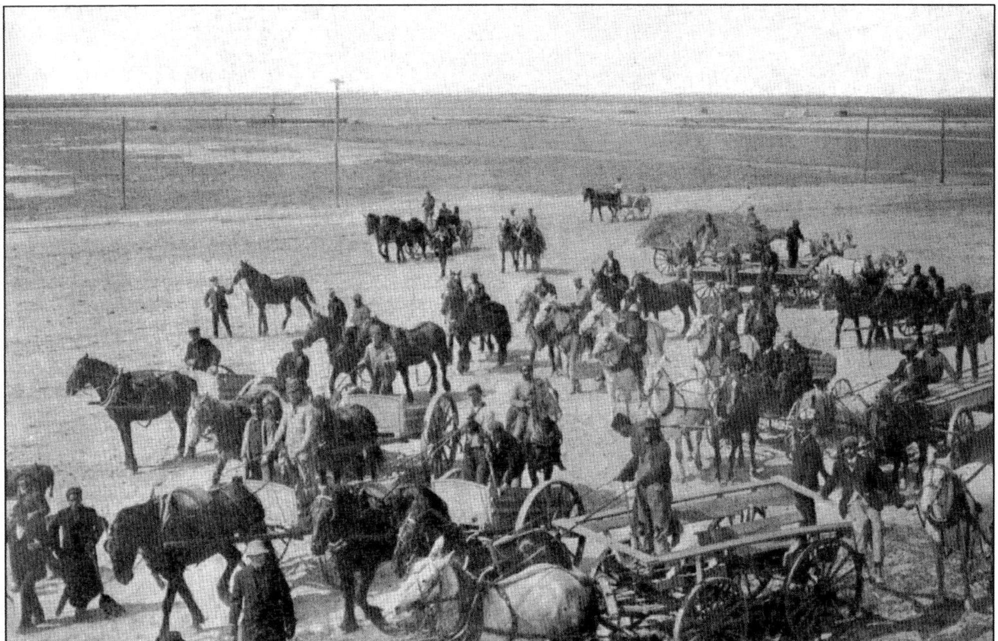

This 1907 photograph depicts how the land of Stone Harbor was developed by leveling sand dunes and grading streets. All this work was completed without the assistance of a bulldozer. Lloyd Seaman supervised the graveling of nine and a half miles of streets. It was his idea to lay nearly two miles of narrow-gauge railroad track, using 20 steel dump cars and a small locomotive to transport gravel from the 96th Street and Third Avenue terminal to where it was needed.

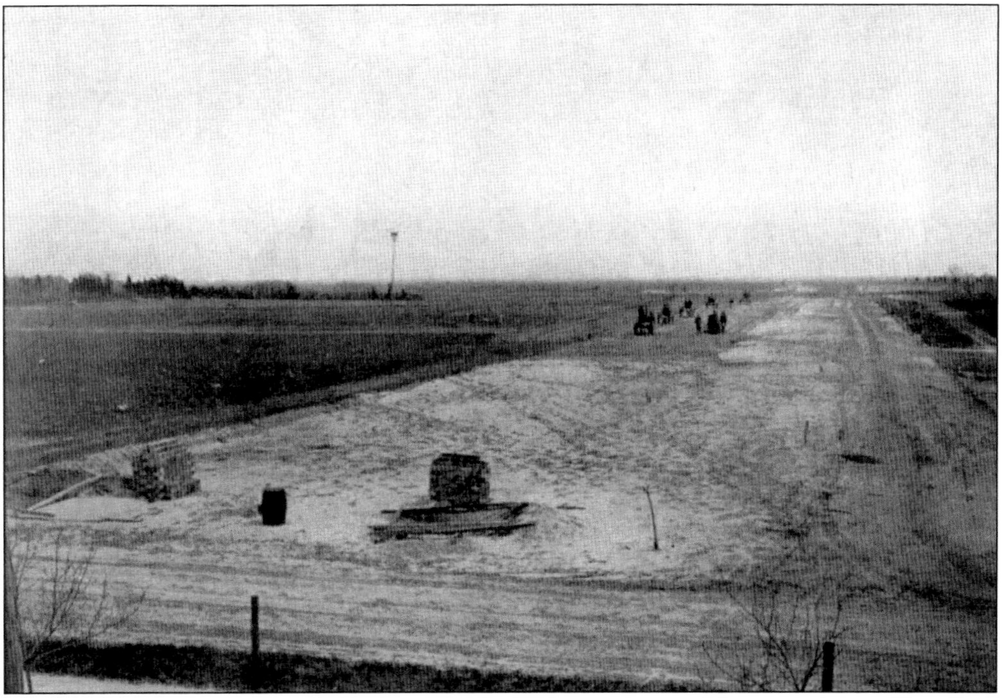

This view is looking toward Stone Harbor from the Cape May Courthouse over the first mile of the Ocean Parkway. At this point, the Ocean Parkway meets the state road now known as the Garden State Parkway.

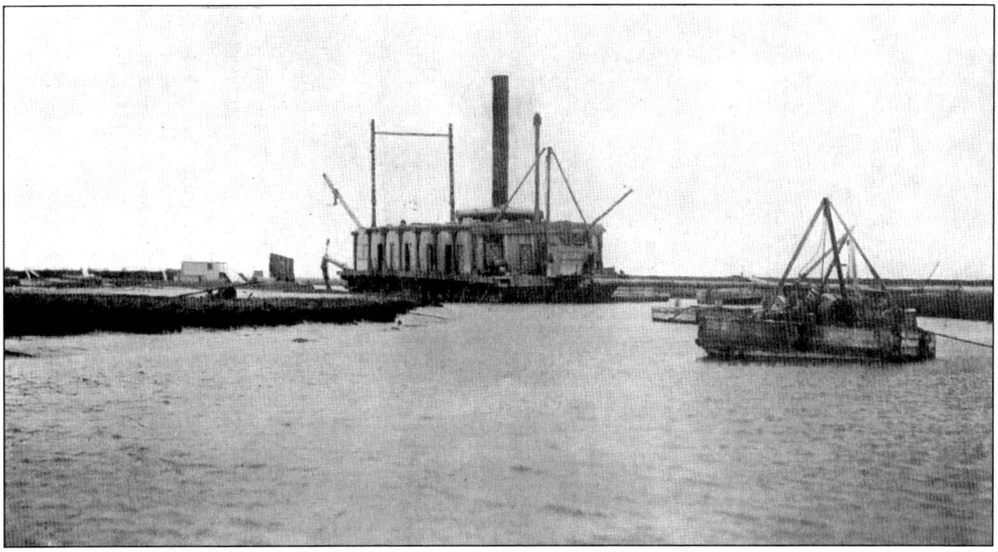

Shown under construction is the first section of the canal between Stone Harbor and the Cape May Courthouse. This magnificent waterway, which is 2 5/8 miles long, 10 feet deep, and 100 feet wide, links two great state operations: the inland waterways and the Ocean Highway. Both operations—the dredging of the canal and the filling of the turnpike, trolley line, and canal lots—were carried on simultaneously. Today, this type of major construction would be under the scrutiny of ecological restrictions. In this photograph, the pipes are pouring sand into the roadway embankment.

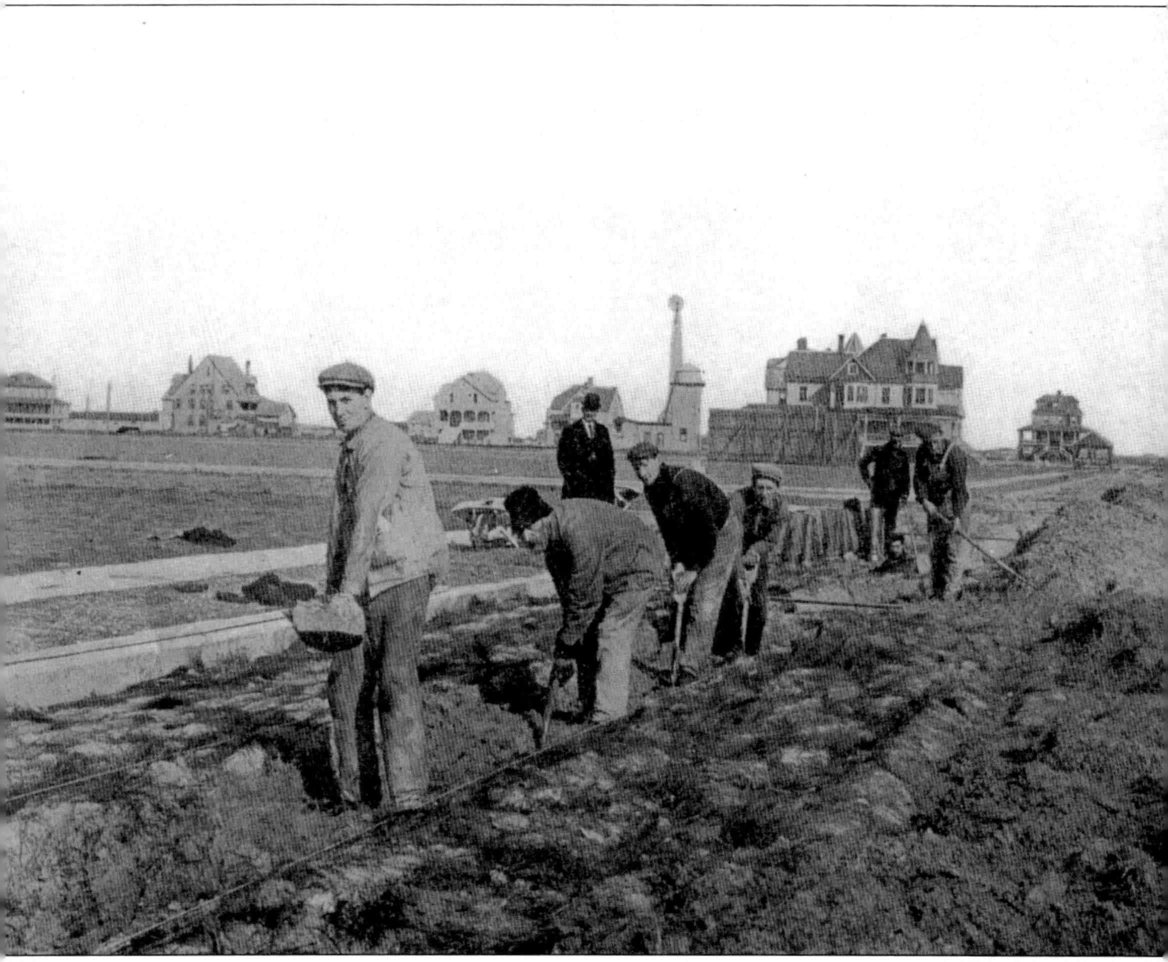

A construction crew is shown laying a sewer pipe on First Avenue. The South Jersey Realty Company put in a sewage and disposal system of the highest standards, complete with seven miles of underground pipe.

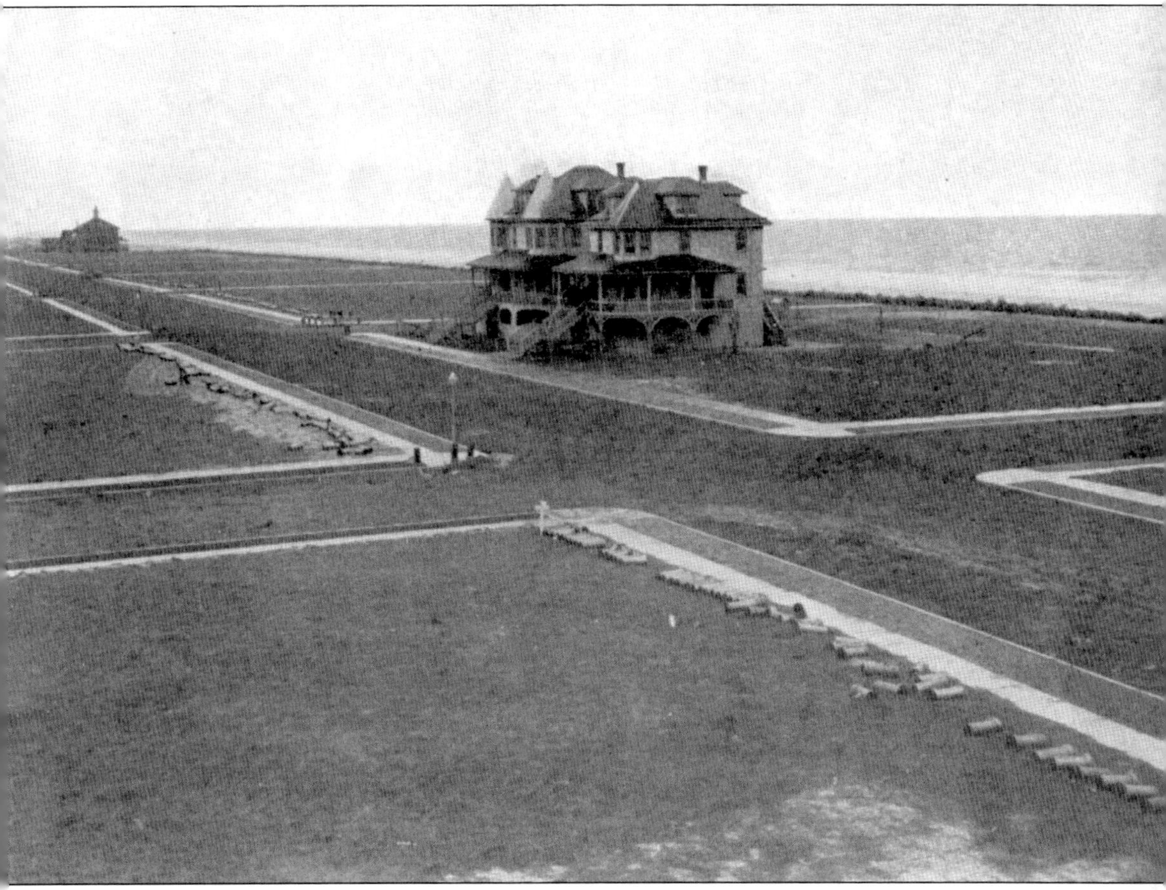

In the early years of development, a cottage in Stone Harbor truly meant getting away from it all.

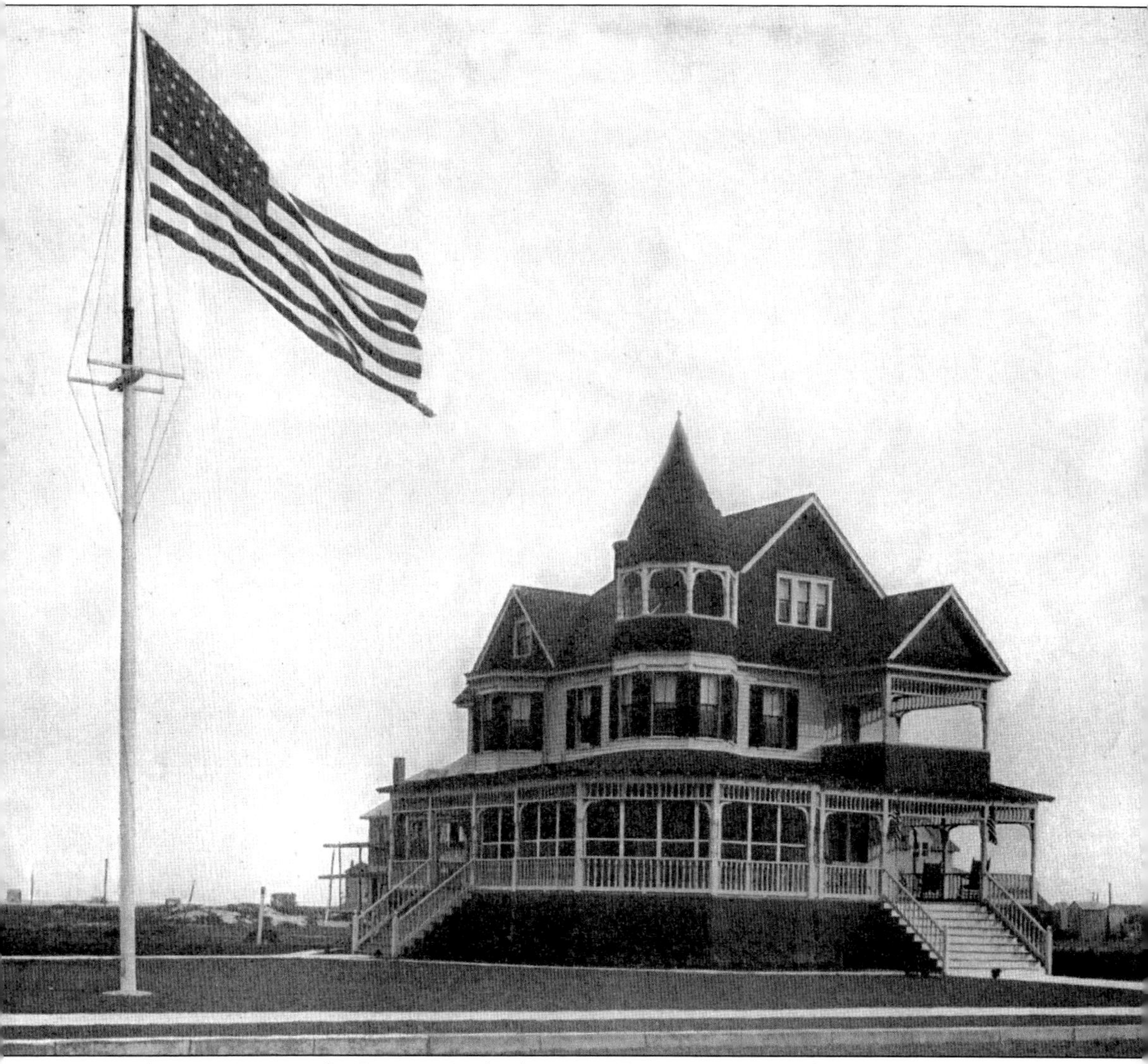

Hydrangea Cottage, the Reese P. Risley home on First Avenue, is a fine example of the Queen Anne style. Reese Risley, along with his brothers Howard and David, developed Stone Harbor. Mary Risley led the women's suffragette movement in the county. With slight alterations, this home is now a bed-and-breakfast.

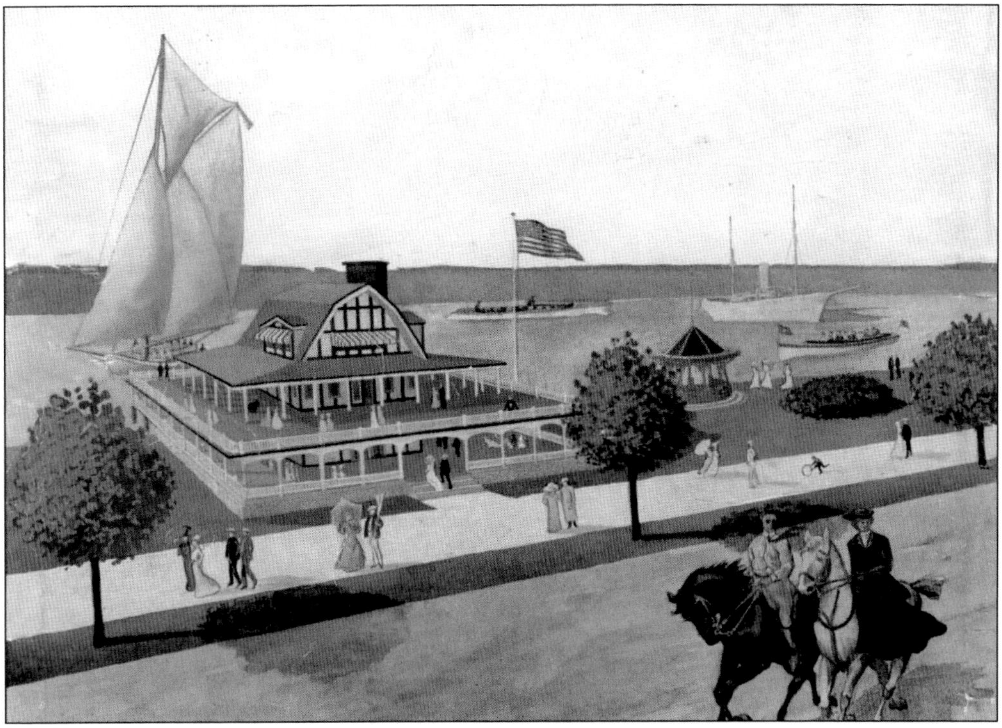

The Risleys bought the Stone Harbor area in 1905 and developed it in a carefully planned manner. This rendering, drawn to promote Stone Harbor, envisions the Risley brothers' grand scheme for the town. It features broad, tree-lined boulevards, elegant homes, and large yachts.

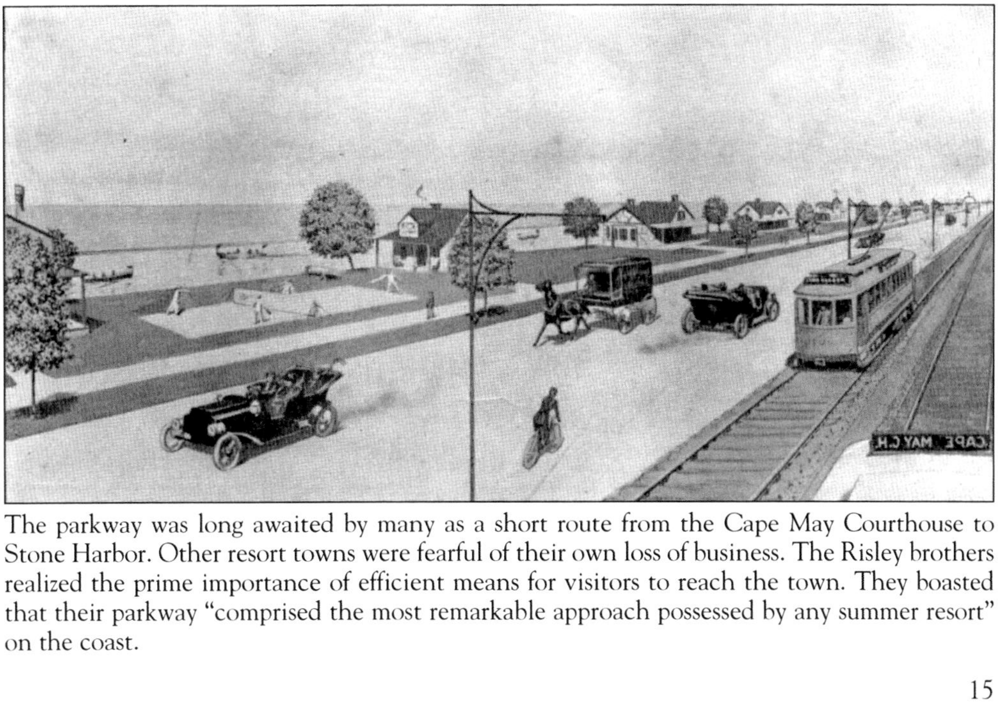

The parkway was long awaited by many as a short route from the Cape May Courthouse to Stone Harbor. Other resort towns were fearful of their own loss of business. The Risley brothers realized the prime importance of efficient means for visitors to reach the town. They boasted that their parkway "comprised the most remarkable approach possessed by any summer resort" on the coast.

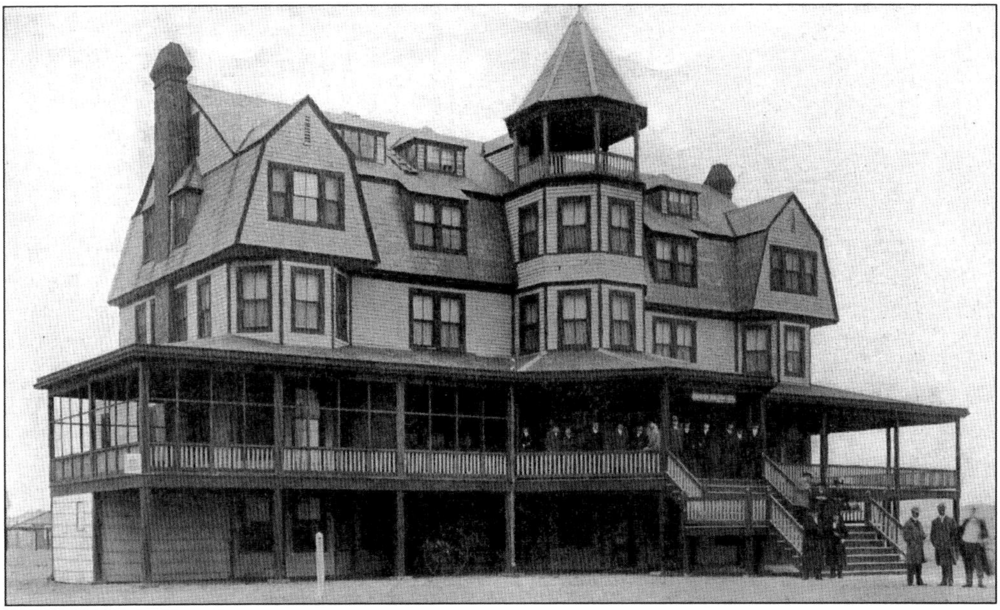

First known as the Abbotsford Inn when it was built by Hugh Holmes, this hotel opened in 1892. Later renamed the Harbor Inn, it was owned and operated by the South Jersey Realty Company, the Risley brothers' organization. It stood on First Avenue near the Avalon border. This hotel was used as an enticement for perspective owners to demonstrate that Stone Harbor was a viable alternative to seaside resorts such as nearby Cape May.

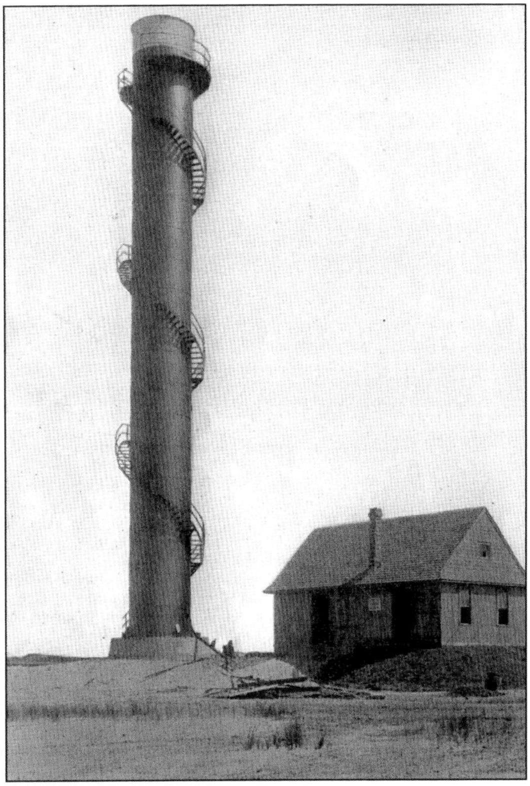

In 1909, the artesian water system was opened at 96th Street and Second Avenue. A well was driven 365 feet deep to reach the Kirkwood sands, which are the source of Stone Harbor's famous drinking water. The standpipe shown here was 100 feet high and 10 feet in diameter, with a capacity of 60,000 gallons.

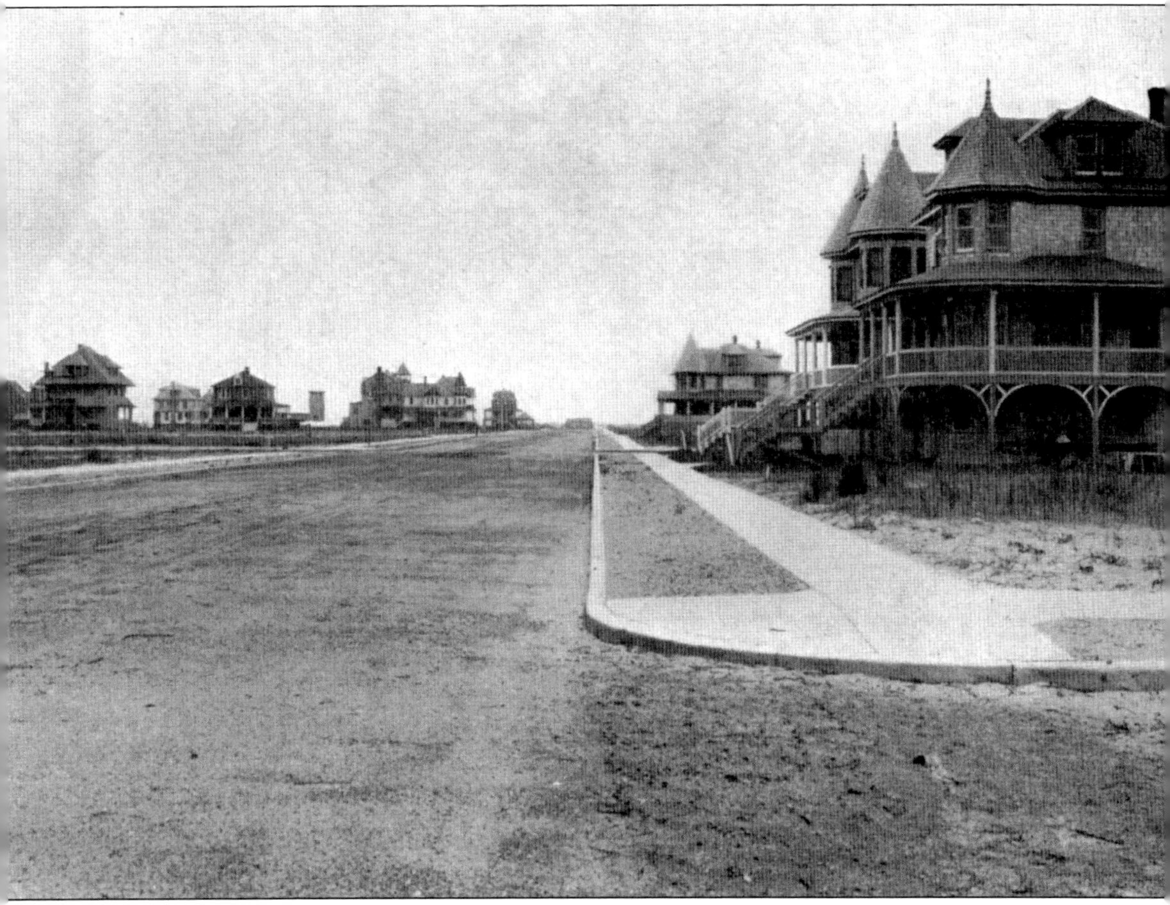

This early photograph shows two large Victorian cottages that were built under the free-lot plan offered by the town. With the purchase of bonds, lots with street improvements were given free to owners. These cottages, located at the corner of 88th Street and First Avenue, were built for August Juergens in the early 1900s. With the exception of one home in the distance, all homes pictured are still standing.

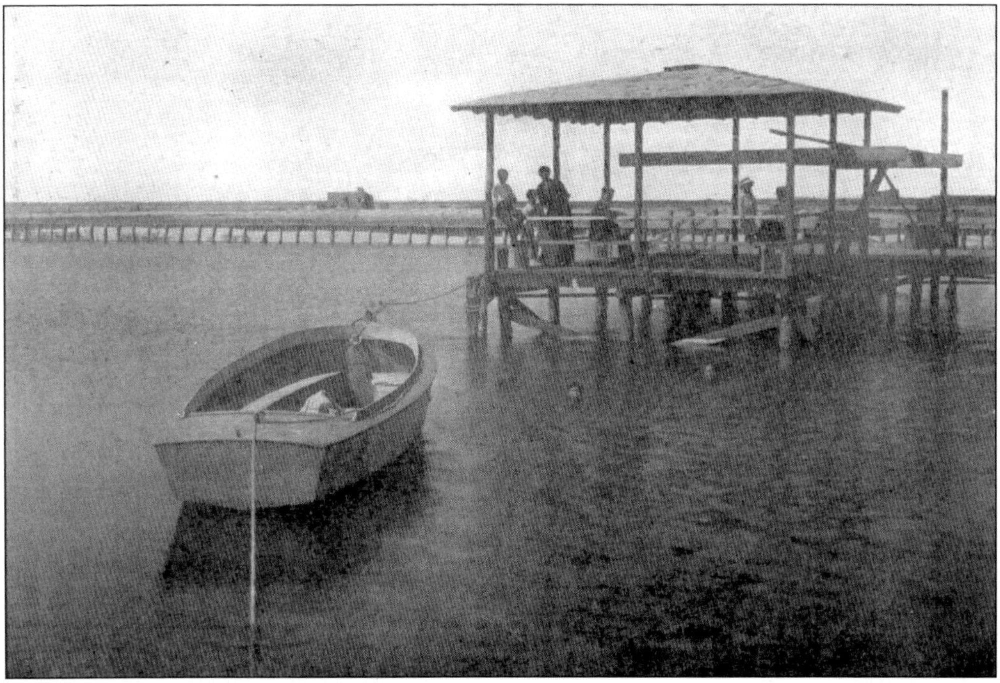

Shown is an early view of the 85th Street Yacht Basin. The South Basin, dredged by the Risley brothers in 1908, was the area's first man-made basin. Snug Harbor and Shelter Haven quickly followed in 1909 and 1910. These well-placed basins increased the number of desirable water-view lots in the growing town.

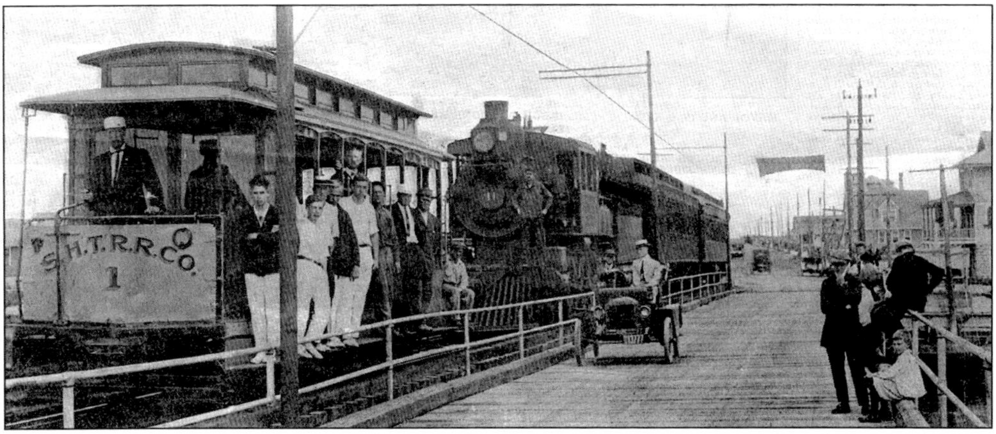

The spirit of transportation is evident in this 1914 view of Stone Harbor from the bridge, showing the trolley, the Pennsylvania Railroad's train, and an early automobile. One of the greatest factors in Stone Harbor's development was the creation of the boulevard and bridge to the Cape May Courthouse. Before then, access to Stone Harbor was by boat from Benny's Landing. The Pennsylvania Railroad was granted right-of-way to the entire Seven Mile Beach. The first train entered via Townsend's Inlet from Sea Isle City in 1892.

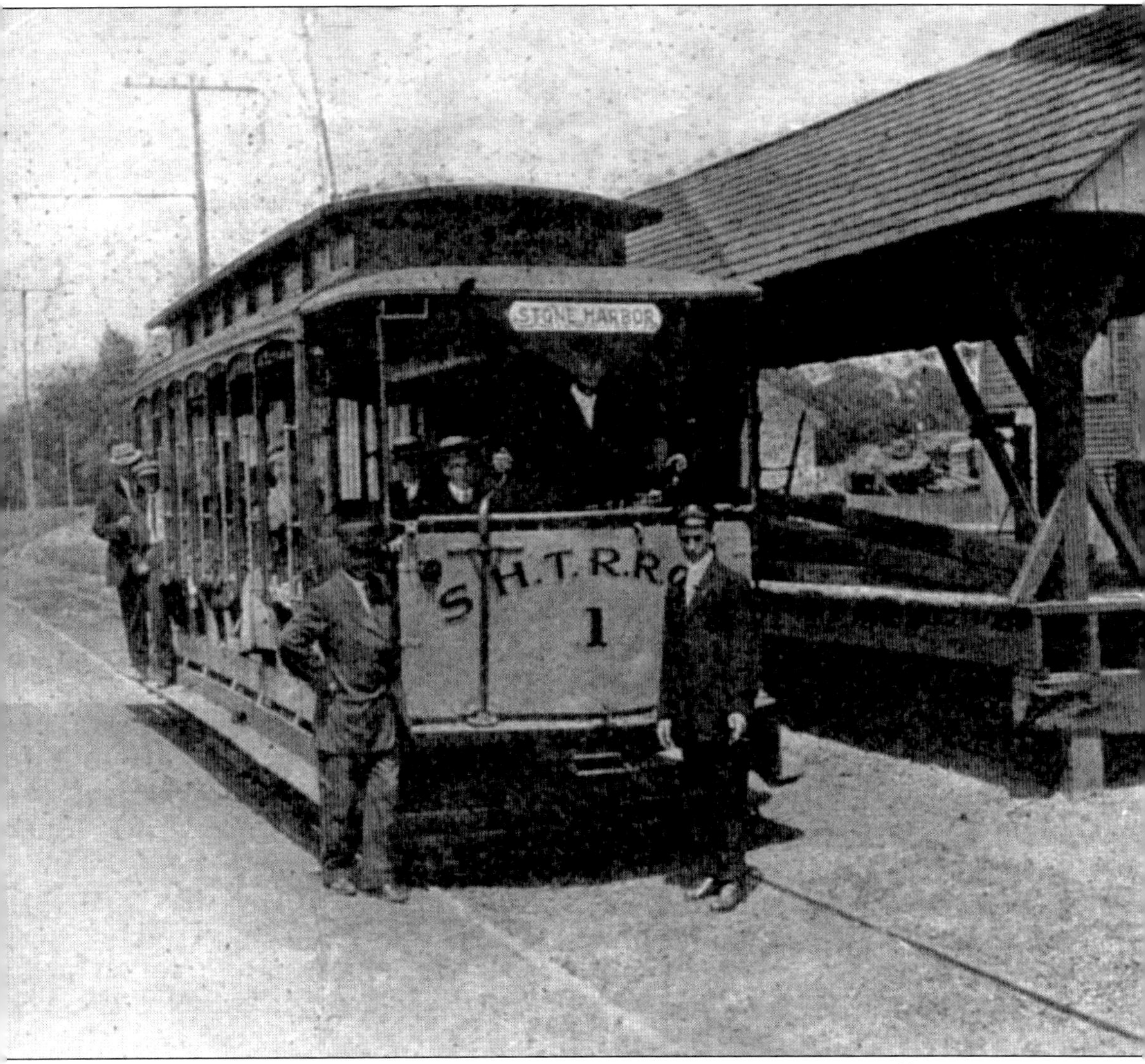

This 1914 photograph shows the Stone Harbor Terminal Railroad Company's trolley preparing to leave the Cape May Courthouse for Stone Harbor. Beginning in 1912, this trolley provided regular service between these two towns for the Reading Railroad. The Stone Harbor depot stood at 96th Street and Second Avenue.

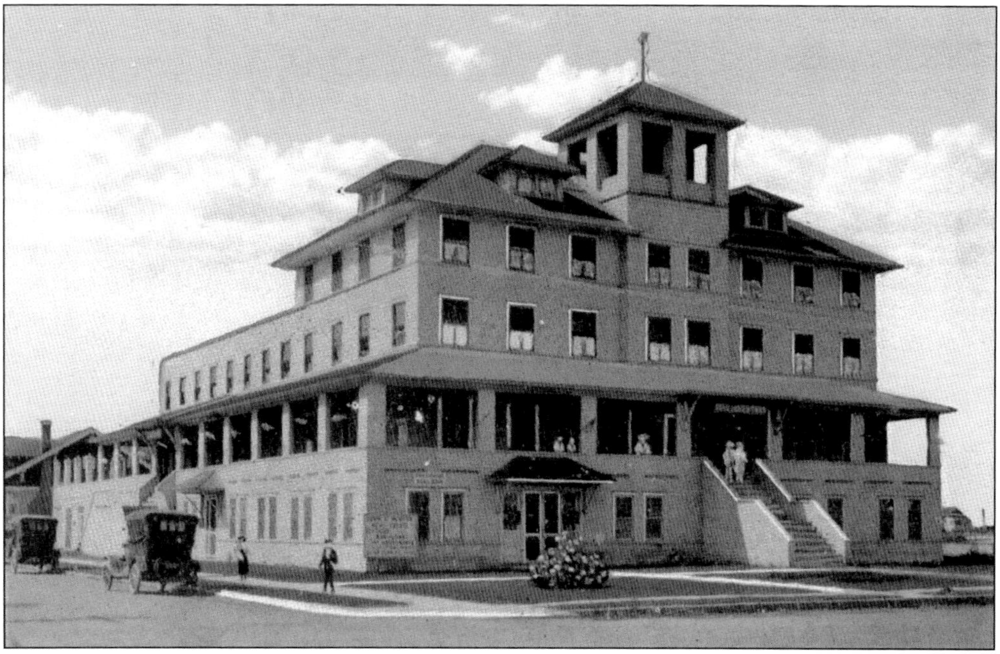

The Shelter Haven Hotel opened its doors on August 1, 1912. It was the largest single building in town, boasting 60 rooms and a roof garden overlooking waterways and the town. The builder and proprietor was F.S. Jansen. Because it was right on the bay, it had a private dock from which excursion boats took visitors around Stone Harbor.

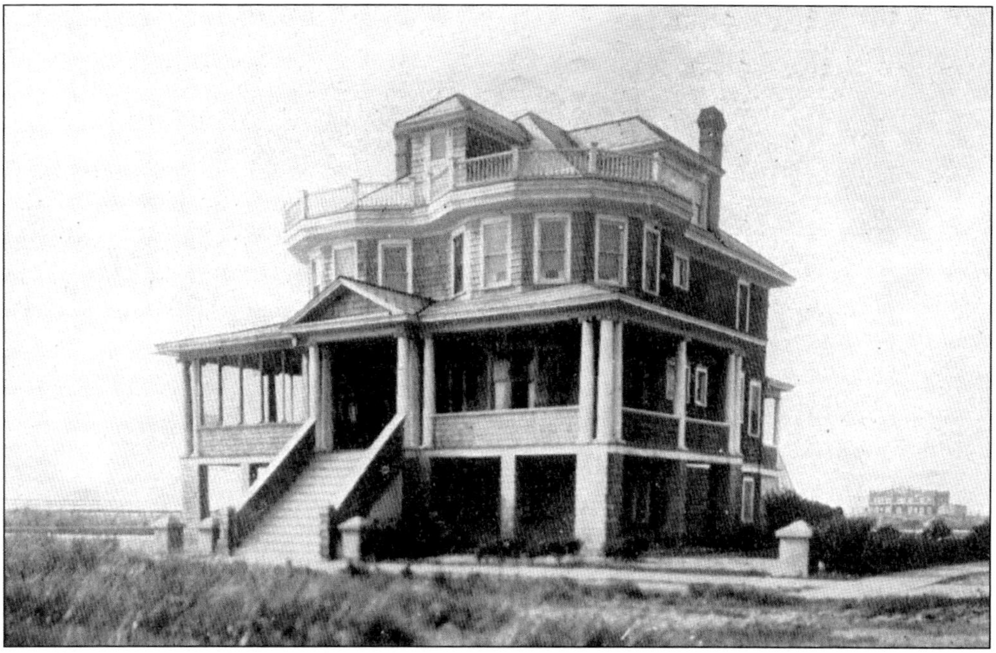

This large home was built in the early 1900s. The widow's walk, wraparound porch, elevated entrance, and shingled siding were typical of summer "cottages" around the turn of the century. In the right background is an apartment house on the beach at 97th Street. Just visible on the left is the old boardwalk.

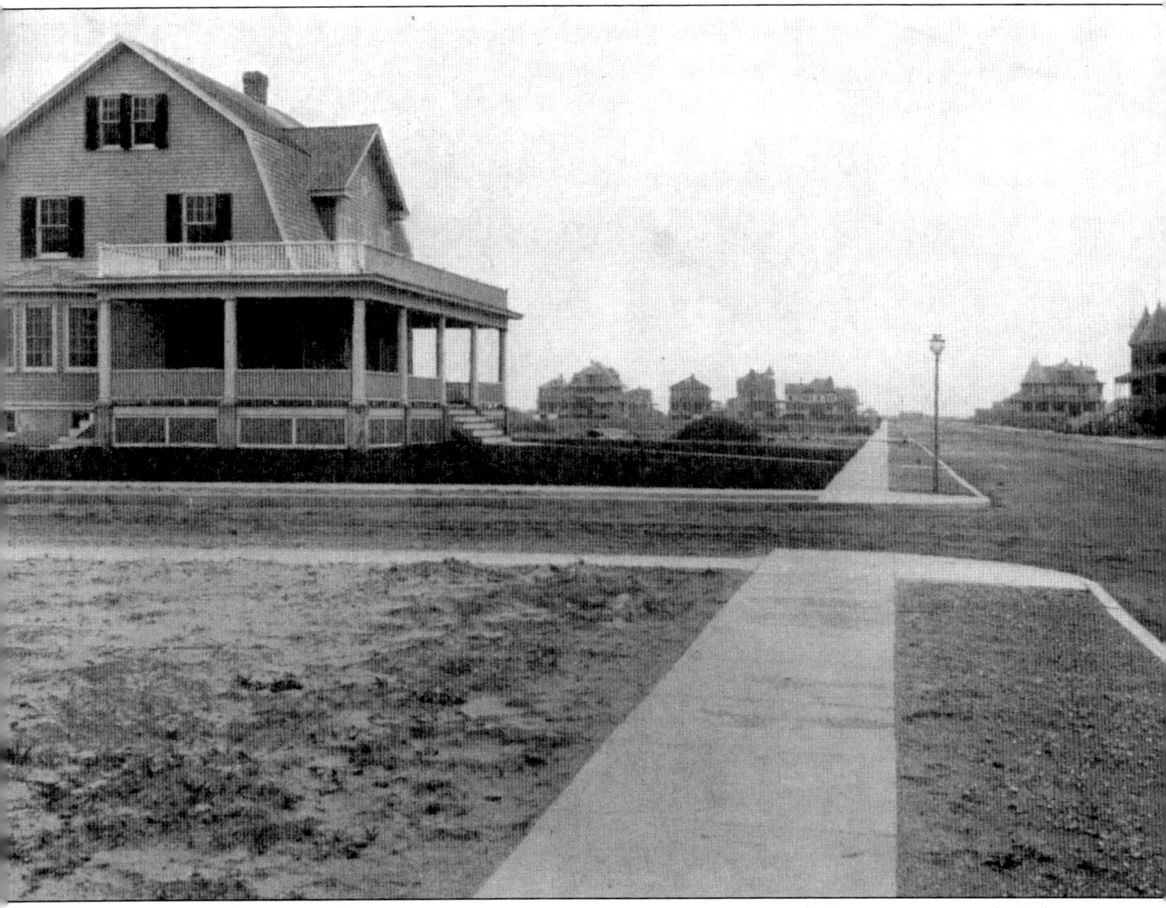

The residence of G. Franklin Davis was located at the intersection of First Avenue and 90th Street. The lot on which it stood, like those on both sides of the avenue, was given to Davis under the free-lot bond plan. In 1913, nearly 100 new homes were constructed. Unfortunately, this house is no longer standing.

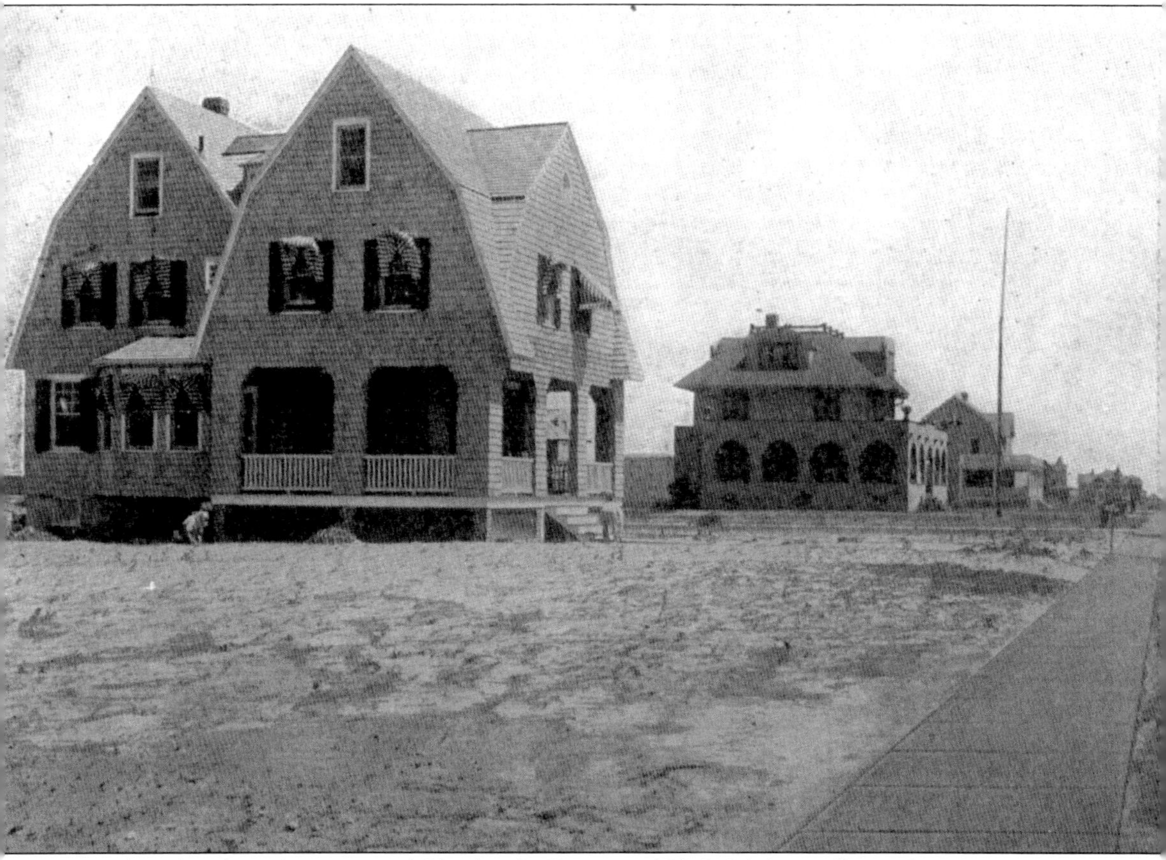

The Shingle-style cottage of Charles A. Farnum of Philadelphia still stands at First Avenue and 91st Street. This house had all the features of the New England summer cottages that were designed by well-known architects *c.* 1900.

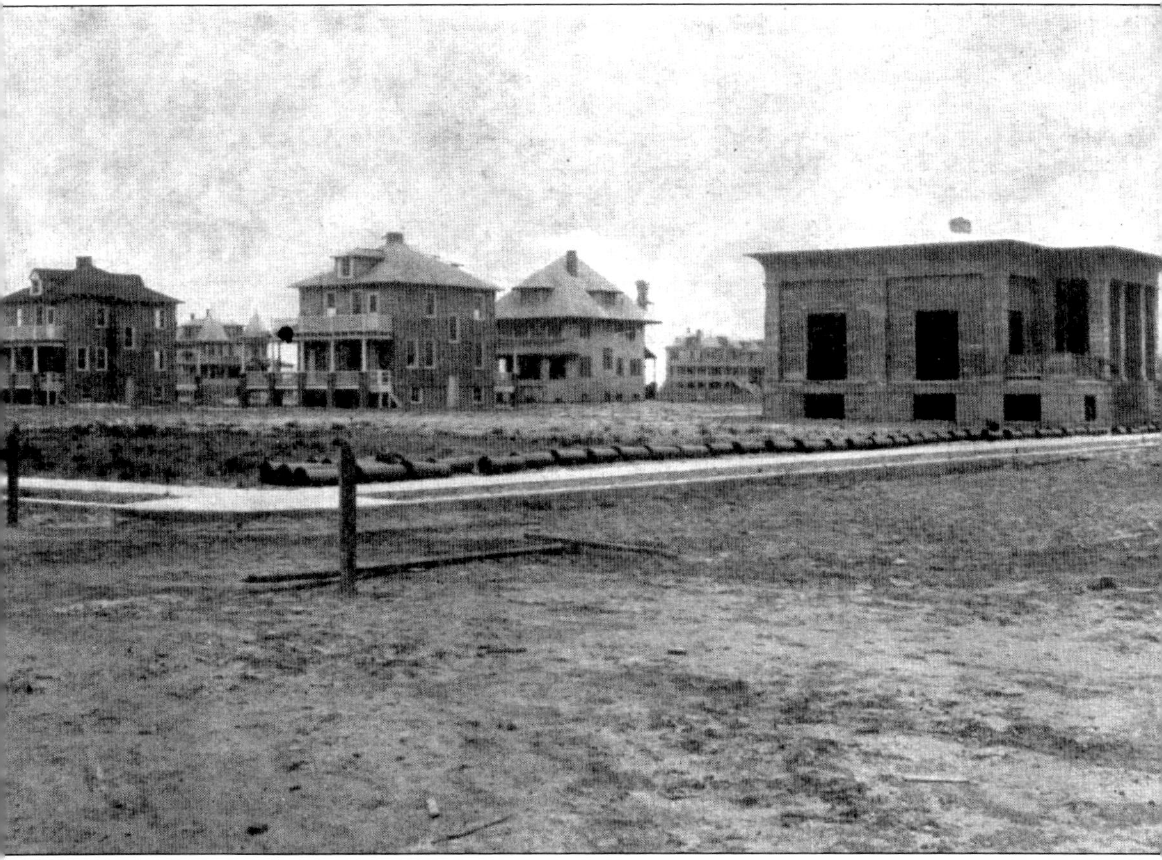

Classified as Egyptian Revival, the all-concrete house at the far right was built by the Gilbert Smith Company of Philadelphia in 1909. What was known as Pennsylvania Plaza was the site of the Pennsylvania Railroad station just across from this house, which is located on 85th Street and Pennsylvania Avenue.

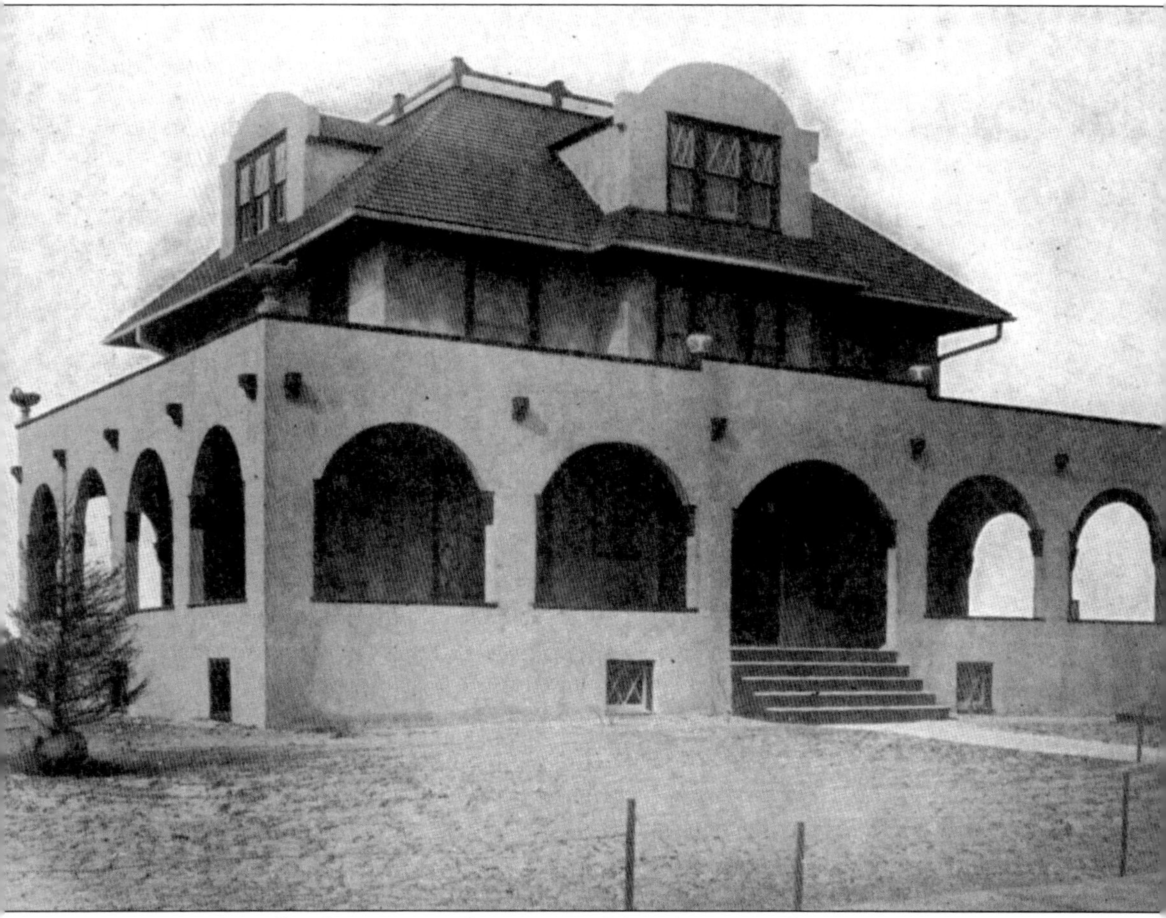

Stone Harbor offered summer residents a peaceful seashore as well as the luxuries of water, gas, and electricity. This rather grand cottage, built in the early 1900s in the Mediterranean style for Charles R. Hall, was located on a 110-by-110-foot lot at First Avenue and 91st Street. The house no longer stands.

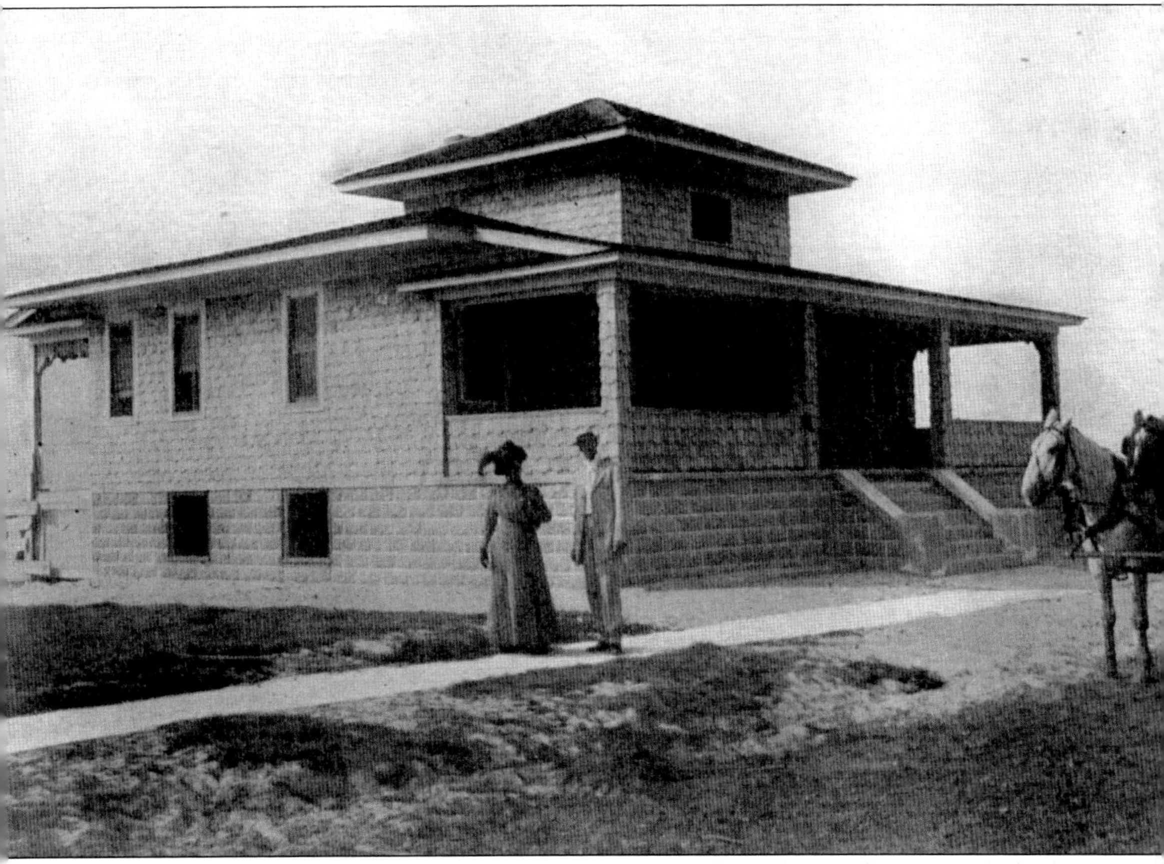

Although its porch is now enclosed, this unusual bungalow still stands at 85th Street and Third Avenue. It was built in the early 1900s for George C. Signor, the superintendent of the old Medico-Chirurgical Hospital in Philadelphia.

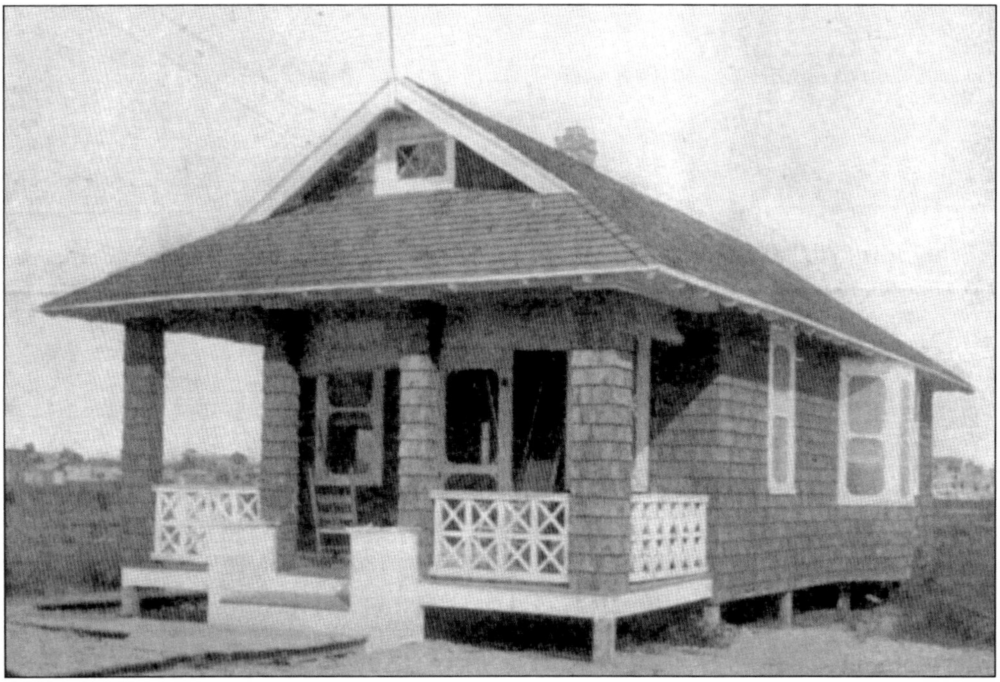

As masters of advertising, the Risley brothers offered something for everyone. Small bungalows complimented larger cottages. Families with children were encouraged to buy properties while Stone Harbor was touted as a town where "you can get a cigar or glass of soda water whenever you want them." This promise was meant to contrast with the restrictions in more conservative resort towns along the Jersey shore.

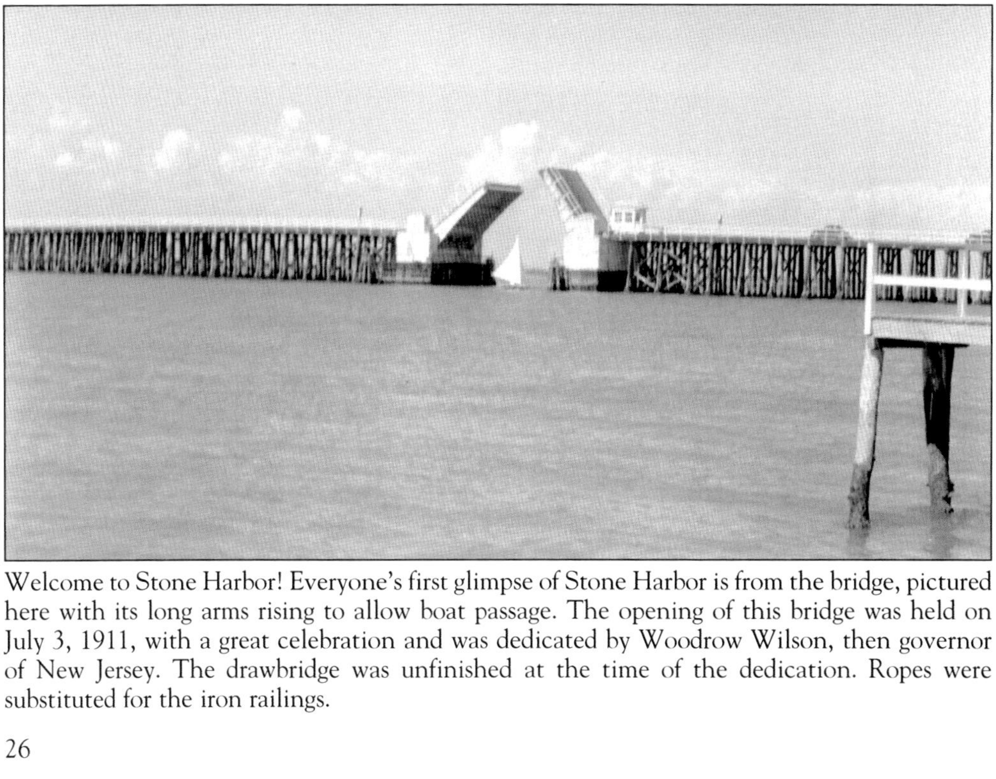

Welcome to Stone Harbor! Everyone's first glimpse of Stone Harbor is from the bridge, pictured here with its long arms rising to allow boat passage. The opening of this bridge was held on July 3, 1911, with a great celebration and was dedicated by Woodrow Wilson, then governor of New Jersey. The drawbridge was unfinished at the time of the dedication. Ropes were substituted for the iron railings.

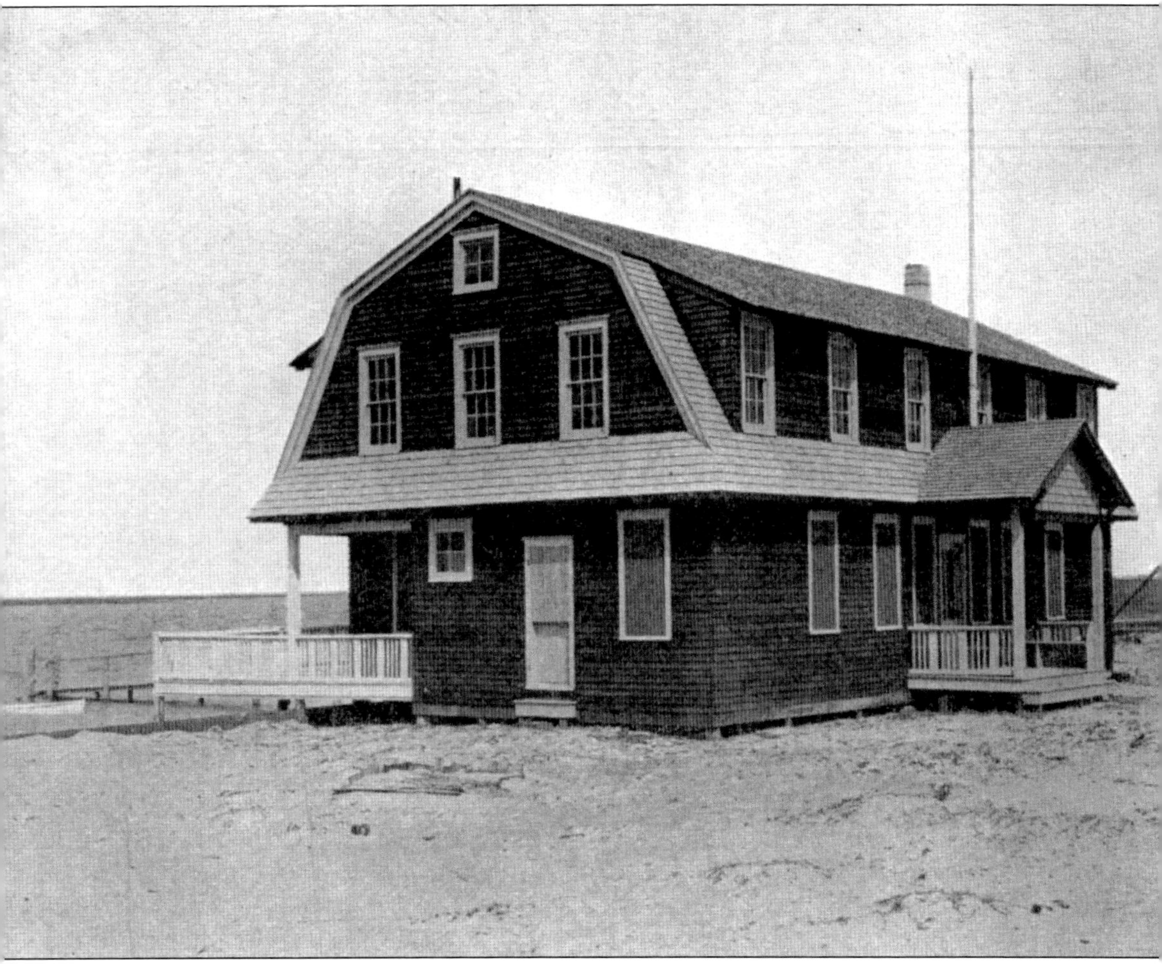

This lovely Dutch Colonial served as the choir bungalow of St. Mary's Church in Ardmore, Pennsylvania. It still stands on a 60-by-100-foot lot on the channel near the Stone Harbor Yacht Club.

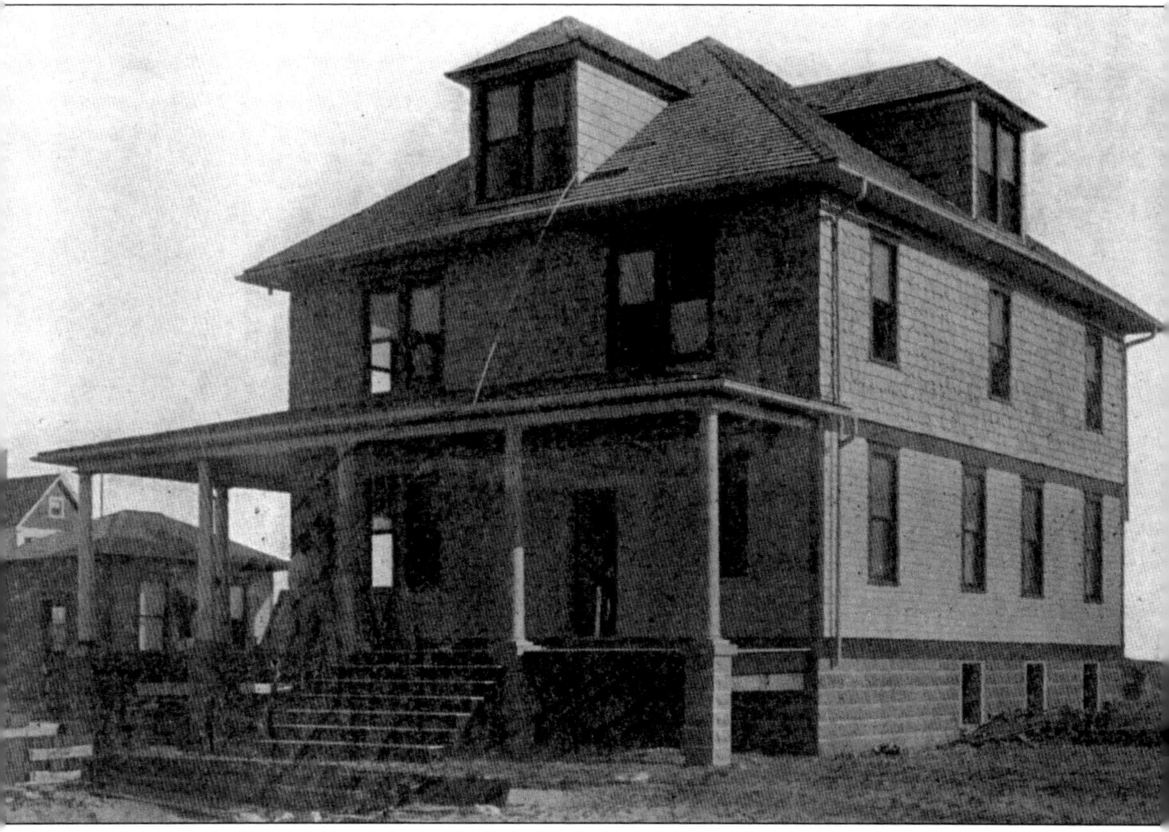

This home, shown under construction for the Simpson brothers *c.* 1909, still stands today. Stone Harbor and other towns of the barrier islands introduced all the modern utilities before many of the established inland communities.

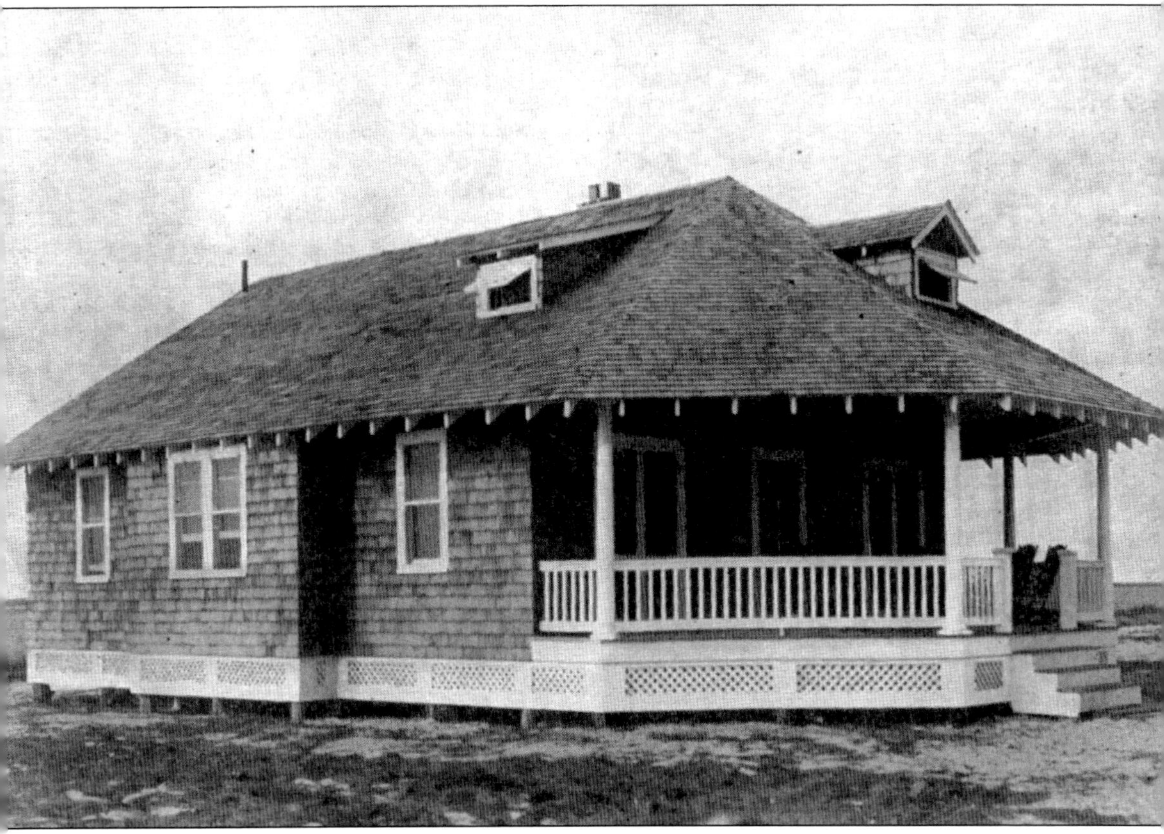

This Shingle-style bungalow on the channel is unique for the half-hexagon front porch. It was built in the early 1900s for Ernest N. Ross of the Tulpehocken section of Philadelphia on a 60-by-100-foot lot.

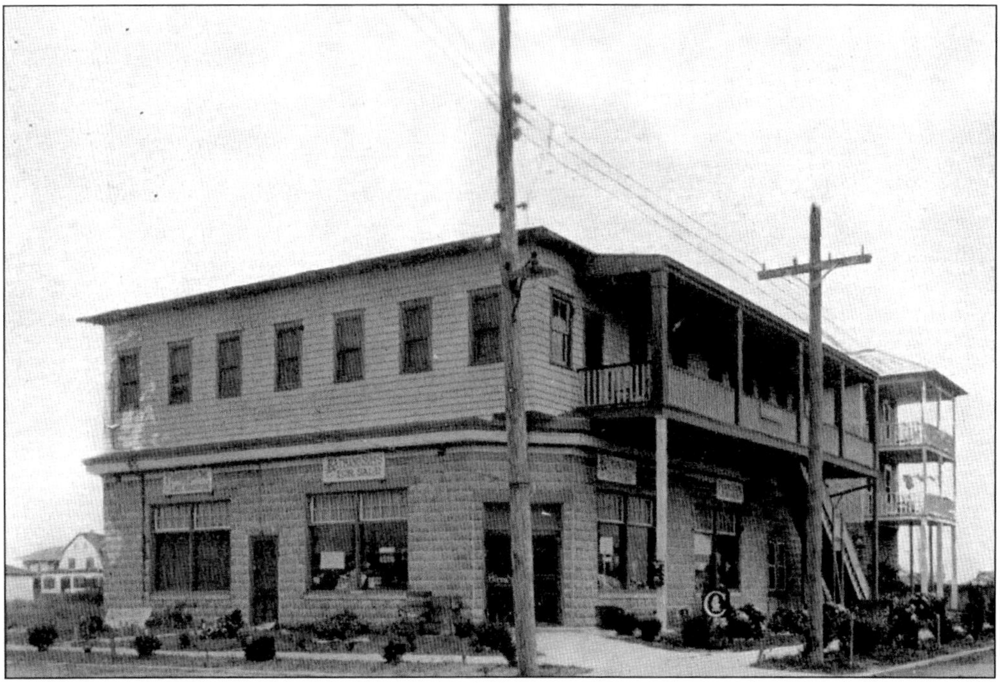

This early view shows what was affectionately known as "Mammy Diller's variety store." This building is still standing behind the water tower on Second Avenue.

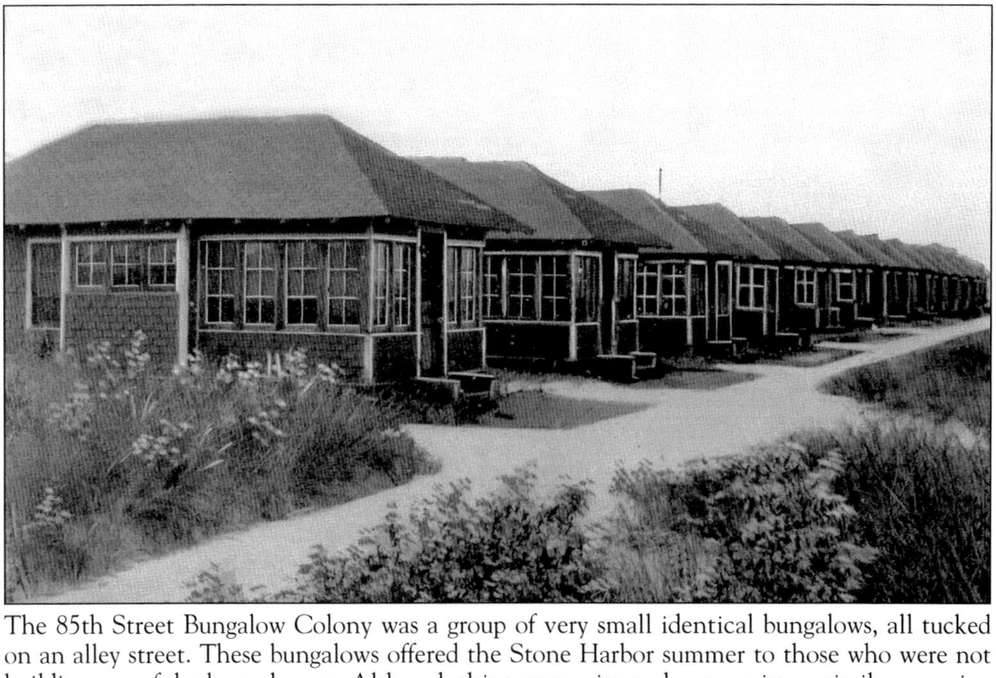

The 85th Street Bungalow Colony was a group of very small identical bungalows, all tucked on an alley street. These bungalows offered the Stone Harbor summer to those who were not building one of the larger homes. Although this community no longer exists, a similar grouping still stands near the bird sanctuary at 110th Street.

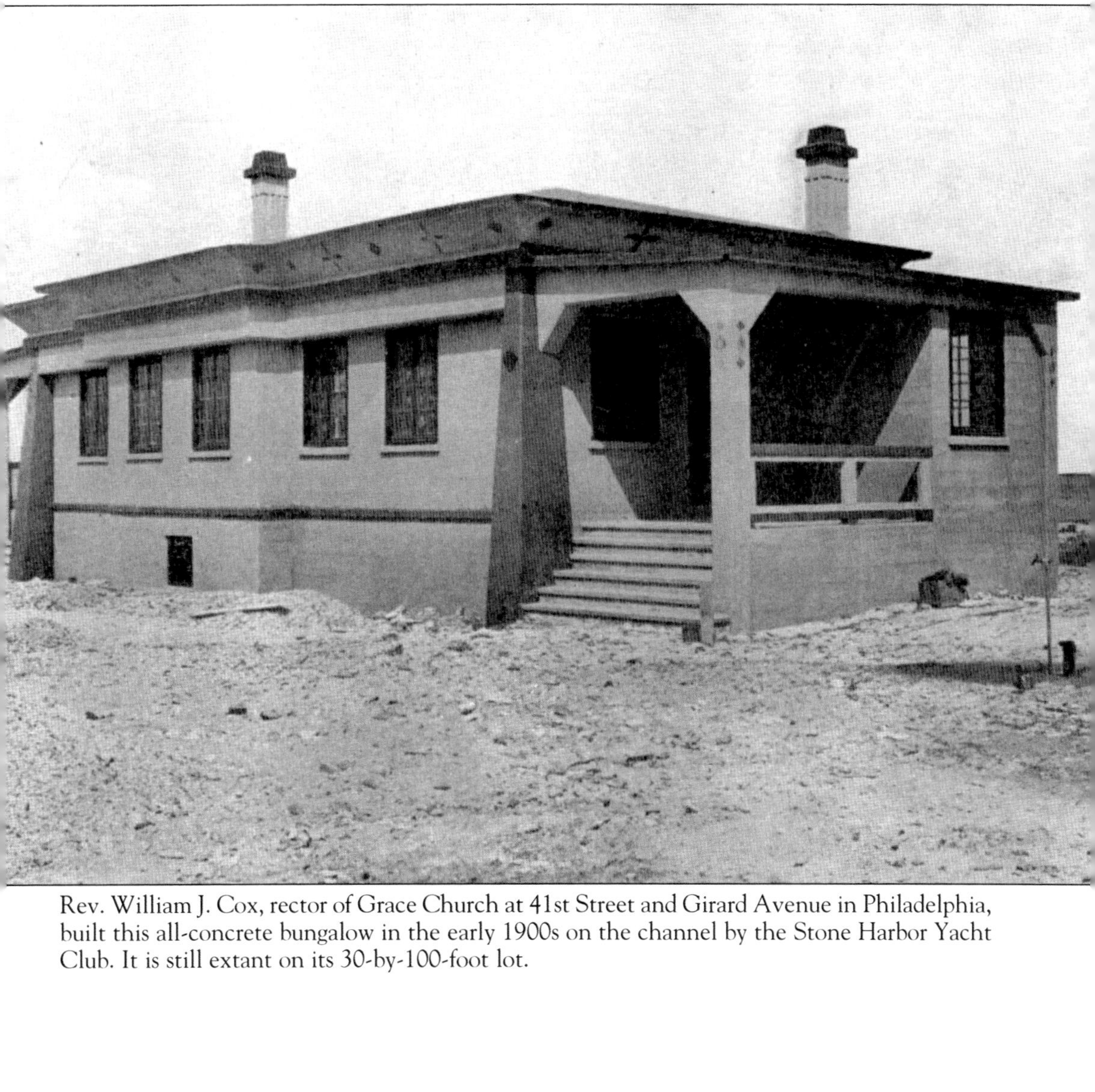

Rev. William J. Cox, rector of Grace Church at 41st Street and Girard Avenue in Philadelphia, built this all-concrete bungalow in the early 1900s on the channel by the Stone Harbor Yacht Club. It is still extant on its 30-by-100-foot lot.

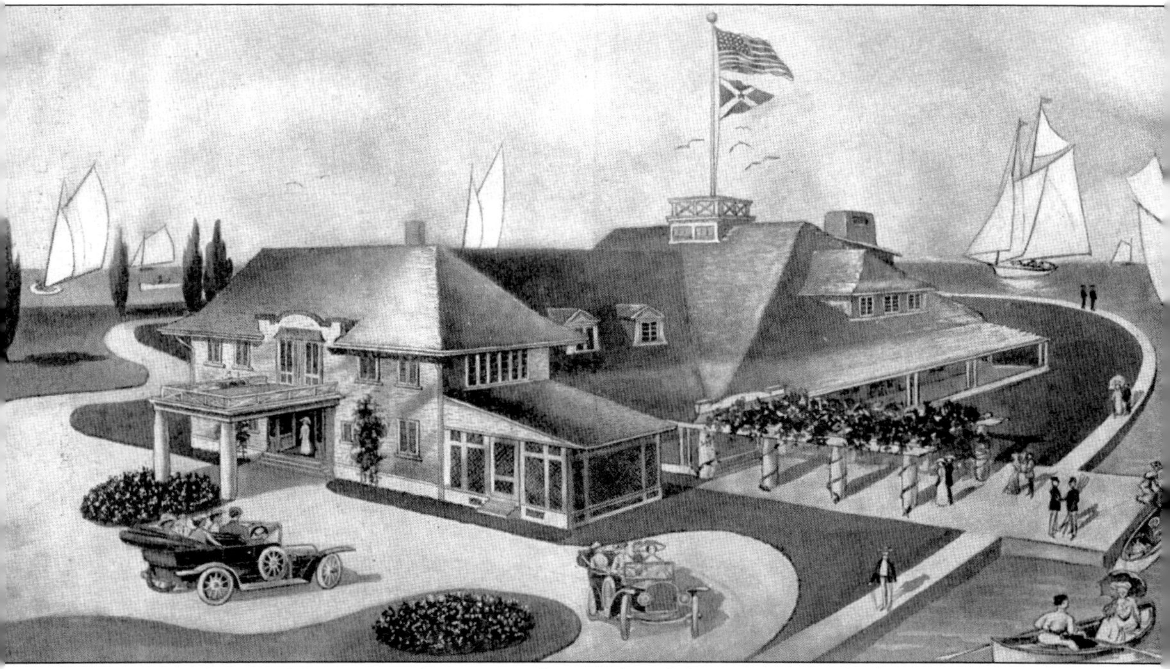

This rendering of the proposed Stone Harbor Yacht Club presents an idealized look at yachting. The Risley brothers formed the yacht club in 1909 and built this $20,000 building in 1911.

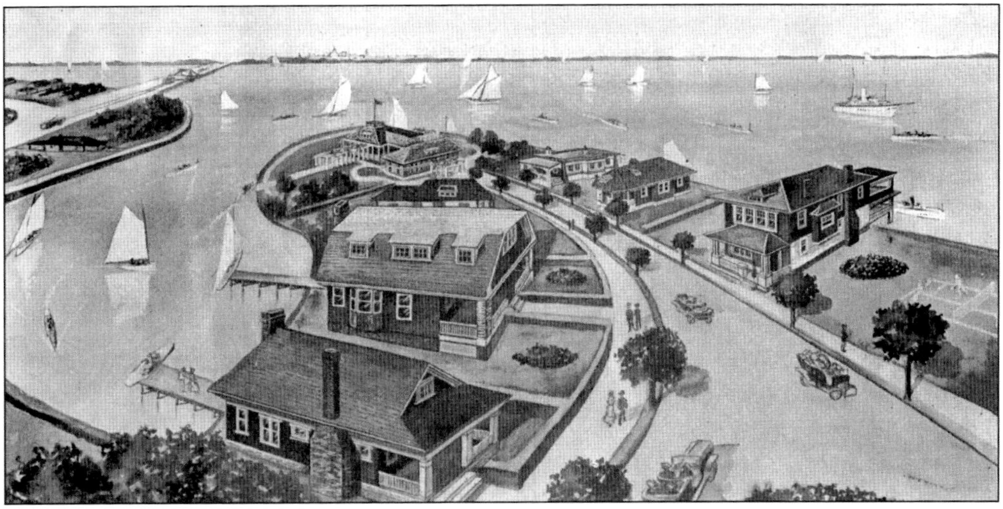

Another conception of the Stone Harbor Yacht Club shows the beautiful homes that would surround the club. In the background is the bridge to the Cape May Courthouse.

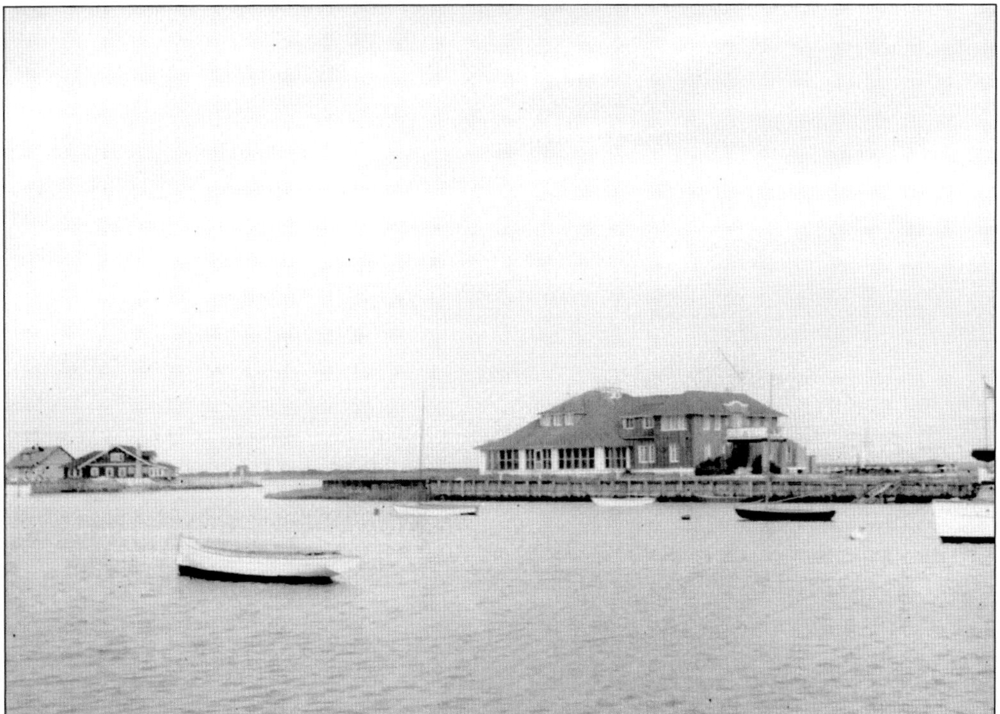

In the beginning, the club was short-lived, as it was closed during World War I. It did not reopen until 1929, when a two-day regatta was held. The Stone Harbor Yacht Club has been a popular place ever since. This shot was taken shortly after it reopened.

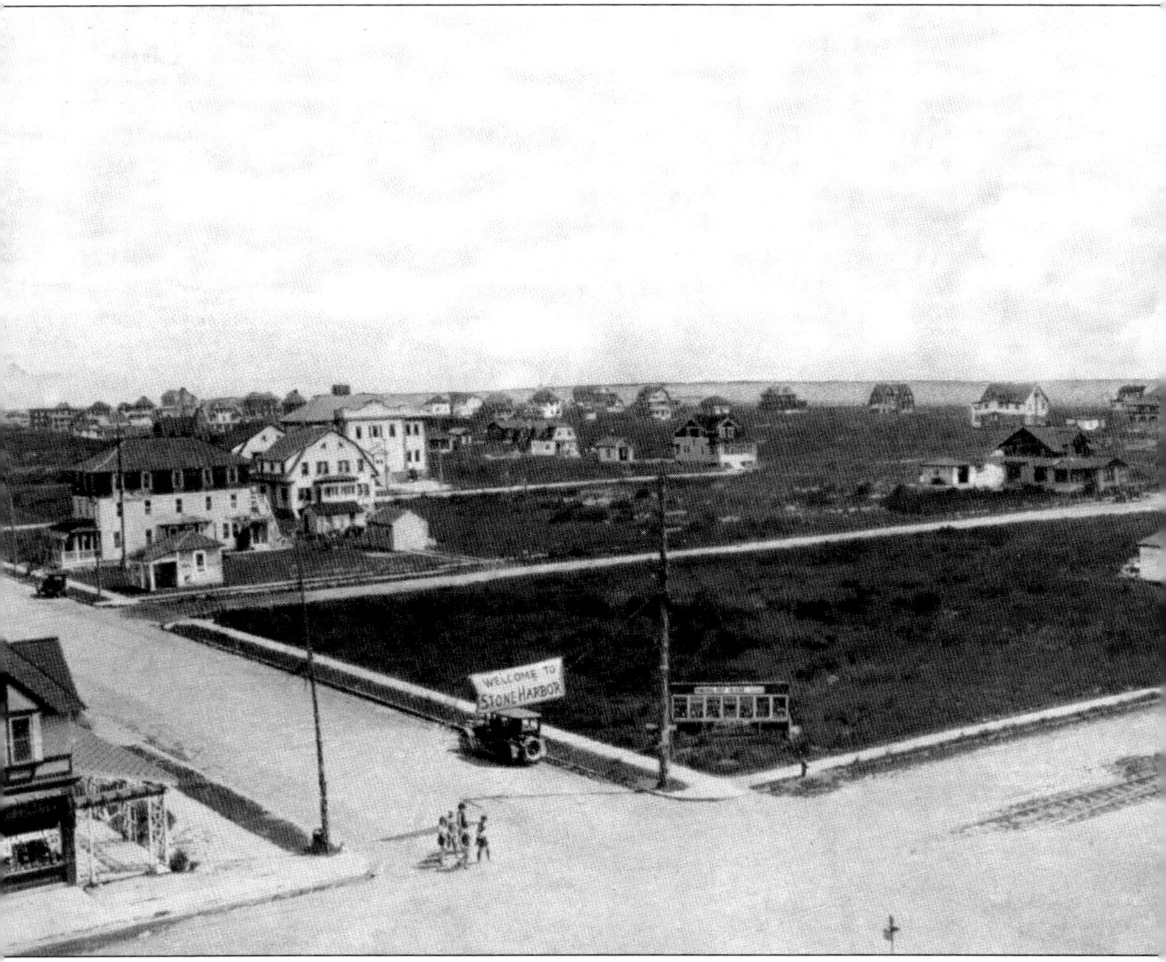

This view, taken from the Shelter Haven's tower, shows 96th Street and Third Avenue in the 1920s. On the left is a building constructed c. 1913 as a block of stores, which became the A & P market in the 1930s. The large hip-roofed building just down the street on Third Avenue is Springer's Ice Cream, a Stone Harbor institution that is still going strong. The large building behind Springer's on 94th Street is Stone Harbor's School No. 1, built in 1915. The view also shows the now defunct railroad tracks, half buried in the sand.

Two

The Golden Season: The 1930s

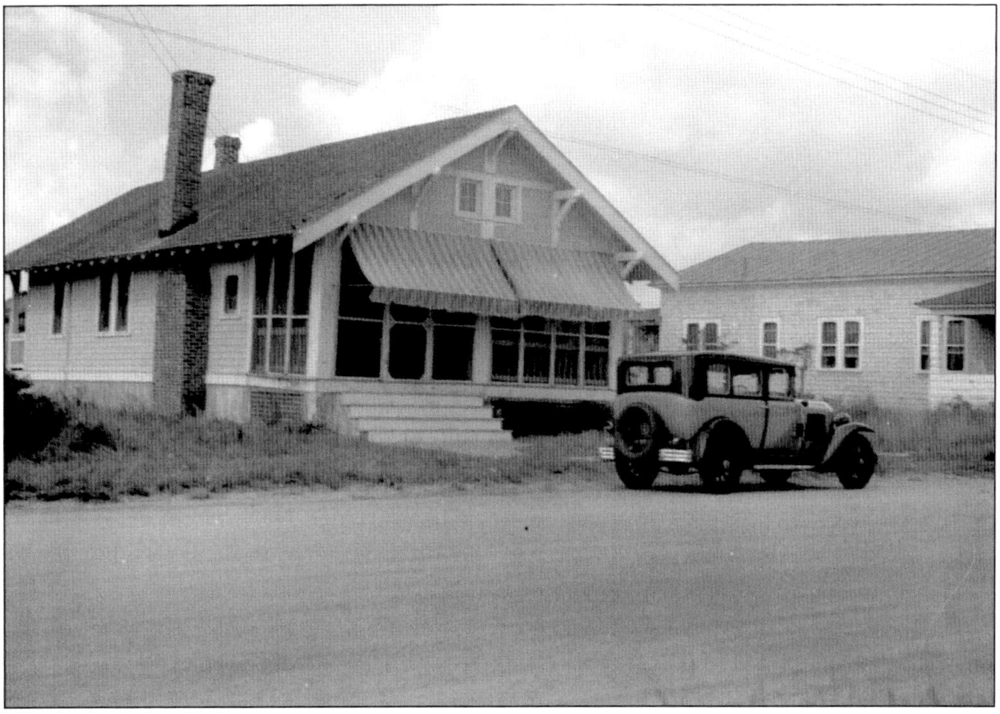

This bungalow near the Stone Harbor Yacht Club was rented by my grandparents in the early 1930s and represents their first summer at the shore. The choice of Stone Harbor was an obvious one, as my grandmother's aunt had owned stock in the South Jersey Realty Company. The sedan in front is my grandfather's Chrysler.

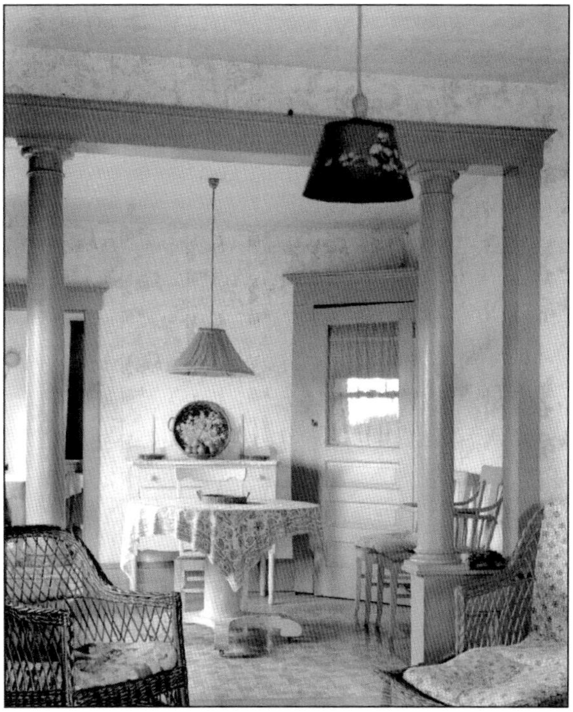

The interior of this rented cottage is typical of most seashore homes of the period.

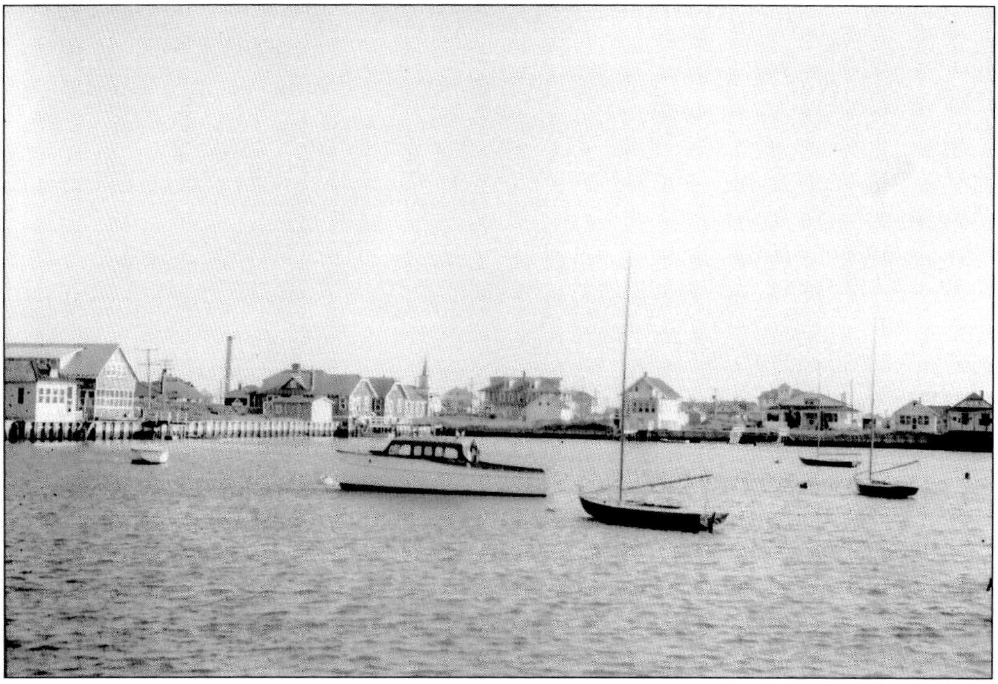

Although not on the bay, the cottage still had a water view from across the street. Taken from the rental, this view of the Stone Harbor Yacht Club basin shows that mooring a boat was more common than docking it. Mingling with Comets, the large cabin cruiser was a 26-foot Owens Dinette. In the background is the old water tower and the steeple of the Lutheran church, which was built in 1917.

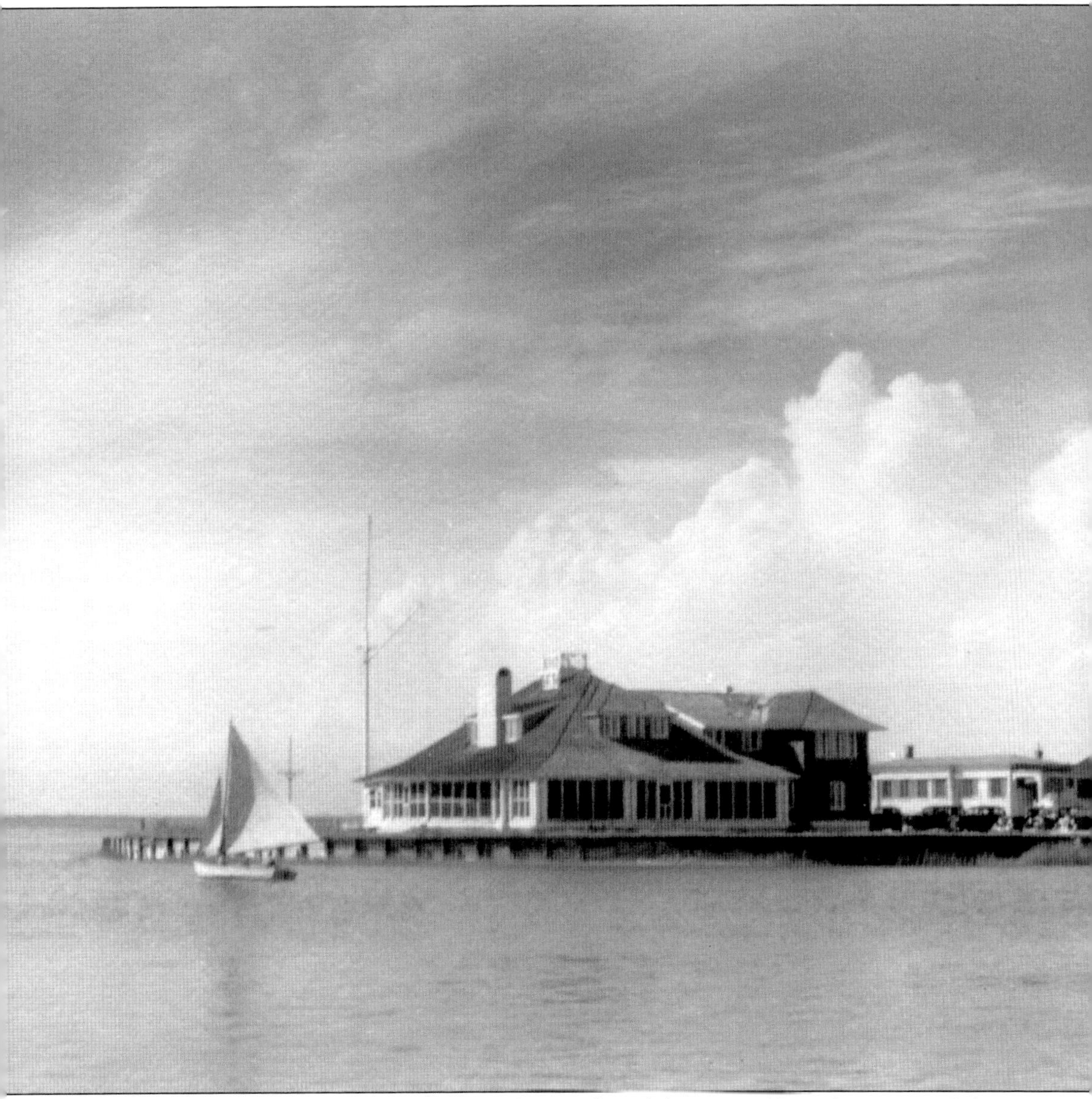

A lone sailboat sets sail from the Stone Harbor Yacht Club on a golden afternoon in July 1936.

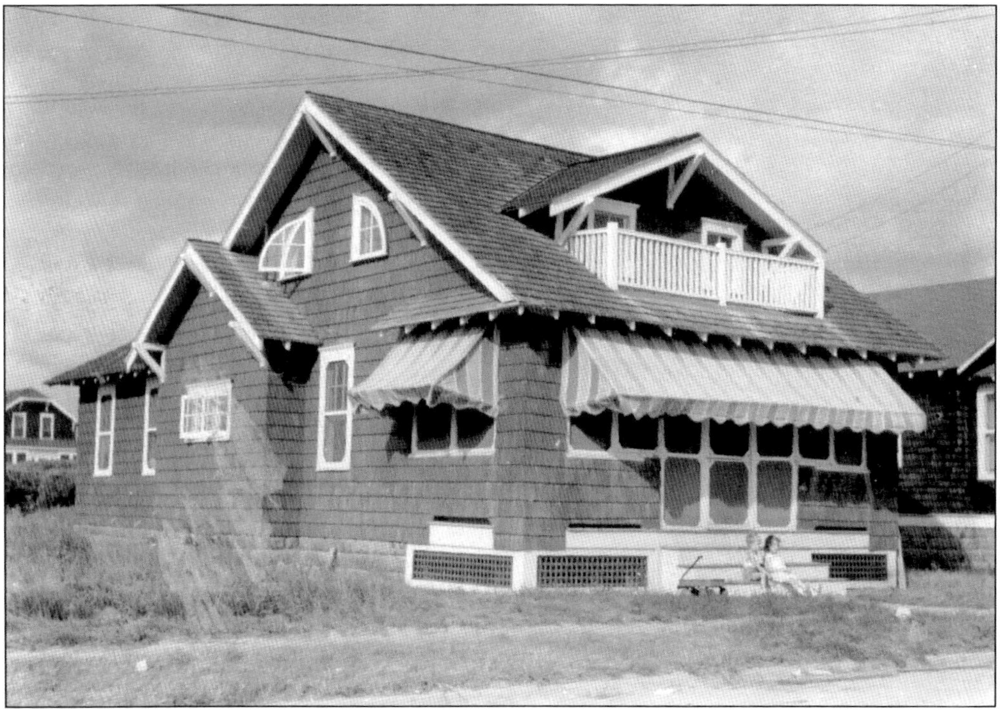

An afternoon visit to a friend leaves the children anxiously waiting the wagon ride home. This typical cottage of the 1920s was much smaller than the earlier, grander homes and reflected the popularity of the California bungalow with its wood shingle siding, deep overhangs and de rigor canvas awnings on the porch.

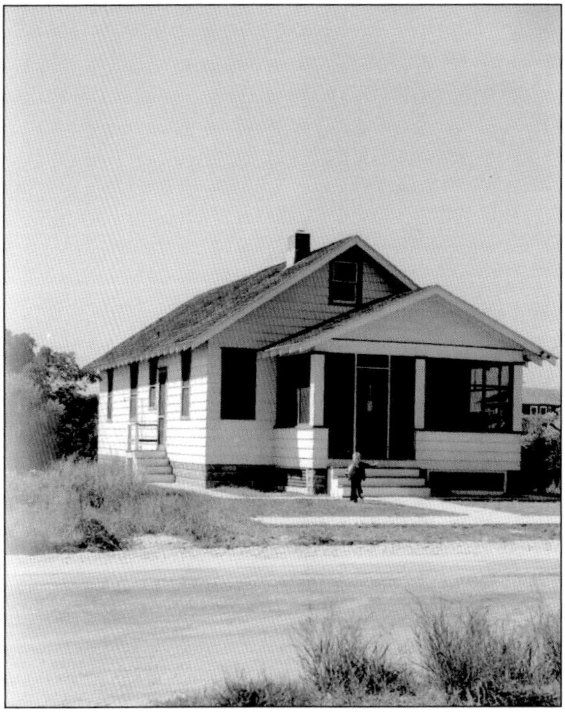

Through my great-aunt, my grandparents purchased this cottage on Sunset Lane and 98th Street in the early 1930s. In the more than 40 years that my family owned this house, no one can ever remember having a bad time there. This shot of the newly purchased house shows none of my grandmother's landscaping that would later make this house our home.

This 1933 image shows a typical interior of a shore bungalow. These rooms remained as they are shown—with the exception of changing tastes in wallpaper, curtains, and paintings—until the house was sold some 40 years later.

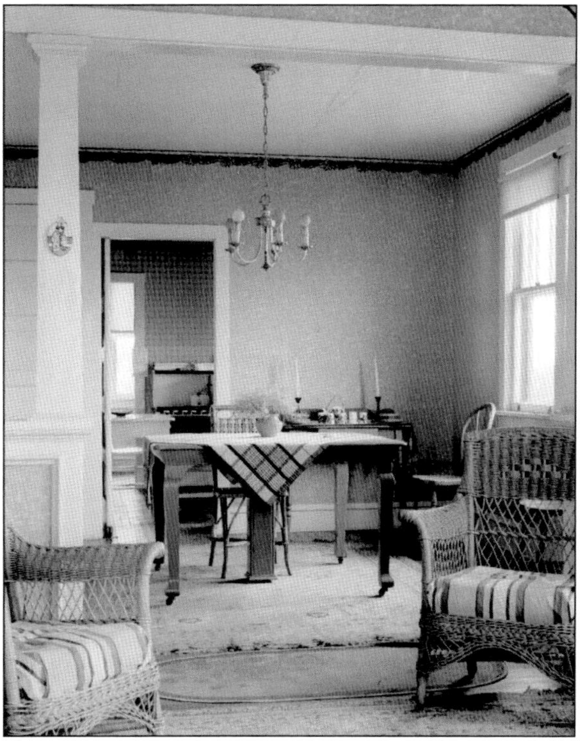

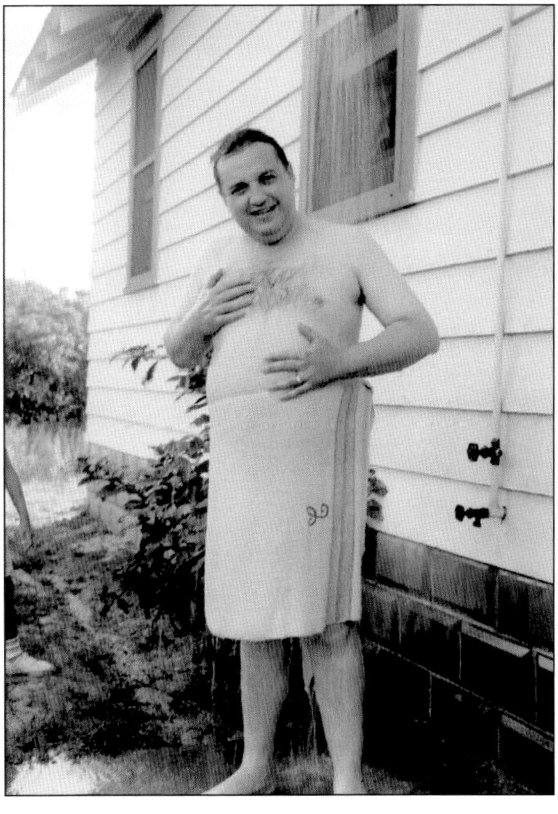

My father's uncle discreetly models the use of our open-air shower. In all the years the family owned the house, it never occurred to anyone to build a shower screen. Not uncommon was an outdoor entrance to the bathroom.

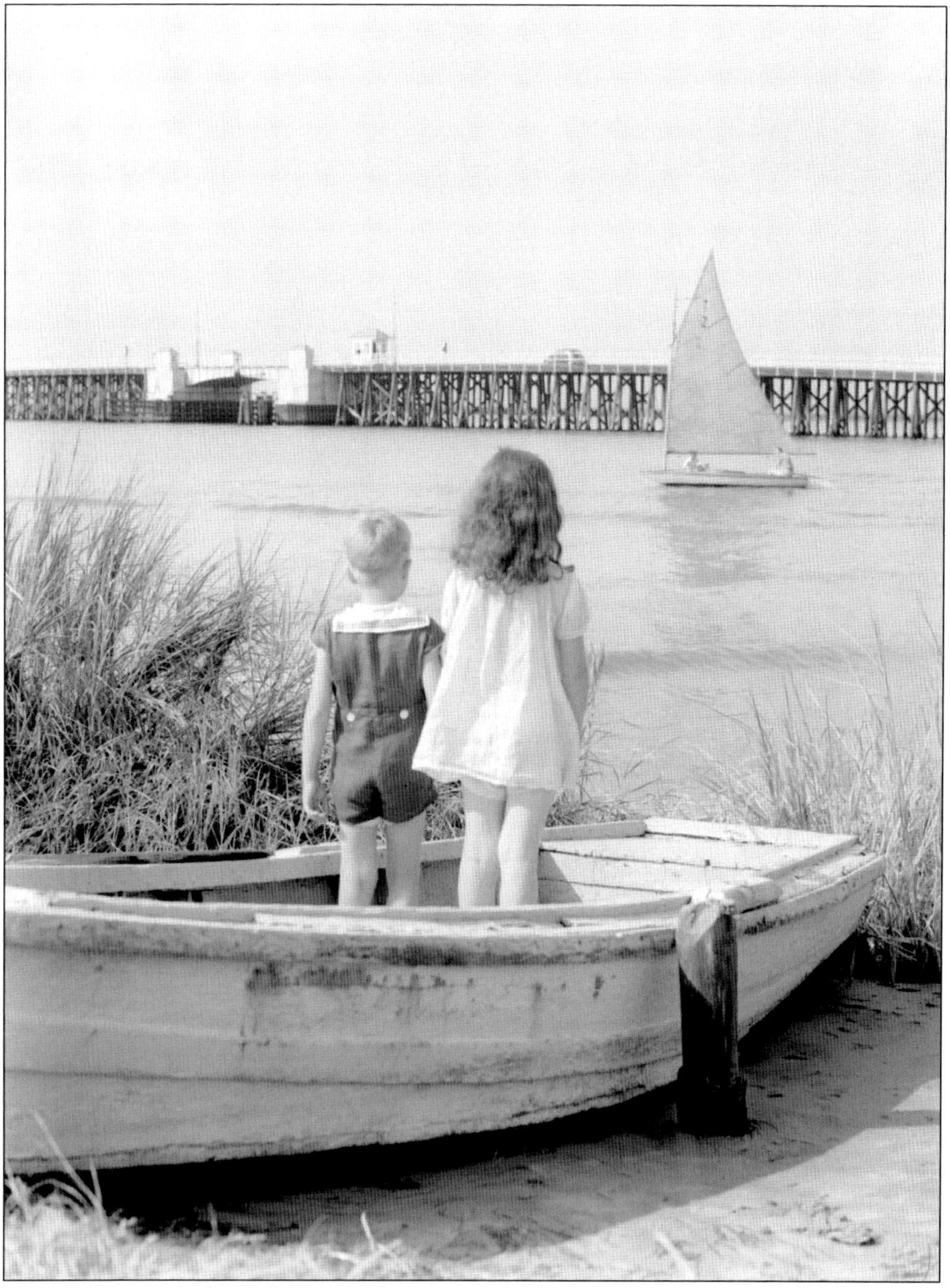

Too young to race, these children look on as a gaff-rigged Barnegat Bay Sneak Box heads out to race past the bridge in the background. This boat, designed originally for hunting in salt marshes, became one of the Moth-class sailboats.

For many years, this model racer sailed the backwaters of Stone Harbor. It was one of a series of always splashy gifts from my father's uncle. Looking to improve upon its maneuverability, my father adjusts the rigging. The little sloop has since been retired to a bookshelf.

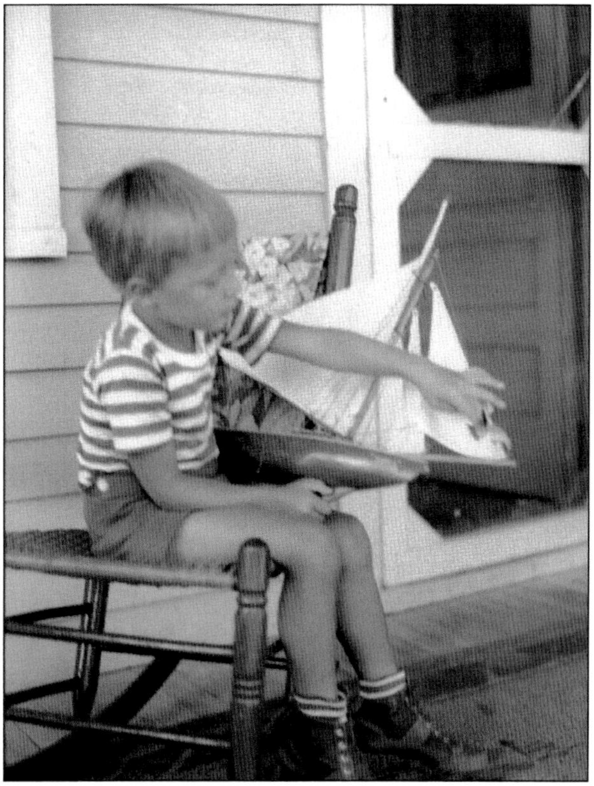

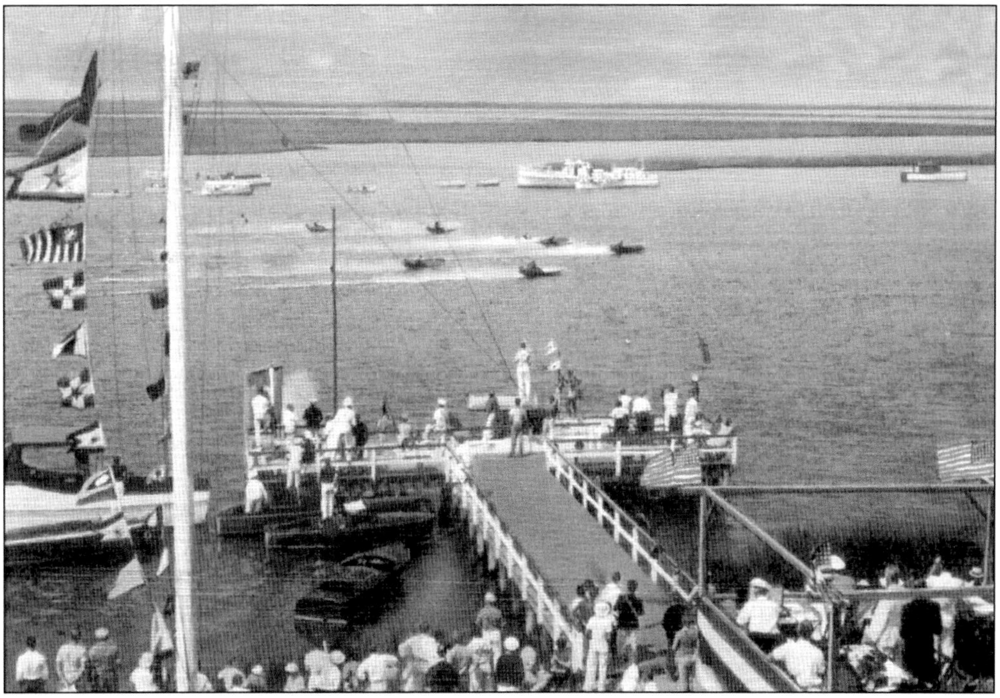

Taken from the roof of the Stone Harbor Yacht Club, this view shows speedboating in the 1930s. In the foreground are some beautiful mahogany runabouts of the day.

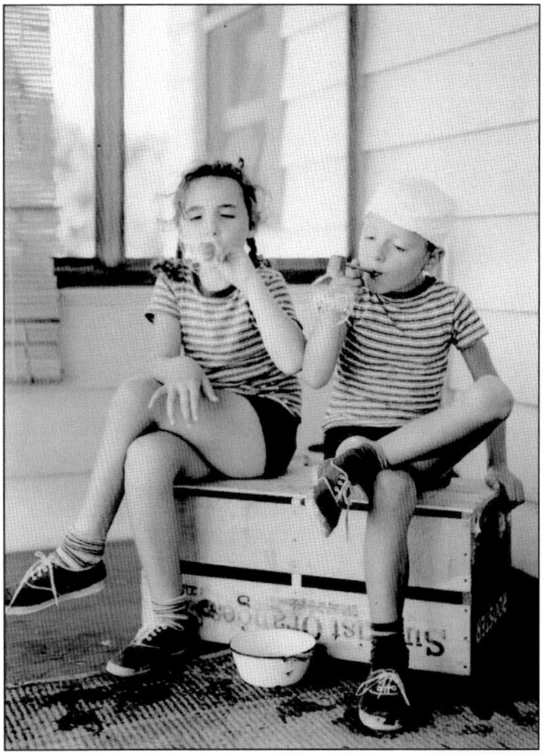

Not every day was sunny in Stone Harbor. What do you do when it rains? Blow bubbles on the sun porch.

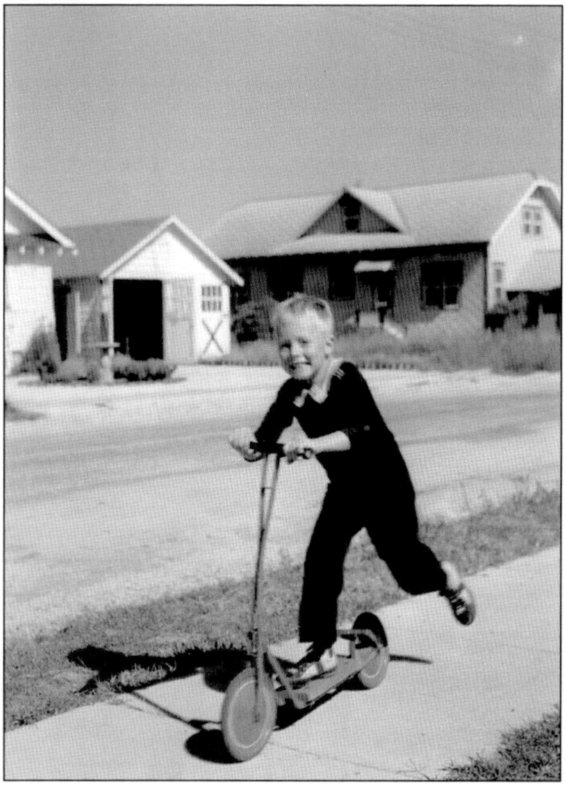

With scooters being the latest rage, this shot could have been taken yesterday rather than in the 1930s. It is an interesting glimpse of an older generation's play with scooters just as a younger generation discovers them.

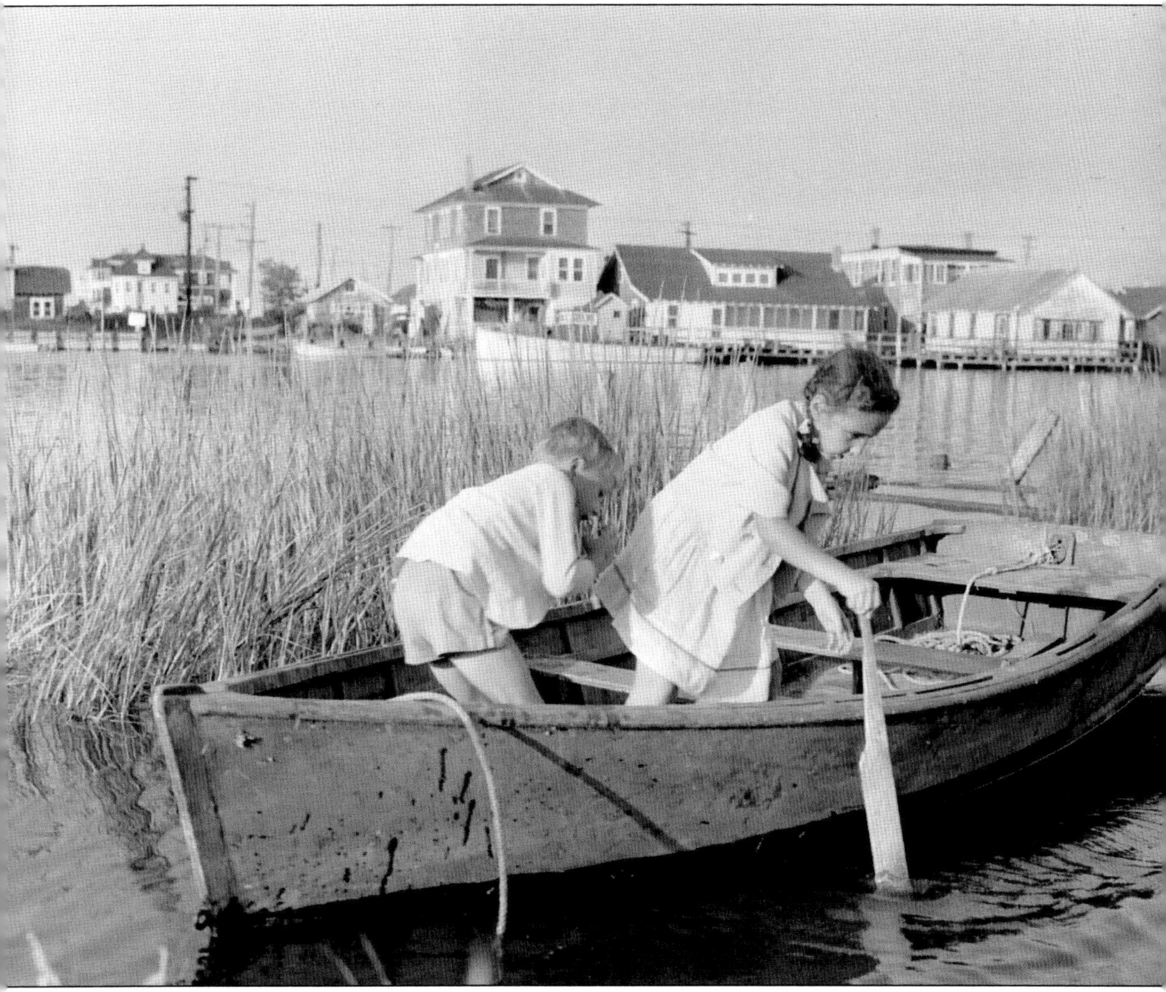

These children are crabbing in the marshes of the Shelter Haven Basin. The little dory was built by Capt. John Stiles, who operated a small boatyard and a charter boat fishing business, seen across the bay.

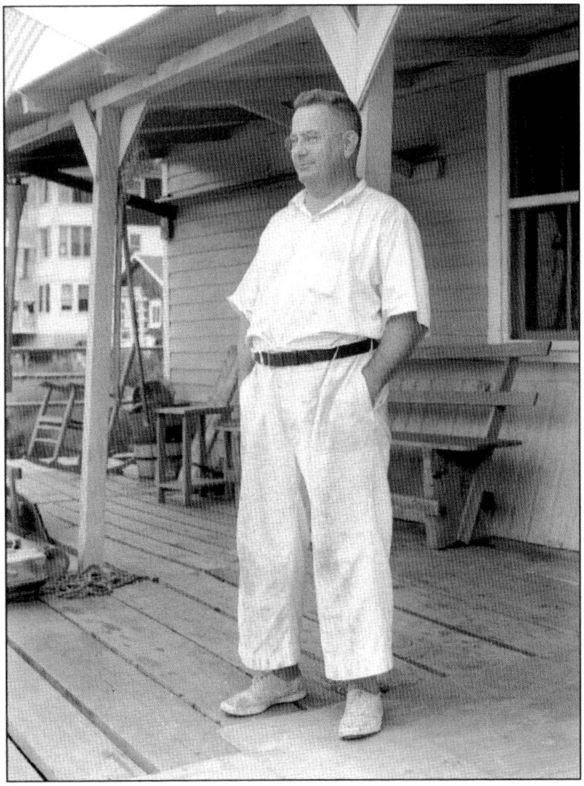

"Bucky" operated a small marina next to the Stone Harbor bridge, where he rented boats and boat slips.

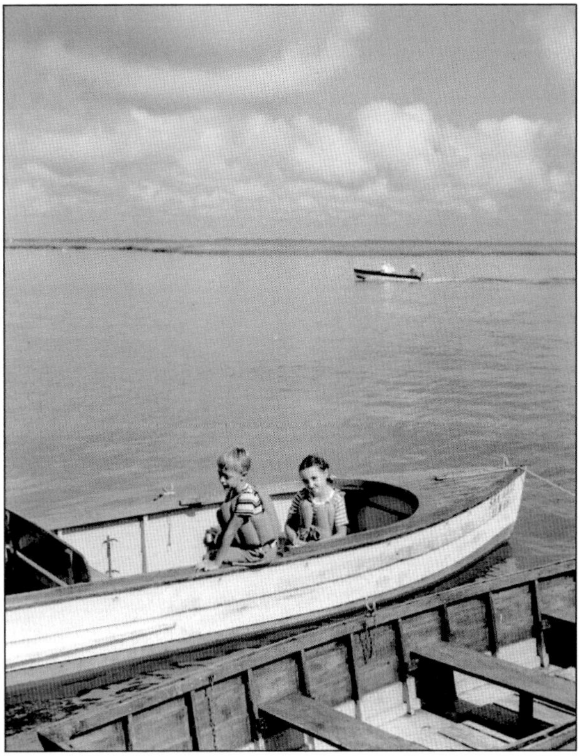

Two children prepare for an outing in one of Bucky's boats.

Playing on the beach was not limited to sand and surf, as amusement can be found on this slide near 87th Street. Swings, slides, and monkey bars were not uncommon along the beach. The large house in the background is still standing.

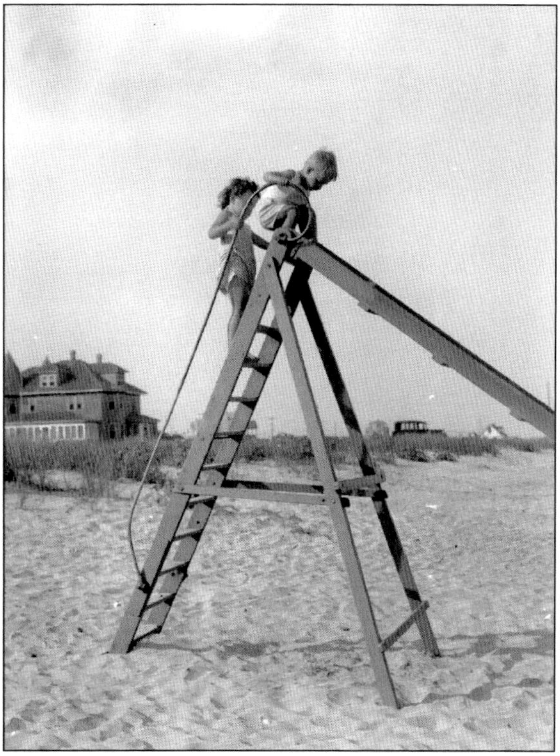

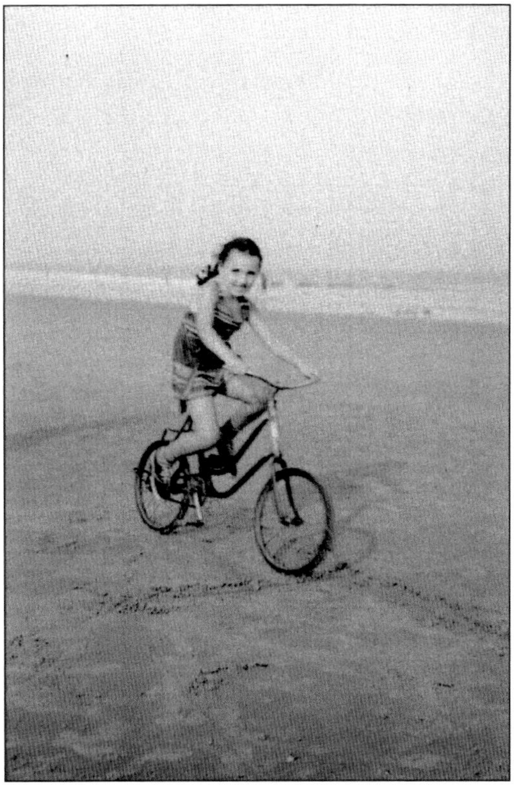

Bicycling on an empty beach during the summer would be an impossible feat today.

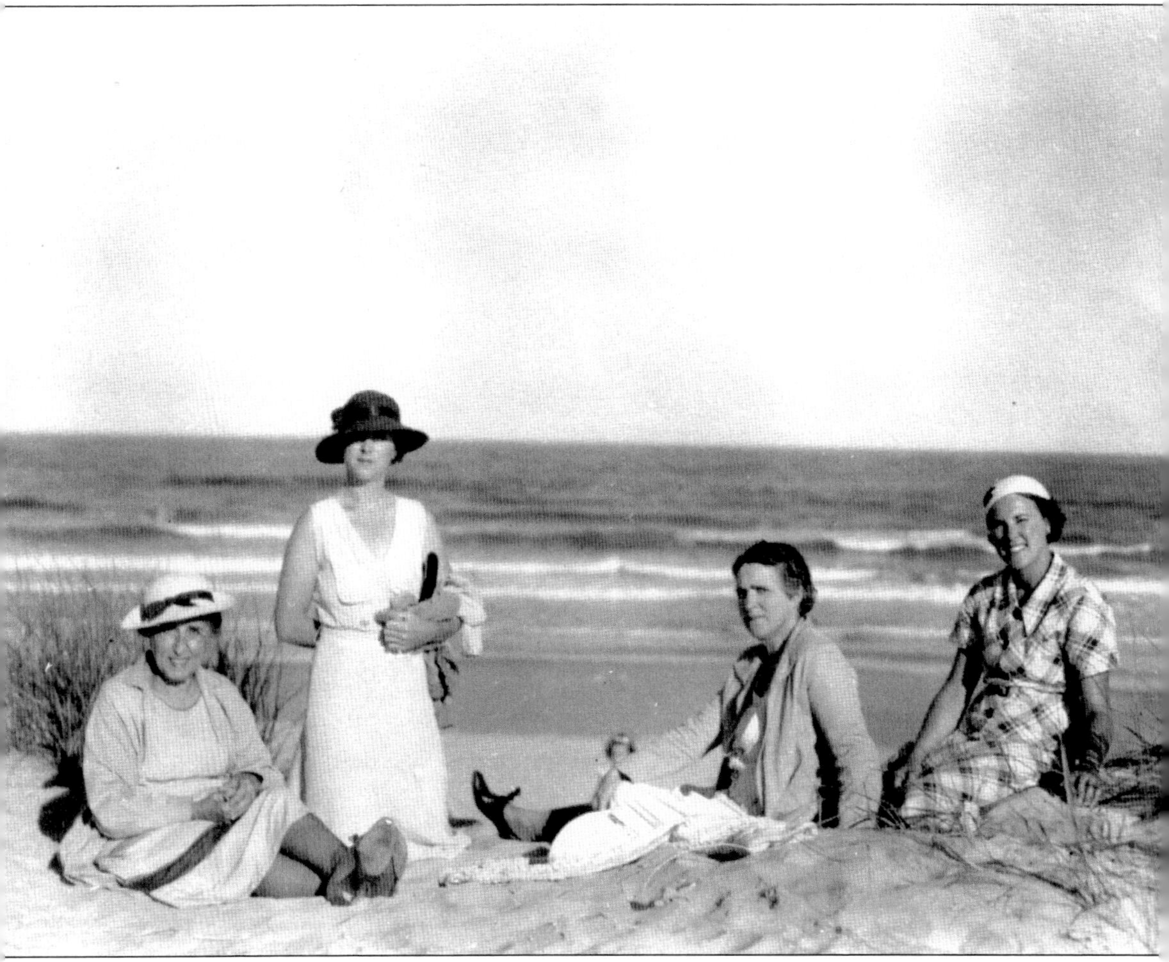

Put on your hat and heels and head for the beach. From left to right are Angie Marké, Angela Ravaud, Mathilda Weiss, and Madeline Cole.

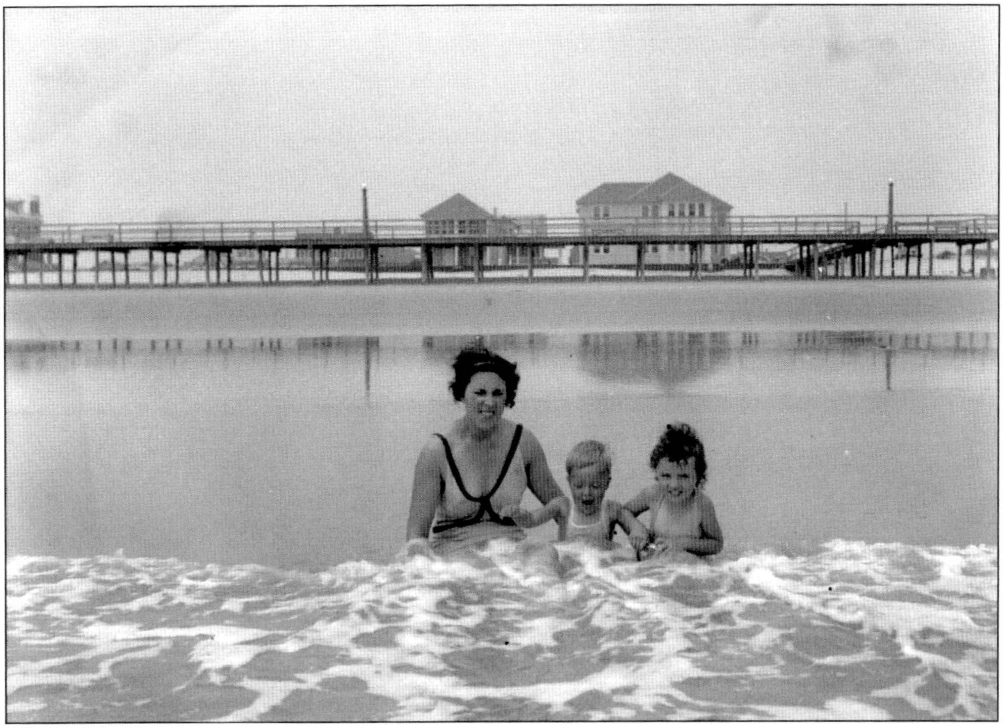

Although the scarcity of beachgoers implies a November day, this shot was actually taken in July. While these people cool off in the waves, the boardwalk provides a background.

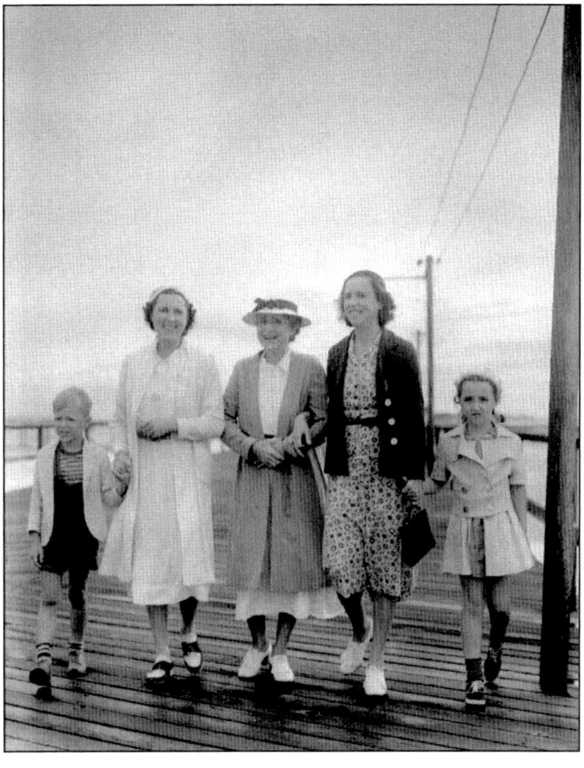

This group is strolling down the boardwalk in the late 1930s. The one-and-a-quarter-mile boardwalk was built in 1914 and was the scene of many family outings until it collapsed in the hurricane of 1944.

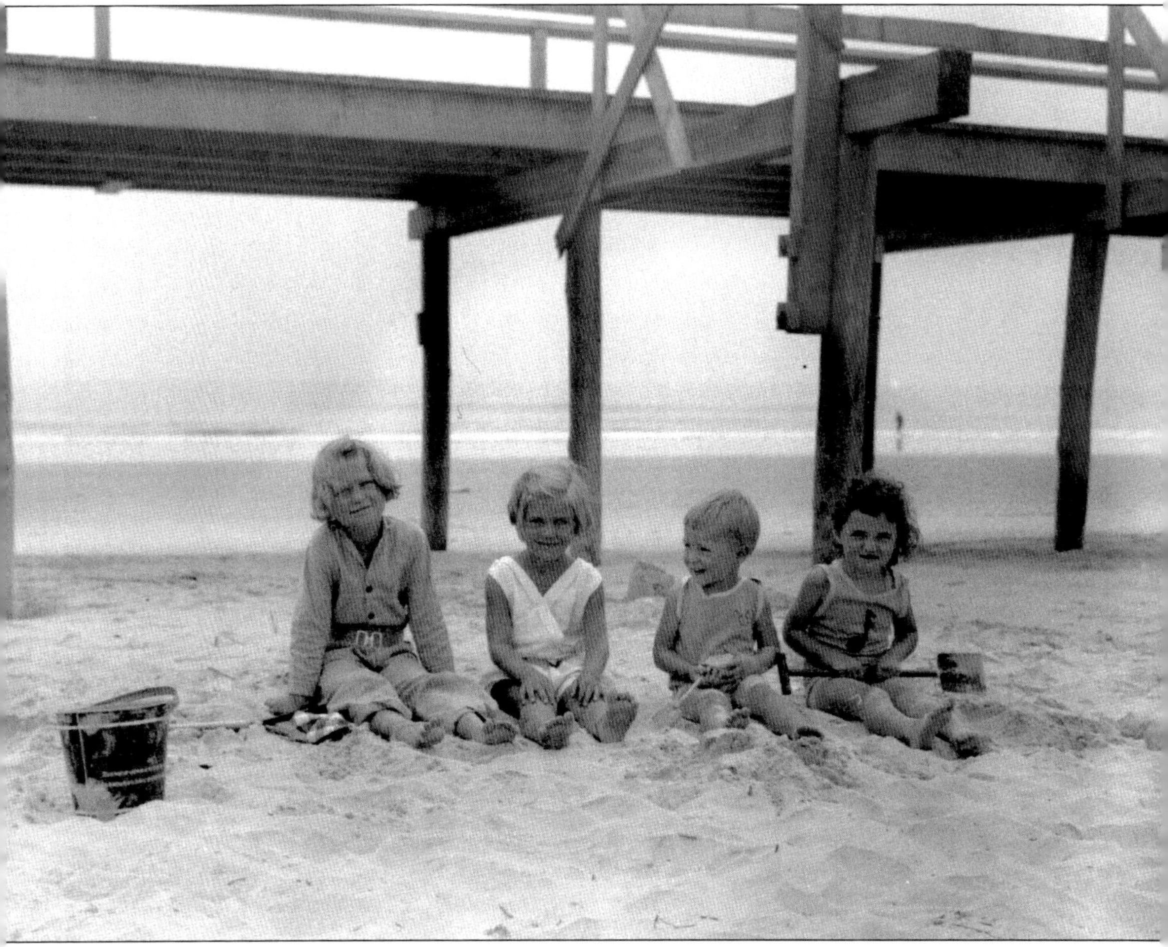

The shadow of the old boardwalk provides not only a perfect place to play in the sand but also a perfect place to pose for a picture on a hot day in July 1935.

Crime was almost nonexistent in Stone Harbor. Mike Lennon was first appointed by the Risley brothers as night watchman in 1912. Starting in 1914, Lennon was named marshall by each mayor until 1951. His police department (which was made up of just himself in the early years) made use of empty boxcars for offenders. Lacking a boxcar, Lennon would simply handcuff the prisoner to himself.

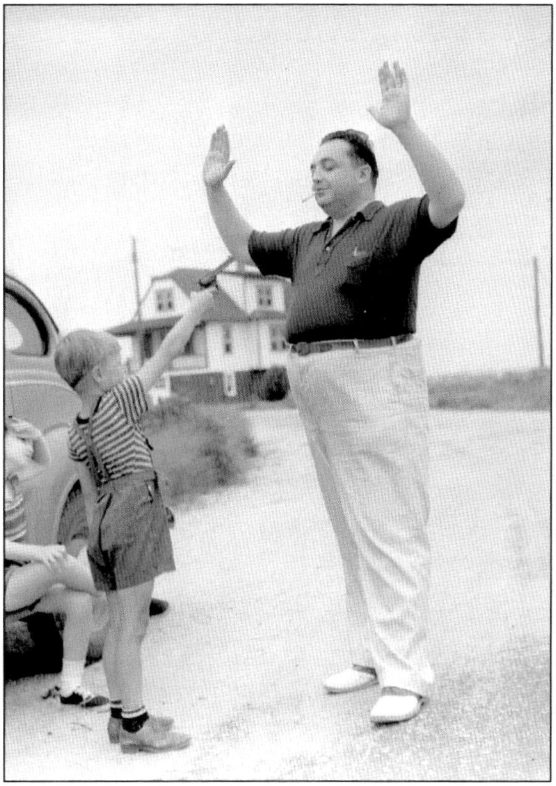

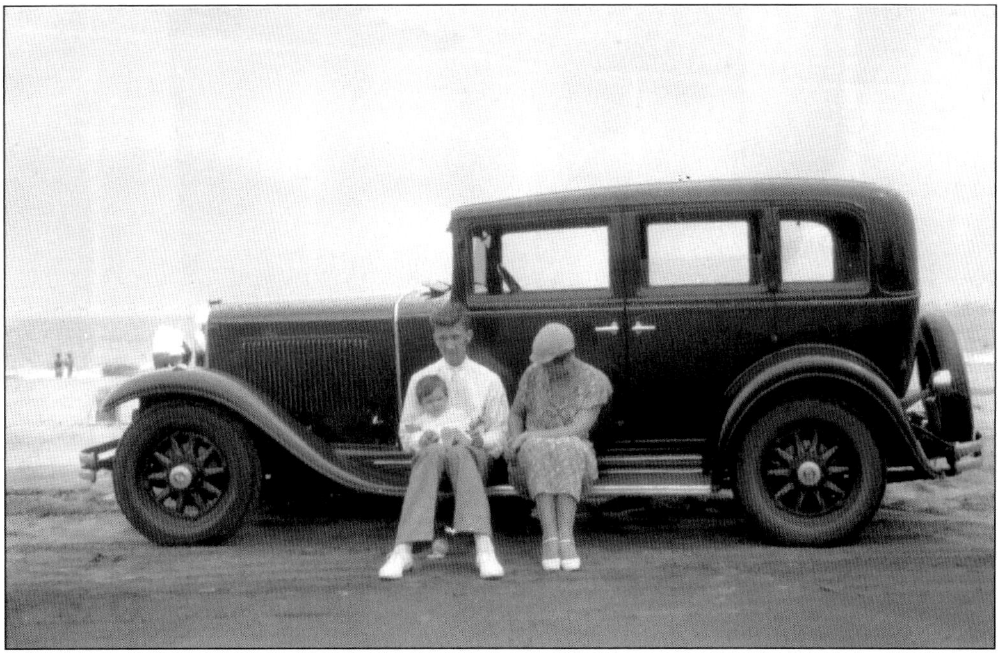

Parking near the beach was not a problem, as seen in this 1933 photograph.

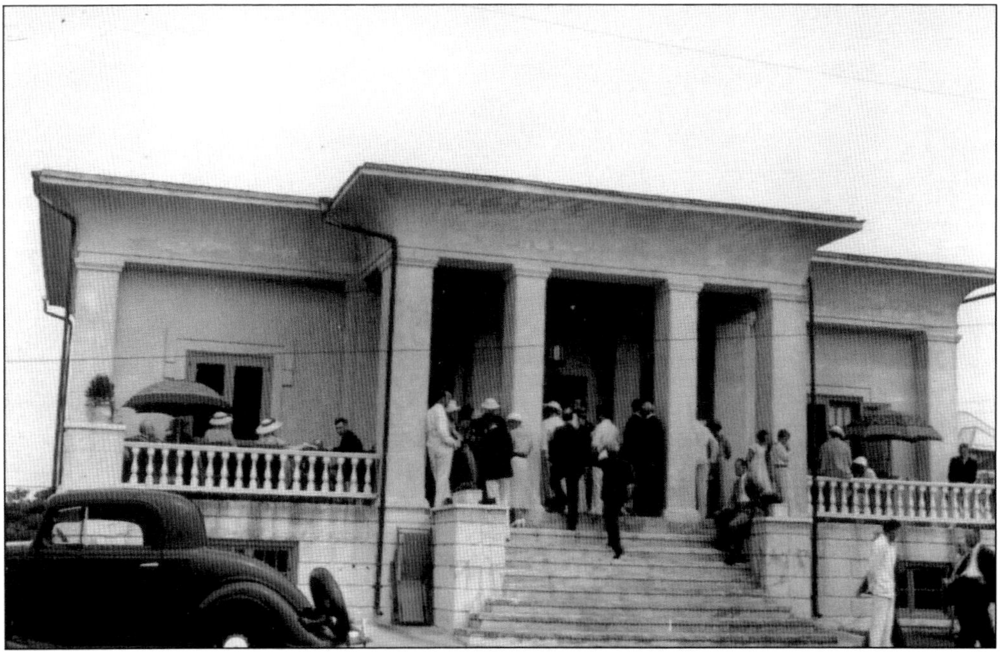

In August 1936, the Crispin family had the wedding reception of their daughter in one of Stone Harbor's more unique homes. This photograph shows the guests overflowing onto the veranda. A view of this house when it was newly constructed can be seen on page 23.

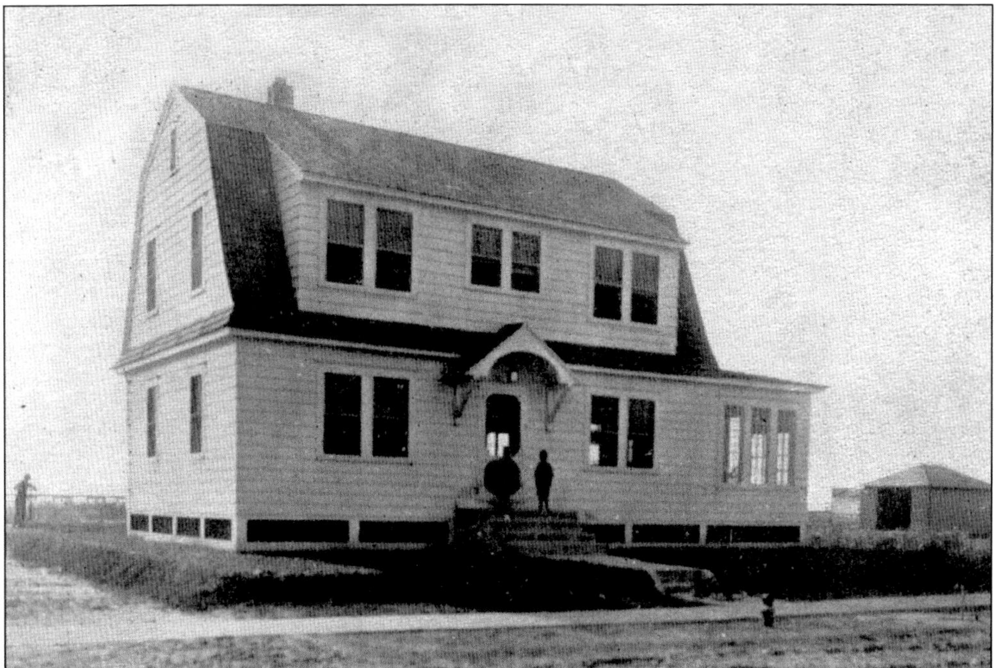

For sale: a home on the Jersey shore. This charming Dutch Colonial offers a living room, a dining room, a kitchen, three bedrooms, a bathroom, and a view of the sea. As the Colonial Revival style became more popular, this home was typical of the houses built in the late 1930s.

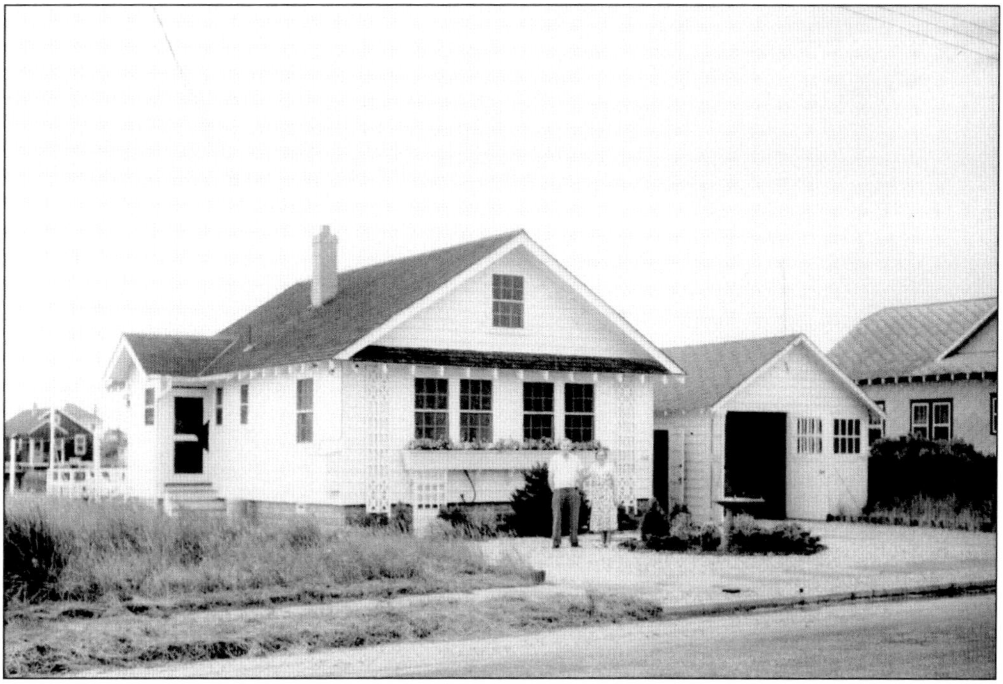

Shown is an example of how shore bungalows lost their Craftsman features as the Colonial Revival style took precedence. The bungalow was built across from my grandparents' cottage on 98th Street by Mr. and Mrs. Miller, who pose in front of their new house.

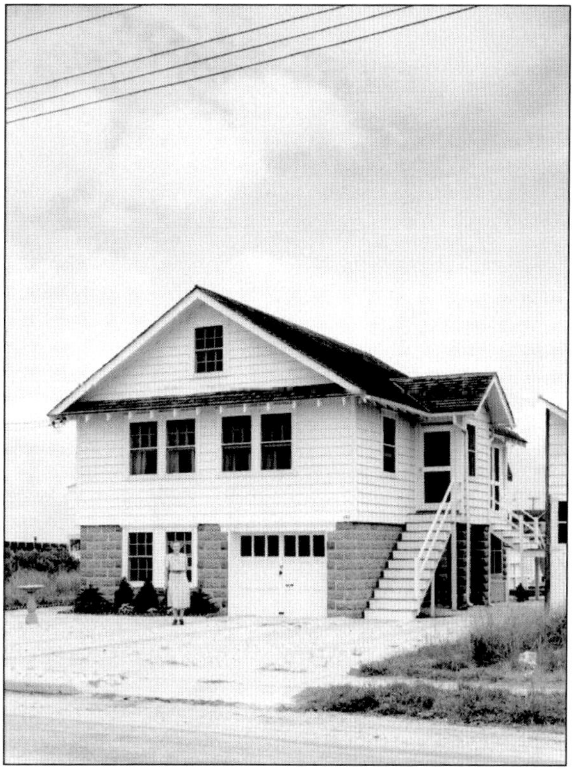

Just a few years after the Millers' cottage was built, the house was raised for a garage ground floor. This would not be its last move. In the 1970s, it was moved out rather than being torn down. It was replaced by a modern house.

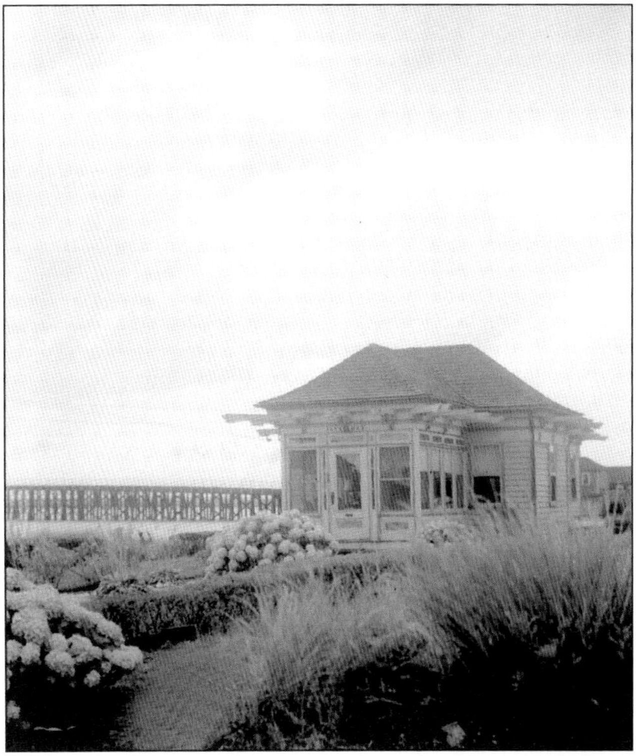

The uniqueness of the Marchiano cottage, with its pagodalike appearance, inspired everyone to refer to it as "the Chinese house." The Marchianos were great gardeners and were very proud of their hydrangeas, seen in this picture. The house first sat along the channel but was later moved directly across the street. Although altered, it survives today.

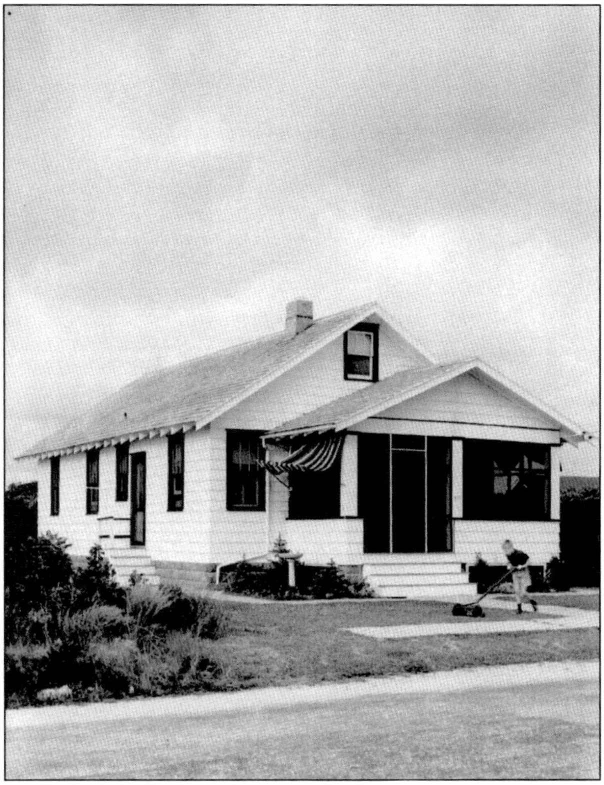

By the end of the decade, the house is becoming a home with the addition of landscaping and awnings. Most importantly, however, the cottage has been given a name—the Colebin.

Three

Changing Times: The 1940s and 1950s

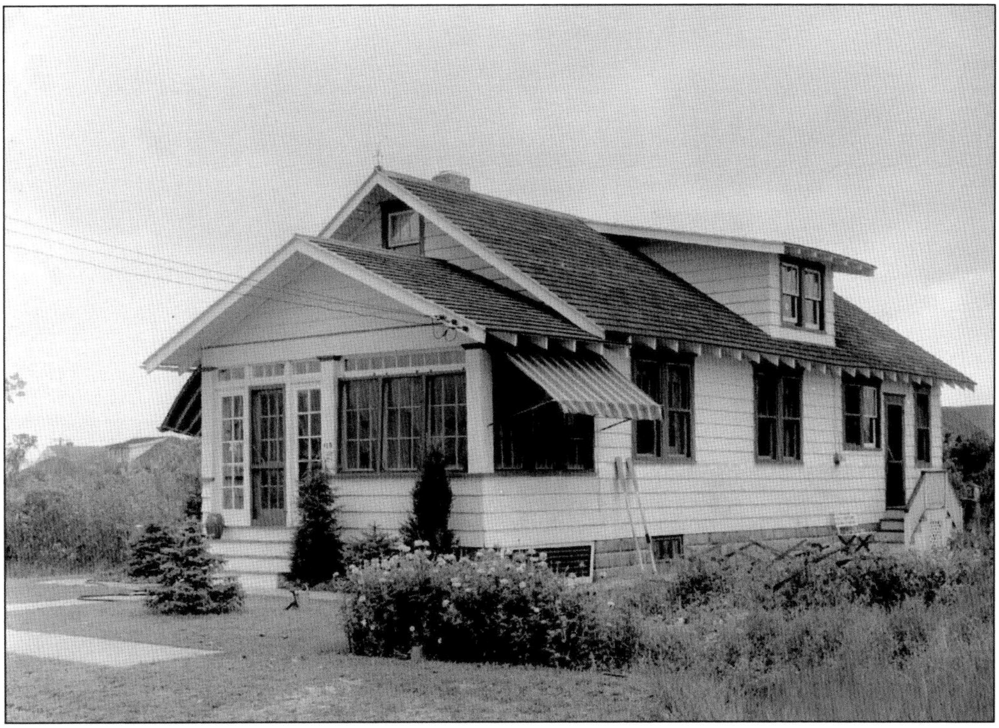

By the 1940s, life was getting sophisticated at the Colebin. Large glass windows were installed on the porch, which could be folded closed on bad weather days. A telephone was installed in case of an emergency with an aging great-grandmother. A small weathervane appeared on the roof peak. This delicate weathervane remained intact until the house was sold.

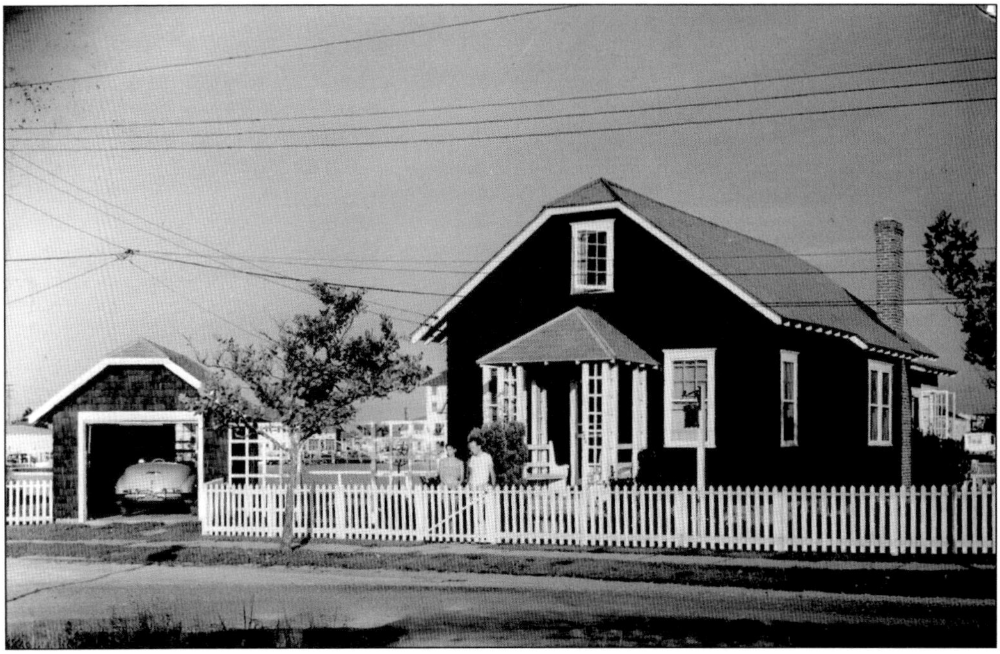

At the corner of the Shelter Haven Bay (98th Street and Corinthian Drive) was the Hoopes' cottage. This idyllic cottage, with its picket fence and trellis, also had a matching garage that afforded their automobile a great view of the bay.

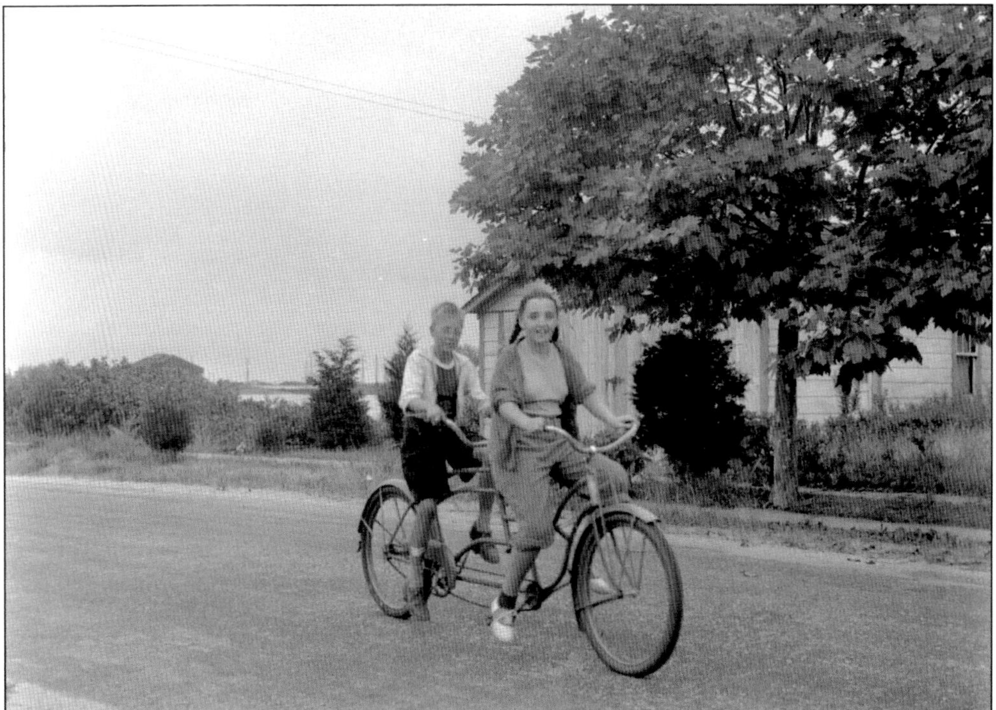

Bicycles built for two were quite popular in the area and can still be rented today. Due to the flat terrain, bicycling remains a popular way of getting around the island.

Fishing off the pier is an ever hopeful lazy-day activity.

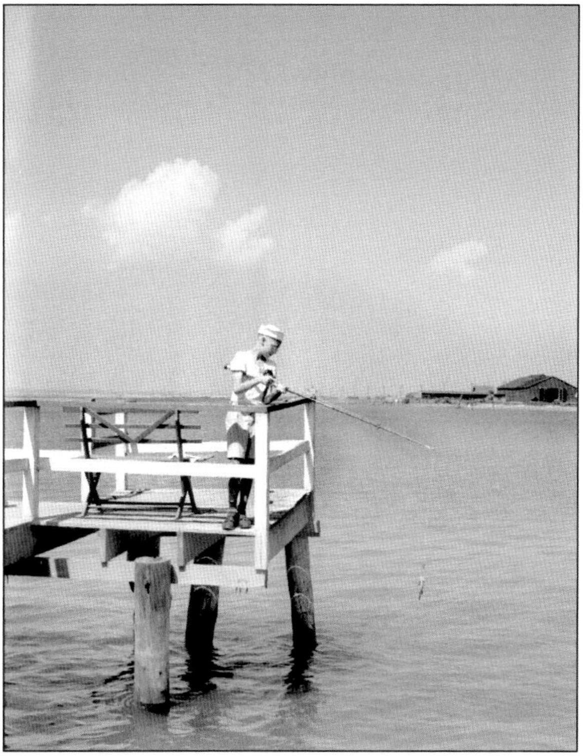

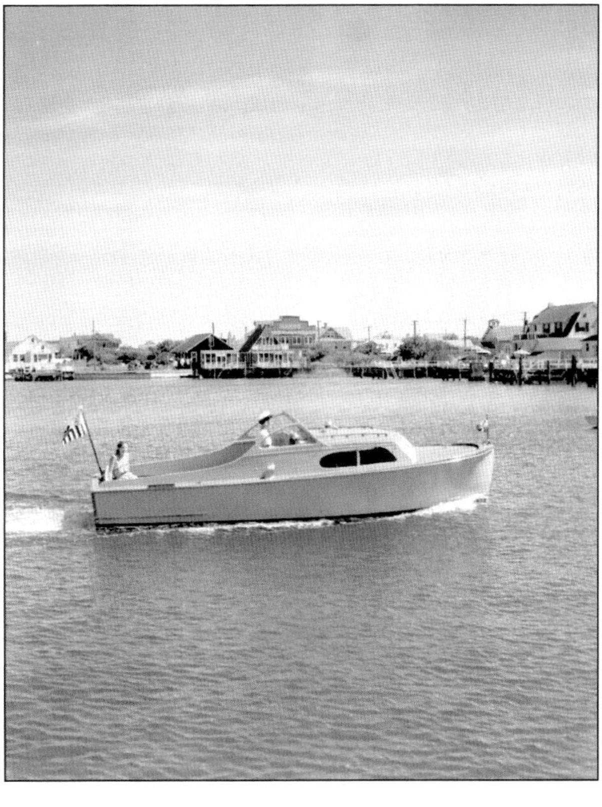

A cabin cruiser of the early 1940s is shown in the Shelter Haven Basin, with the old St. Paul's Roman Catholic Church in the background. In a few short years, builders would cease production of pleasure boats for wartime construction.

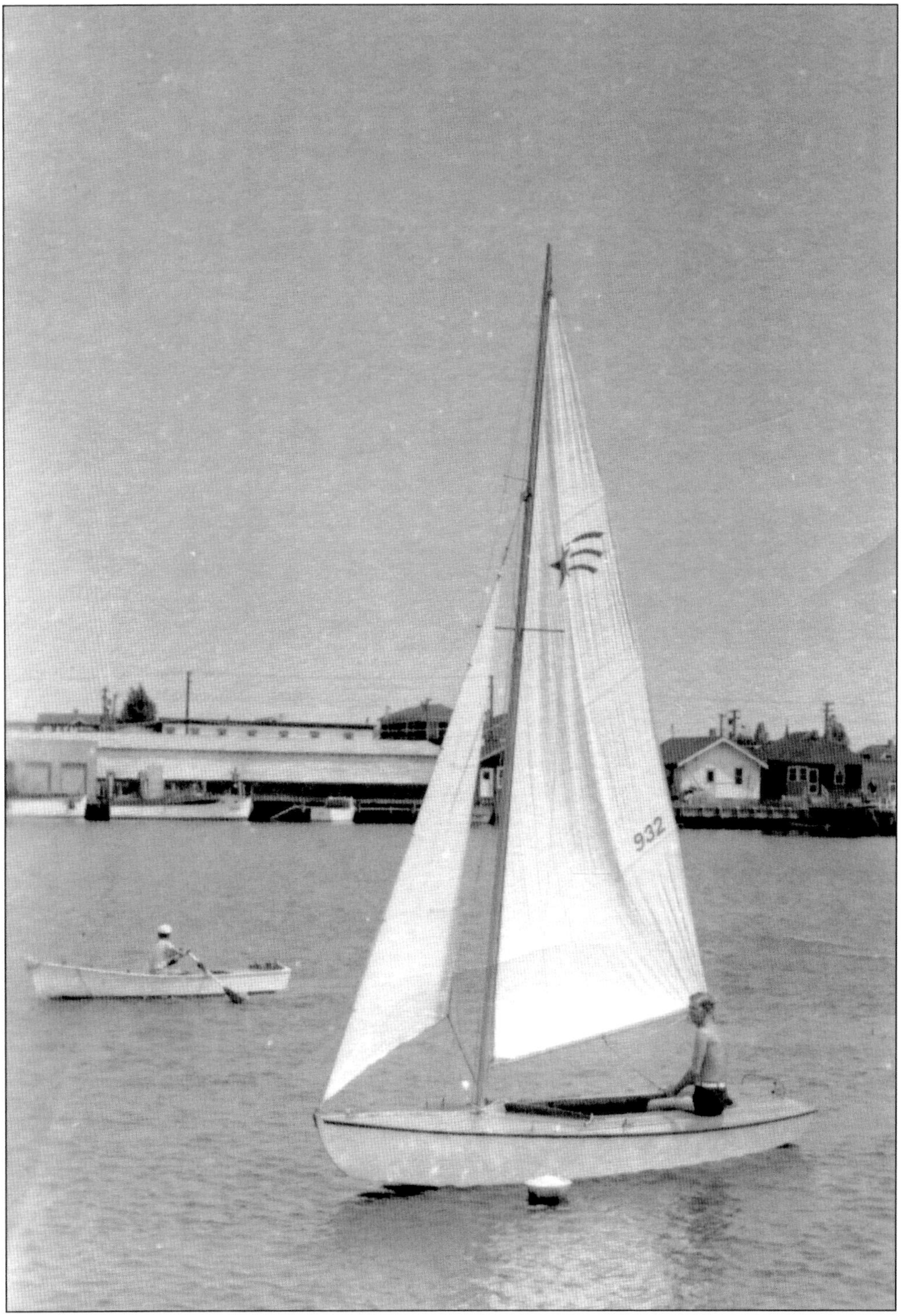

The waters of Stone Harbor were home to many skillful sailors such as Mr. Johanson, shown sailing his Comet-class boat. This photograph was carefully timed to show Johanson as he sailed past the buoy.

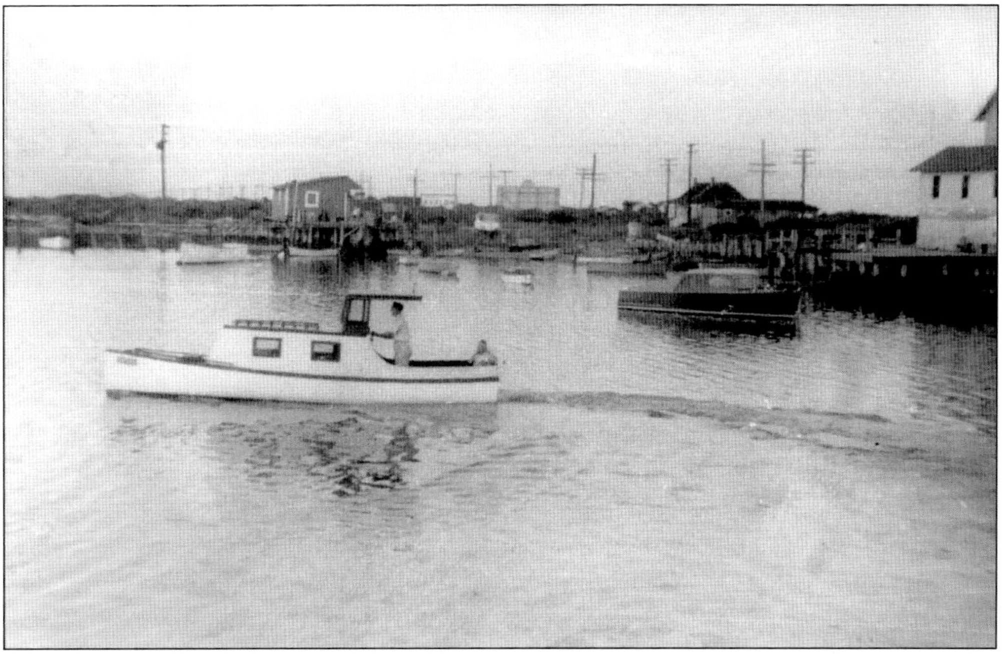

In this 1940s view of the North Basin, the white boat under way was the creation of my grandfather, who had the cabin built onto an open launch. Moored behind him is a Chris Craft motorboat. In the distance stands an old shanty, which was part of the Deschamps boatyard. This basin contained the marinas with a public boat launch and fueling stations. Today it is surrounded by condominiums.

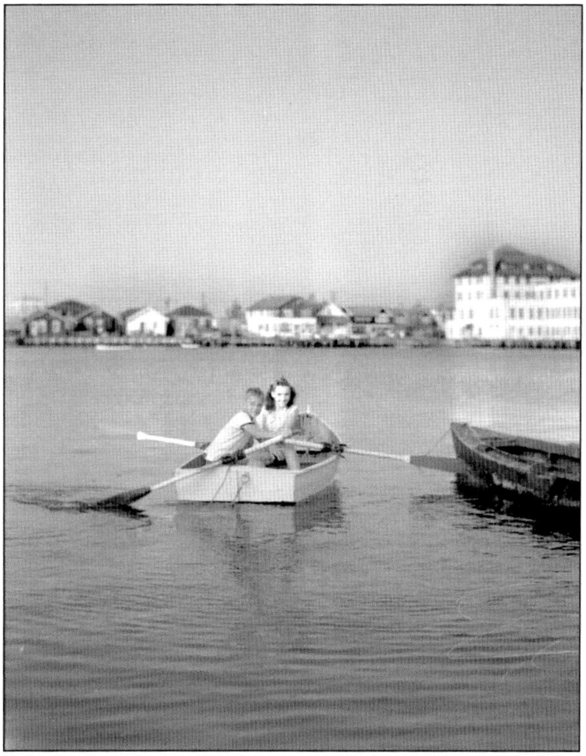

A motorboat was not a necessity to get around the bay. Rowing was not only a great means of transportation and exercise, but it was fun. Seen here in the Shelter Haven Basin, as the girl rows, a boy is using a third oar as a tiller to negotiate around other boats.

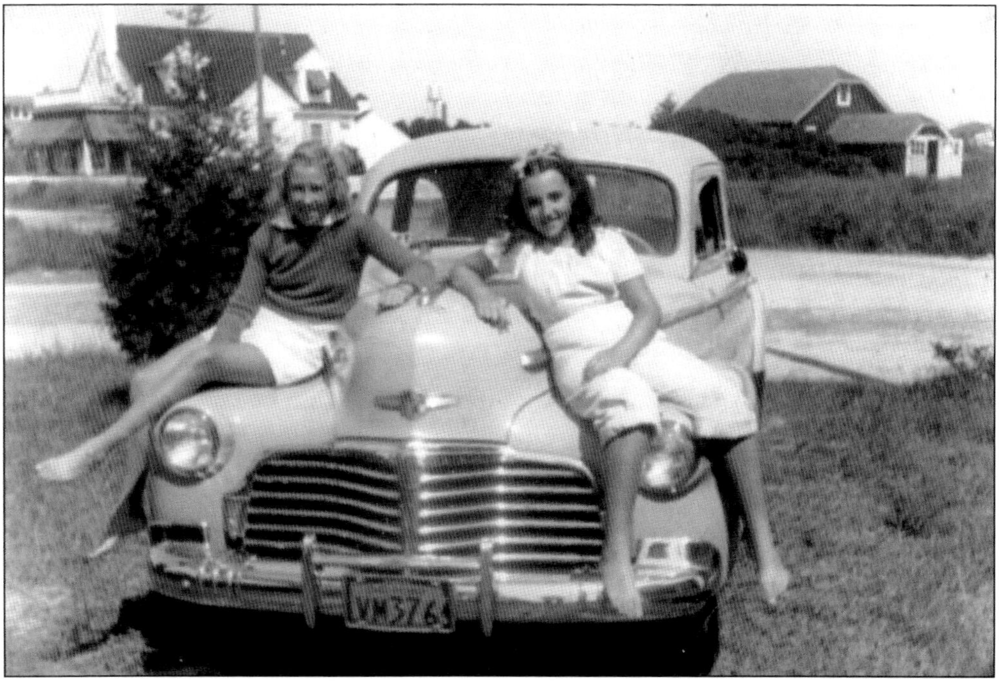

Because of gas rationing during the war, this 1940 Chevrolet would be tucked up on the lawn for the duration of a visitor's stay, but people could easily get around Stone Harbor by foot. This picture was taken in the summer of 1942.

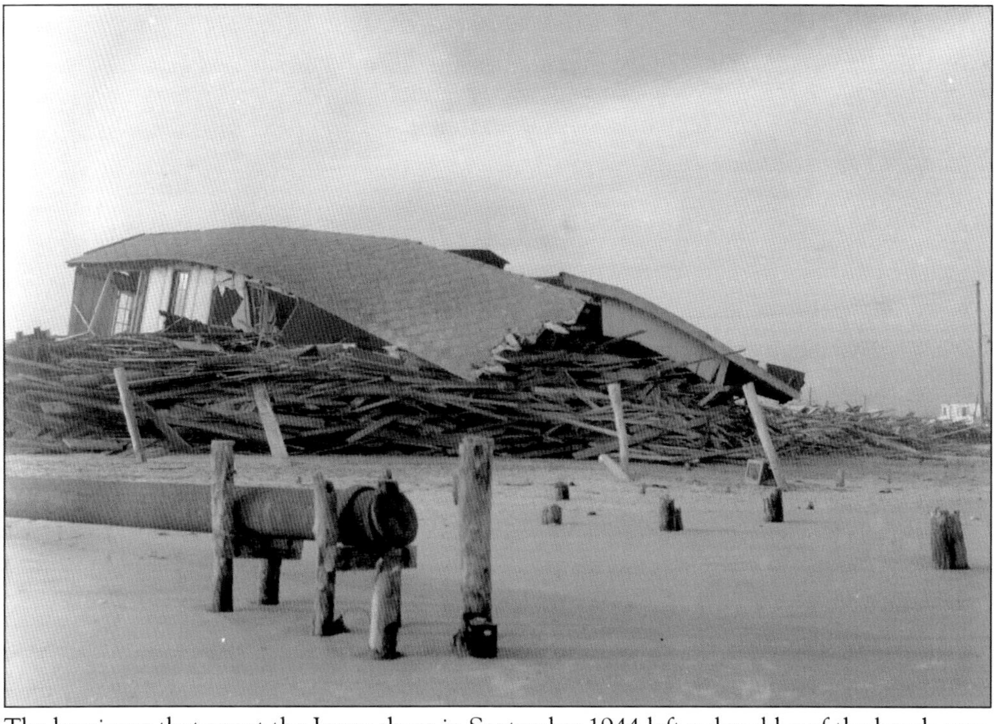

The hurricane that swept the Jersey shore in September 1944 left a shambles of the beach area. This view shows the remains of a beachfront home.

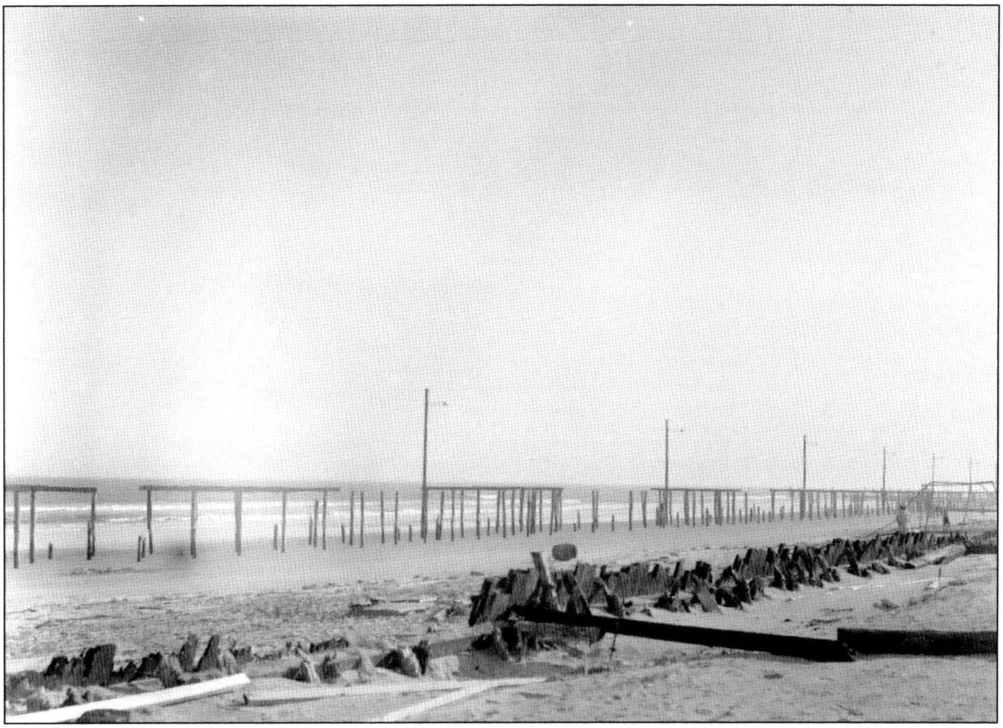

Pictured is all that was left of the boardwalk after the 1944 storm. Along with the boardwalk, two fishing piers were wiped out. They were never rebuilt.

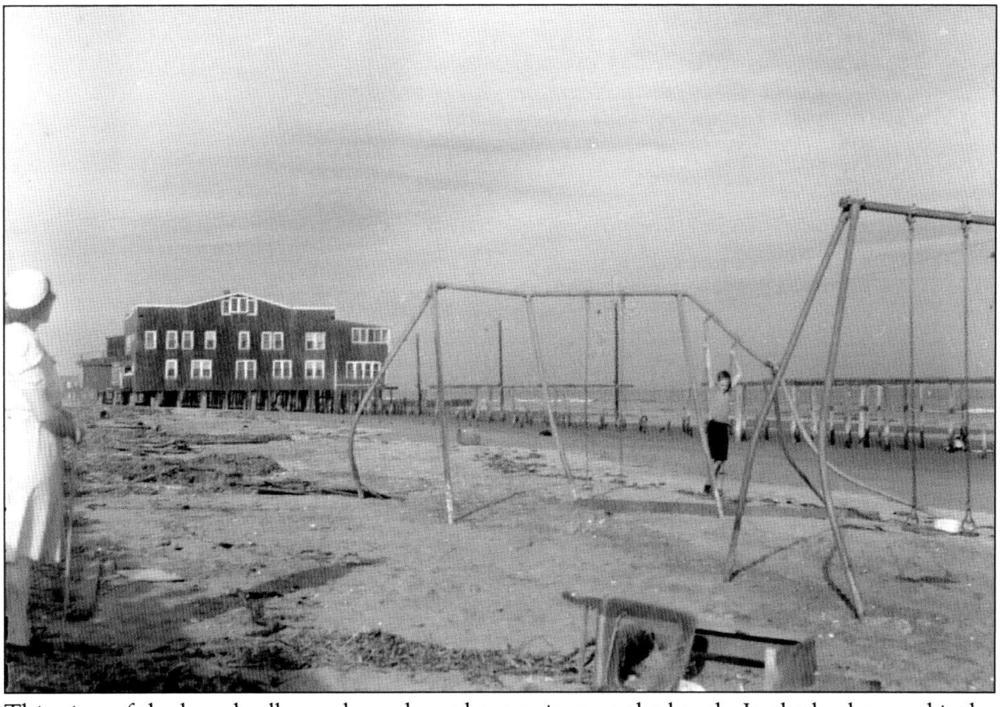

This view of the boardwalk wreckage shows bent swings on the beach. In the background is the 97th Street rooming house, which survived until the storm of 1962.

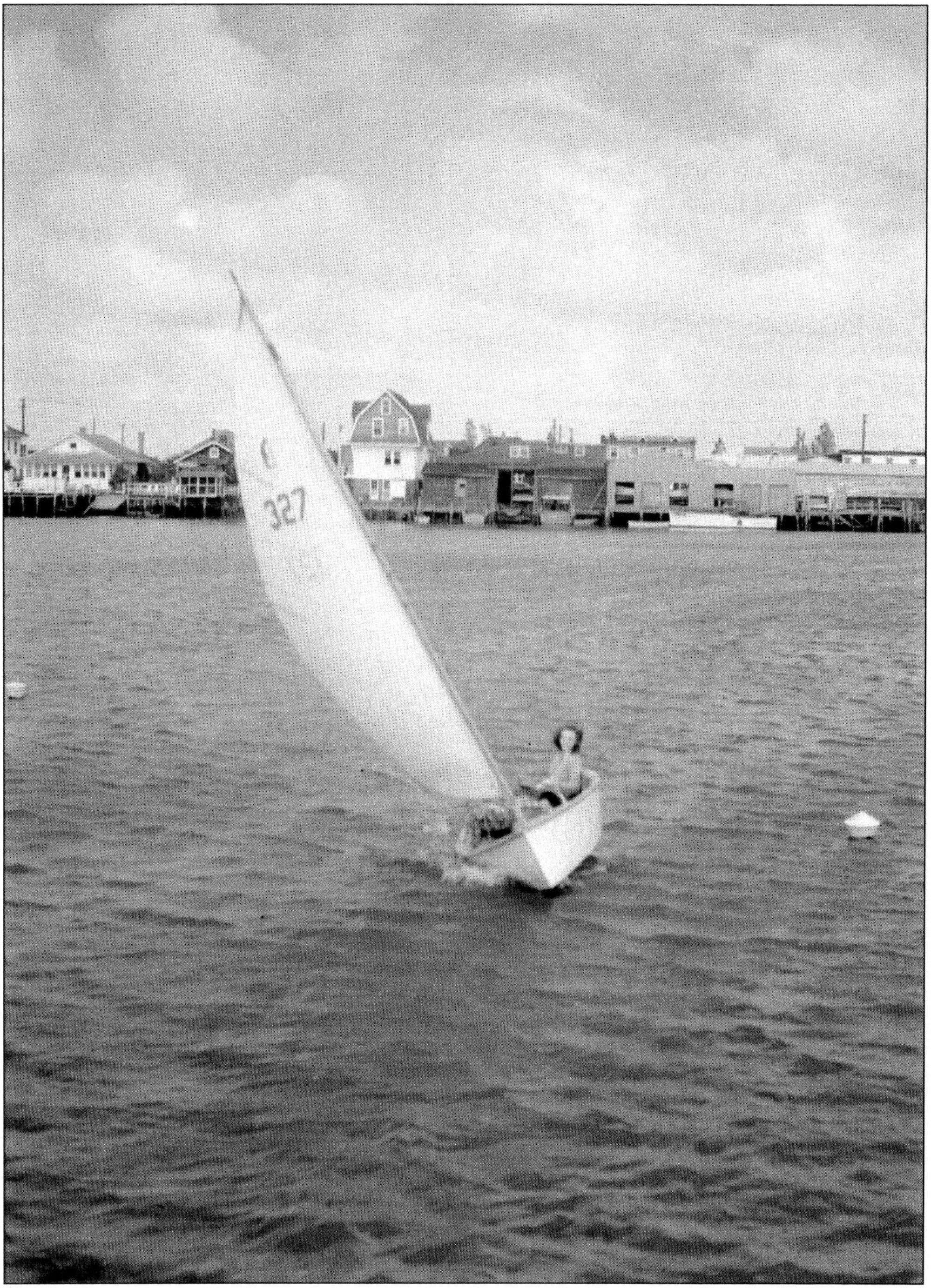

Penguin-class sailboats such as this one were common in Stone Harbor. They were one of three types of boat raced at the yacht club.

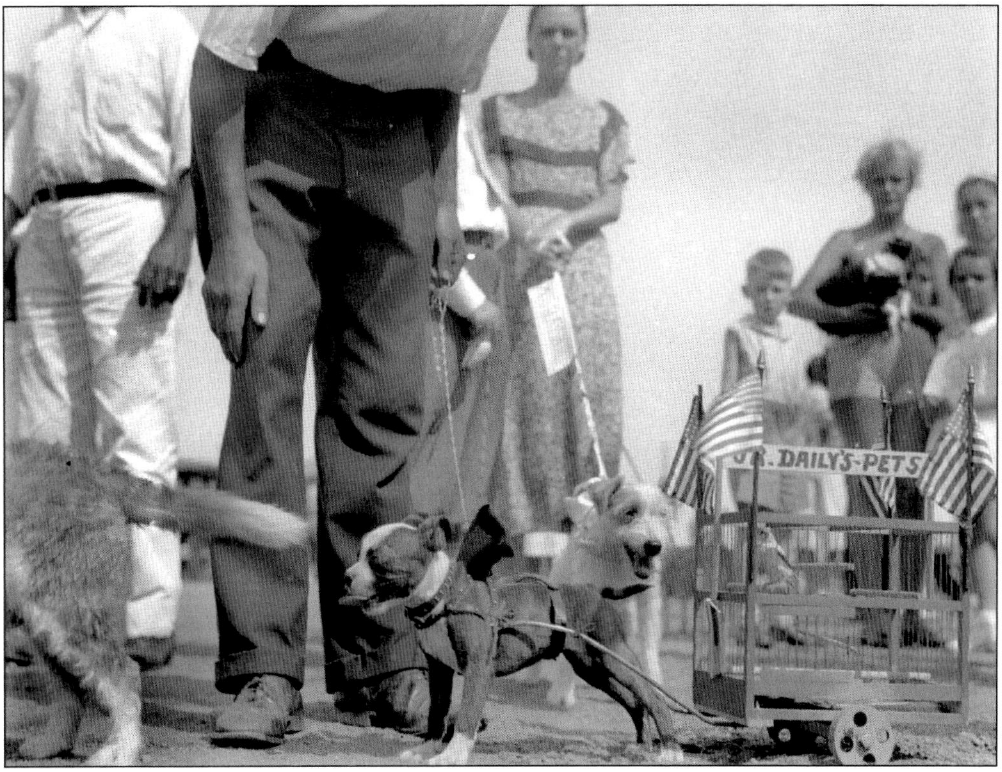

Town activities were extended to pets, whose proud owners led them in the annual pet parade.

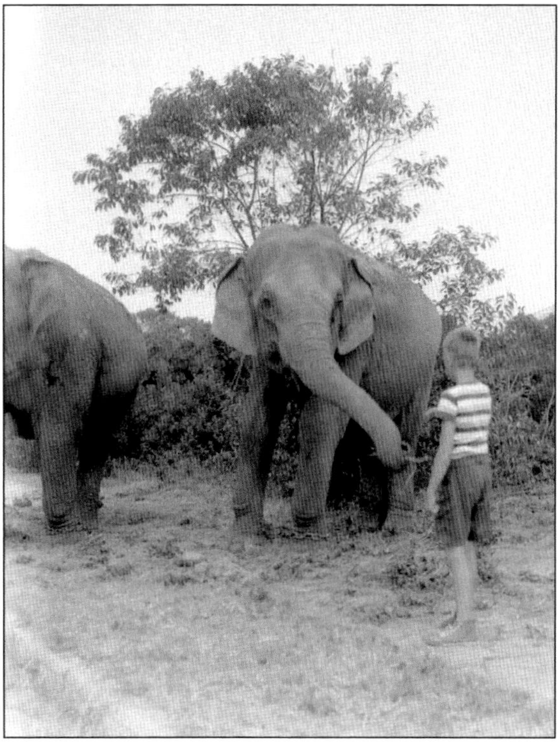

Elephants were an uncommon sight in Stone Harbor, except during the annual Hunt Brothers' Circus.

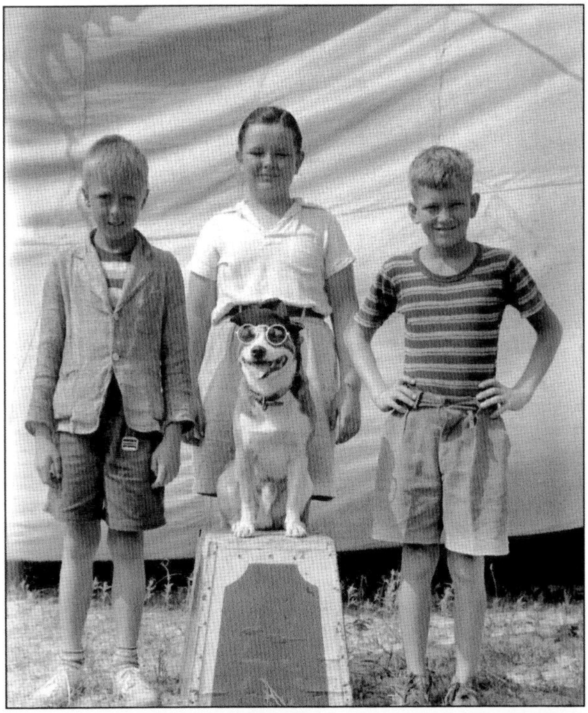

More common than circus elephants (but worthy of a photograph) is this caped and sunglassed circus dog.

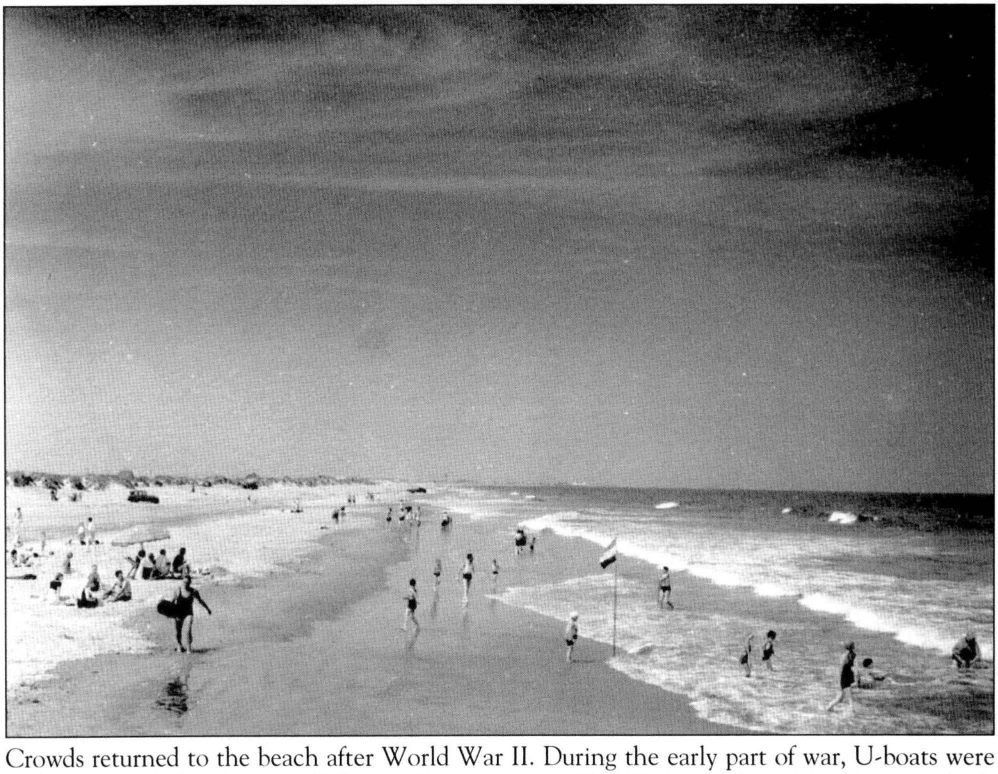

Crowds returned to the beach after World War II. During the early part of war, U-boats were sinking enough freighters in Delaware Bay to create oil spills in southern New Jersey, which made the beach an unpopular place to be.

The dory gets a motor—no more rowing. With the gas rationing of World War II, the number of motorboats decreased. After the war, motorboats began to reappear.

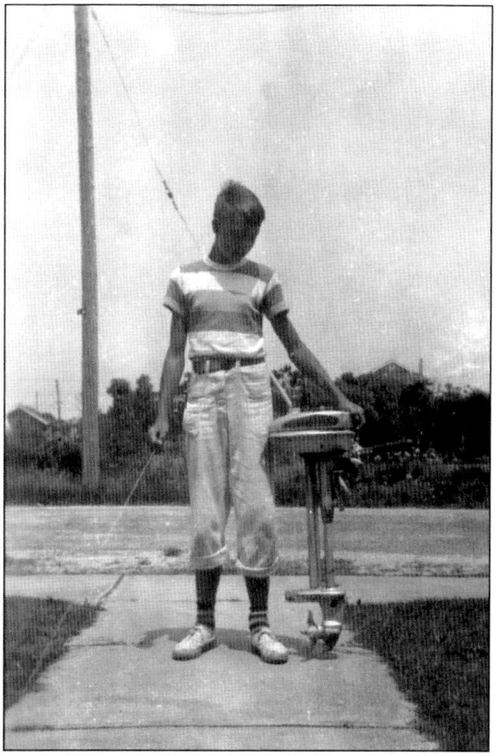

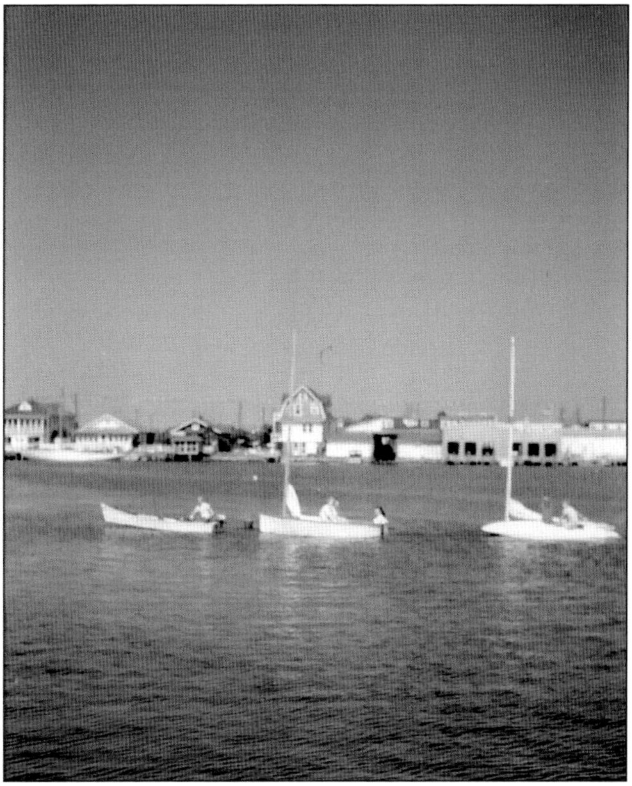

A little dory with a new outboard tows a Penguin and a Moth.

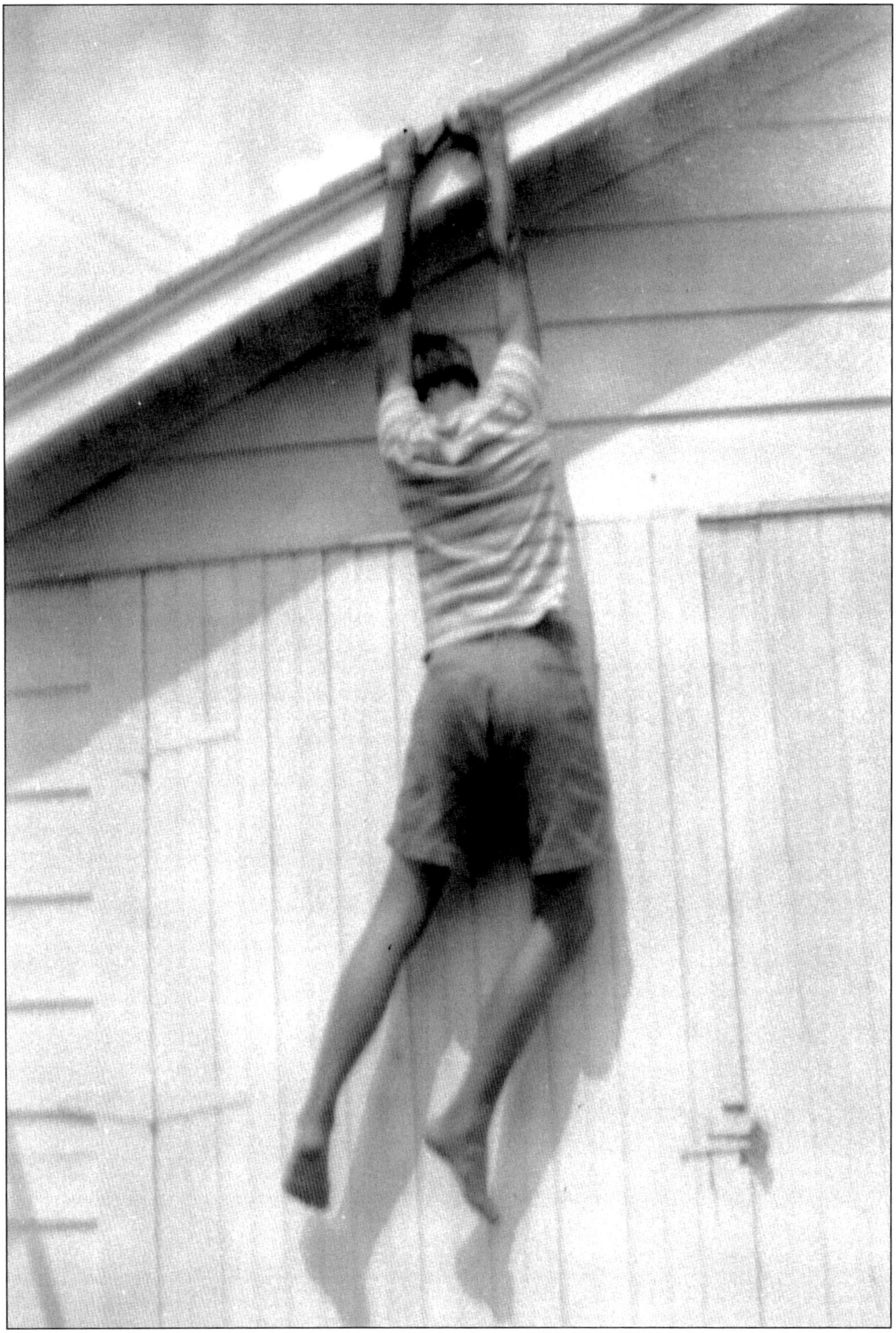

When you have had enough of swimming, fishing, rowing, or cycling, there is another popular summertime activity—just hanging around.

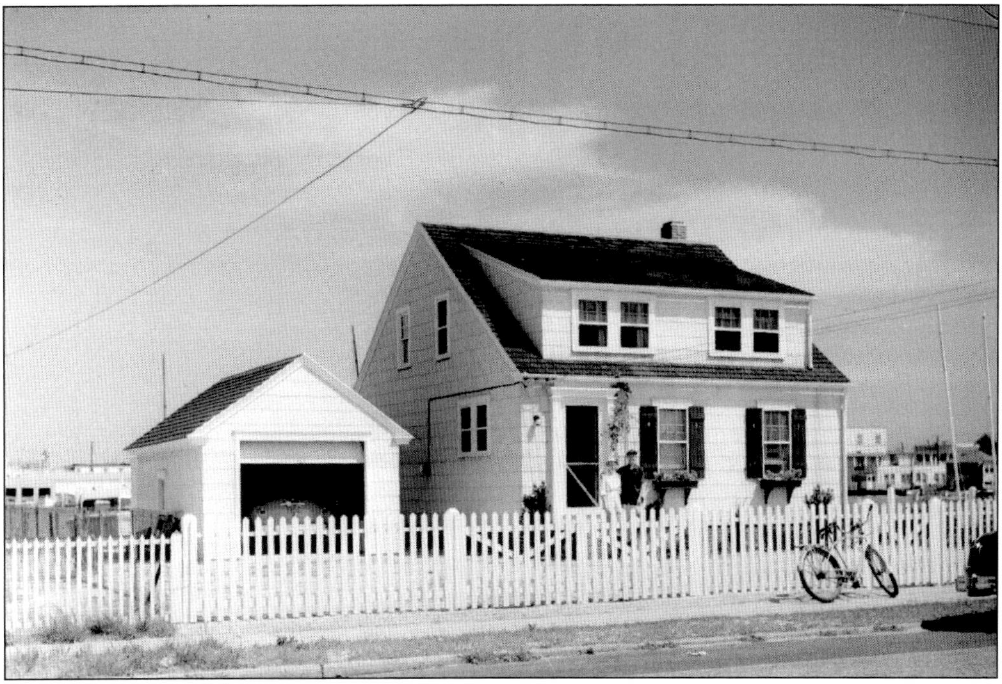

A Cape Cod–style cottage, built in the 1940s, is shown complete with a garage and even a white picket fence.

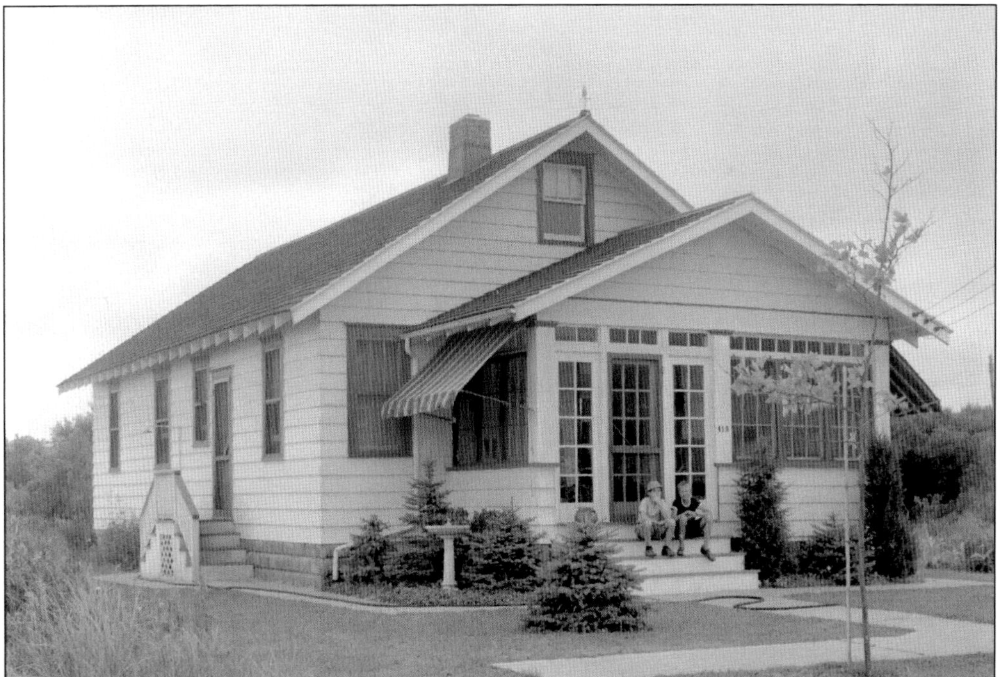

The Colebin, with its new plantings, sits in stark contrast to the wildlife around it. In this back bay area, street improvements only extended to a developed property, resulting in an abrupt ending of the sidewalk at the property line.

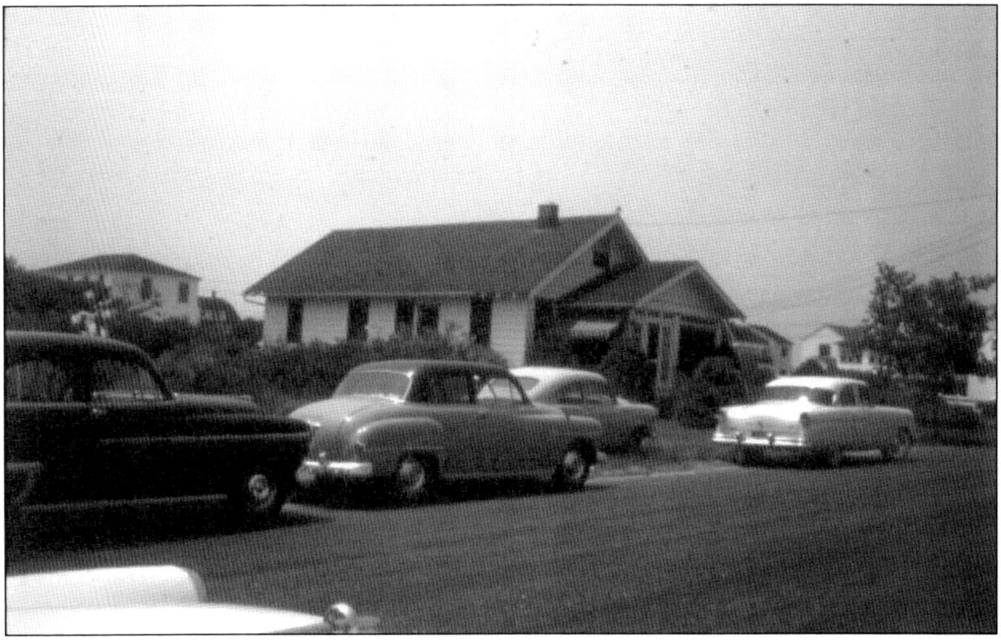

In the prosperous 1950s, people were able to afford more than one automobile. This shot shows an early view of what is now familiar to visitors—streets crowded with cars.

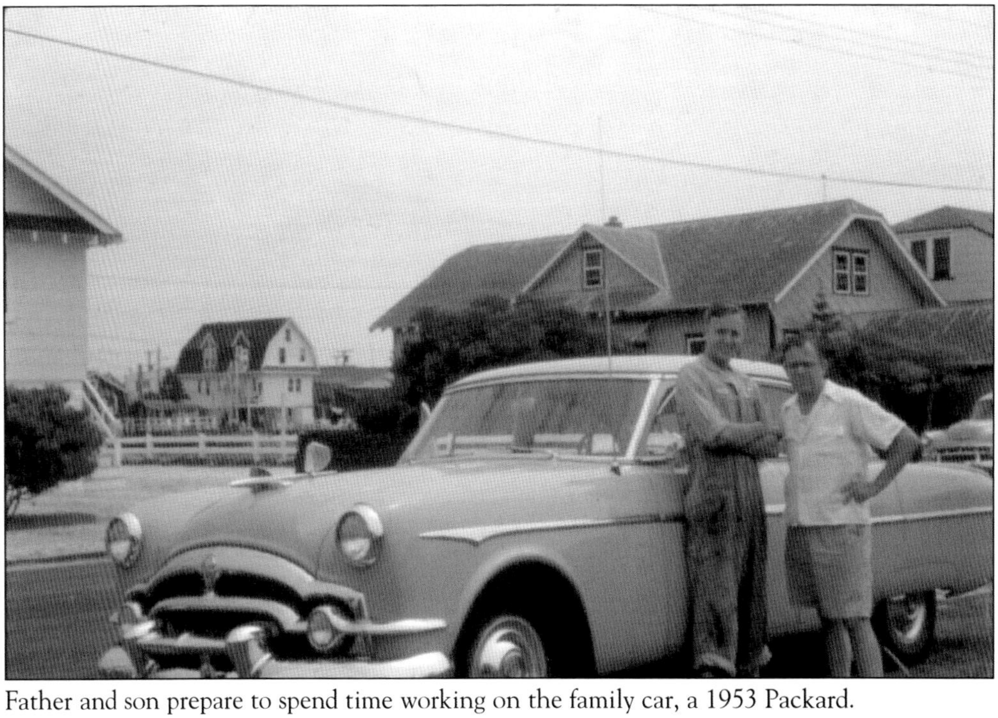

Father and son prepare to spend time working on the family car, a 1953 Packard.

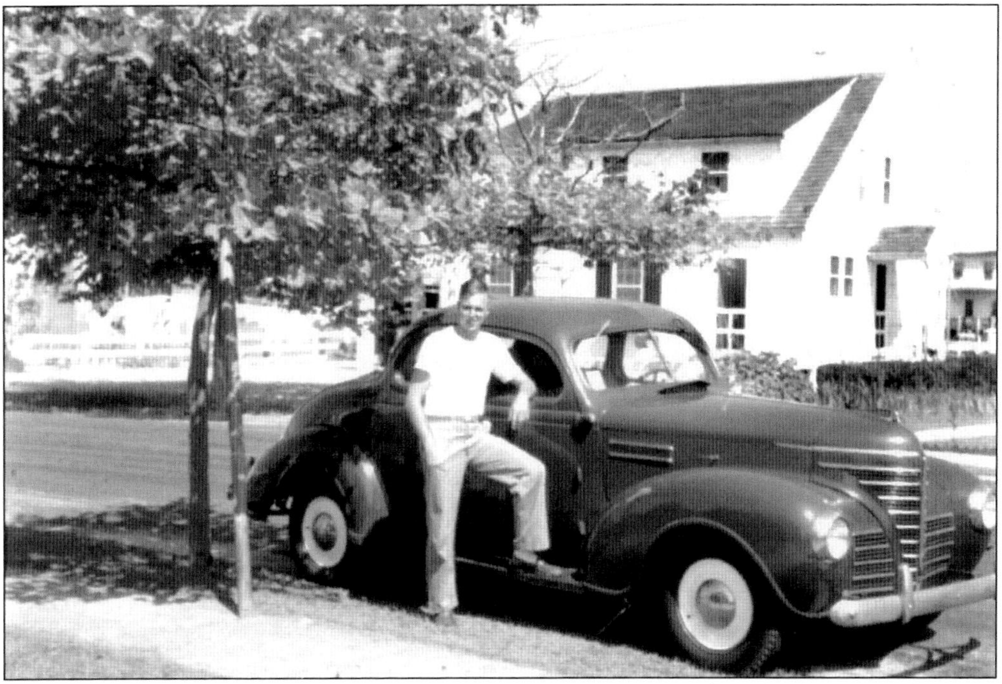

With my father's savings from his job at the Esso station, he paid $50 for this 1939 Plymouth coupe, his first car. He had his heart set on the 1939 Packard convertible, but it was $50 more than the Plymouth—$50 more than he had.

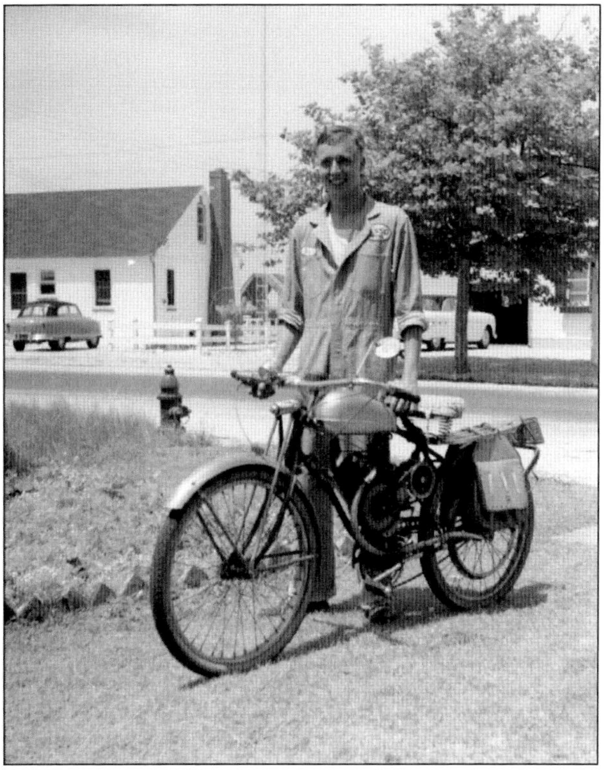

With cheap gas, even bicycles had a motor, as seen with this 1950s Whizzer motorbike.

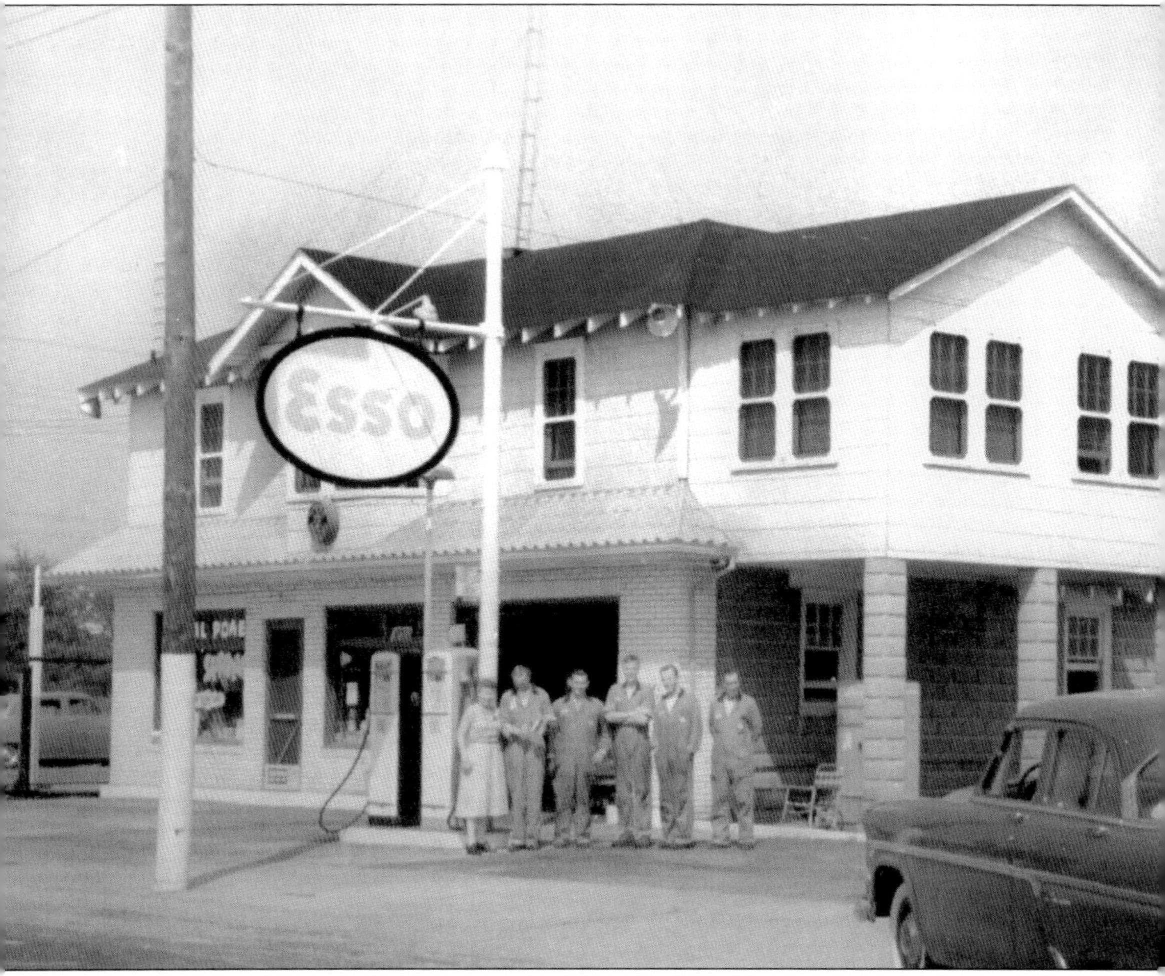

Matthew's Esso was a full-service station with an ideal location behind Springer's Ice Cream, where everyone hung out. My father, who always enjoyed cars, worked at this station during summers in the early 1950s, as did other young men before being drafted for the Korean War. The owners were Mr. and Mrs. George Matthews, shown on the left.

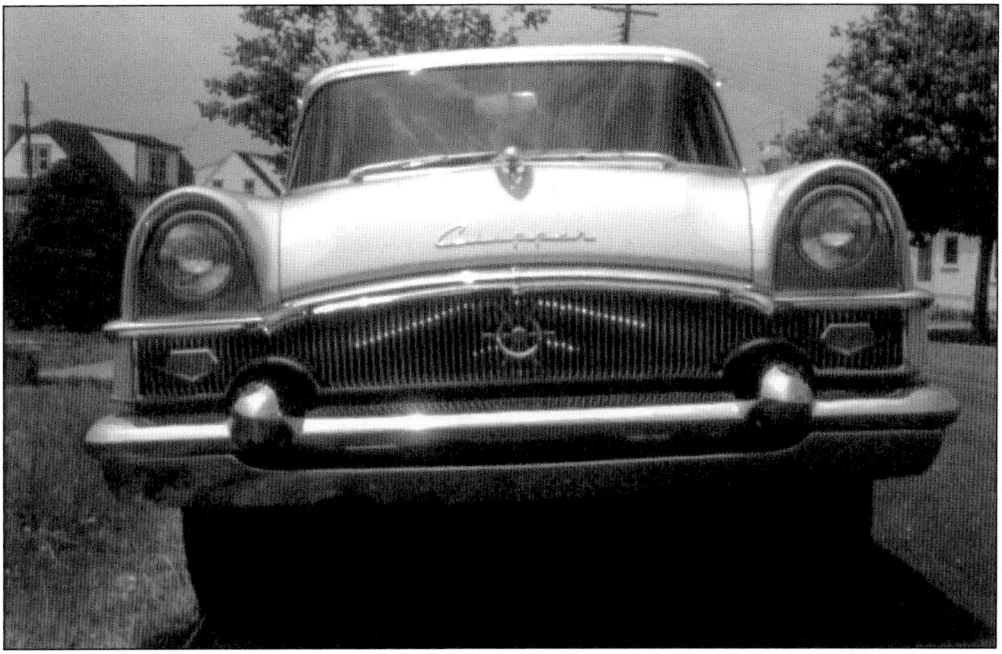

The fascination with all the chrome of the 1950s automobile extended to my grandfather's photography. Here the grill of the 1956 Packard serves as a study in modern styling.

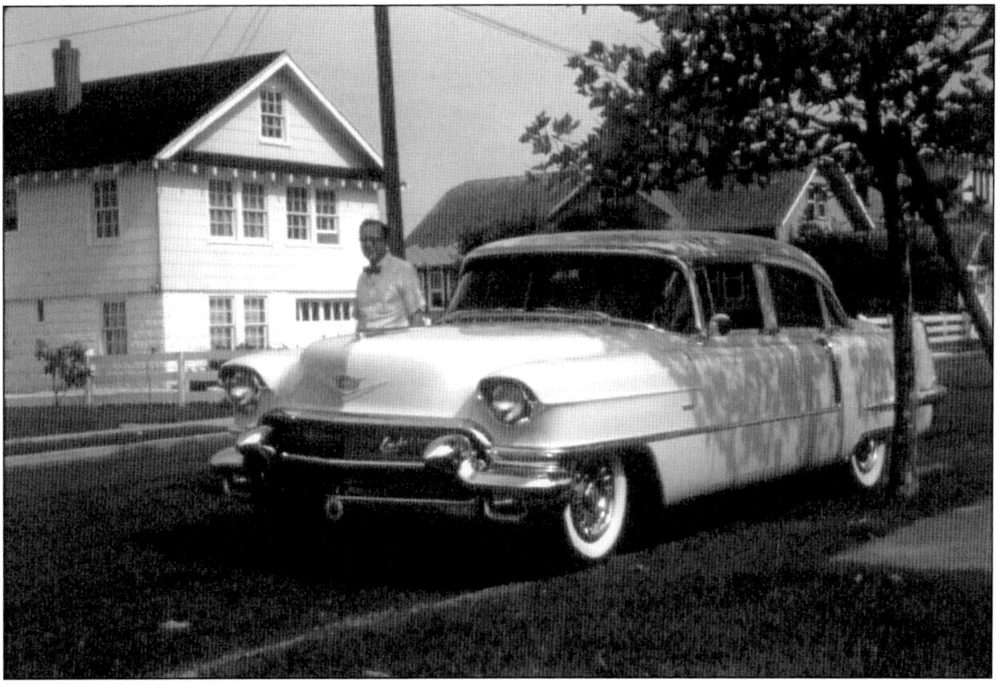

The Packard is out, and the Cadillac is in. This giant Cadillac was so large that curb feelers were added to it.

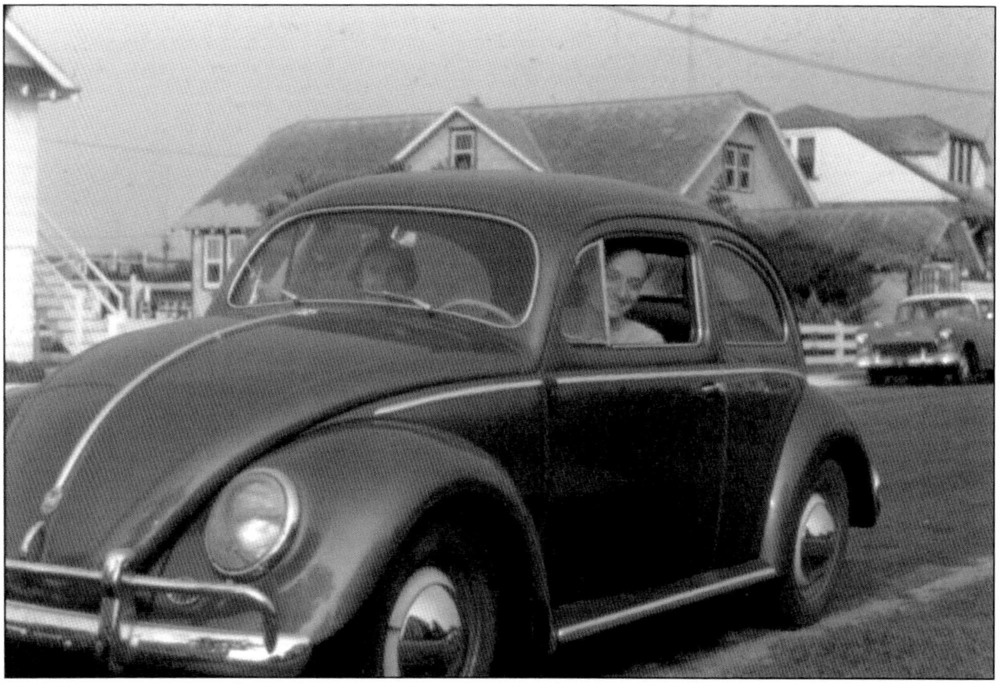

In the 1950s, the Beetle made its appearance everywhere in the United States—even in Stone Harbor. Johnny Falco of Philadelphia shows off his brand-new 1953 model, driving it down to the shore from Philadelphia.

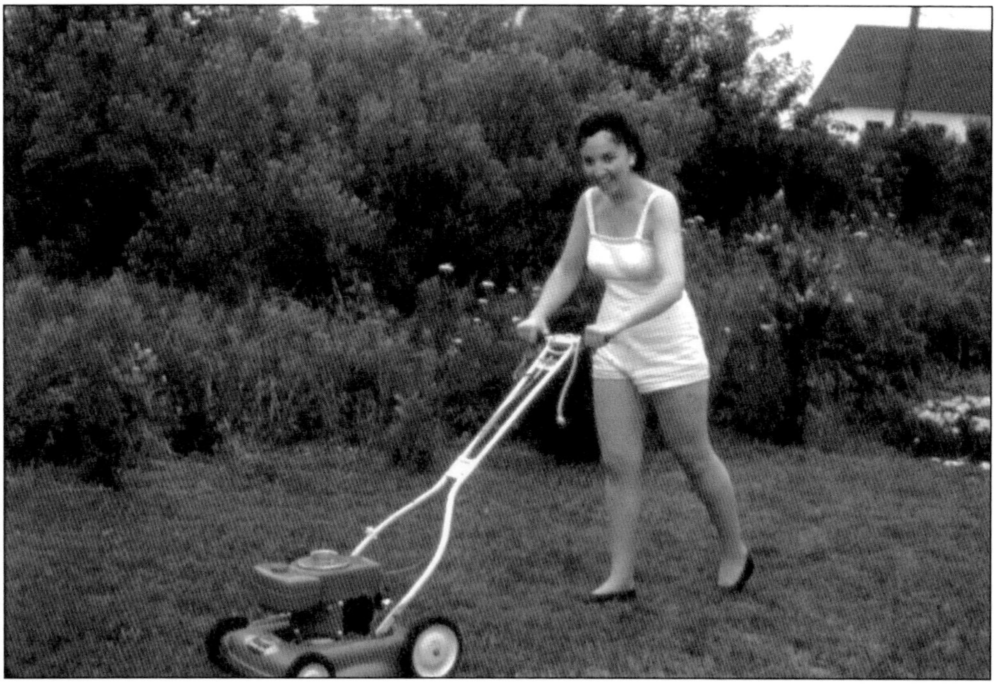

Even the lawn mower became motorized and reduced time and labor. More importantly, it was a prop to pose my aunt mowing the lawn in her bathing suit.

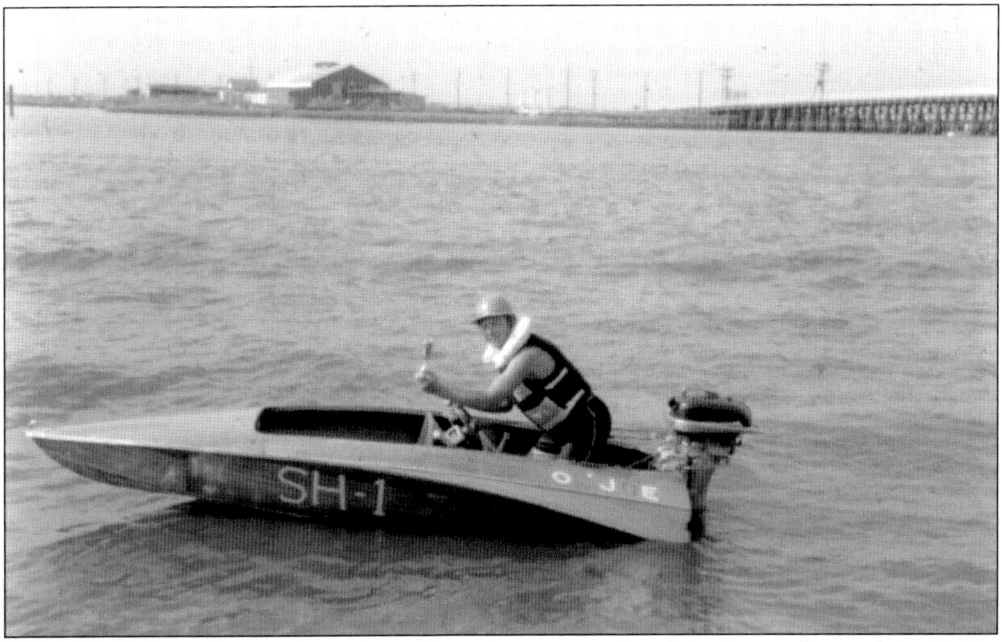

Carroll Brooke, showing off a very small trophy, poses in his father's speedboat of the 1930s. Racing speedboats became popular in many communities along the Jersey coast in the 1930s, with a revival after the war.

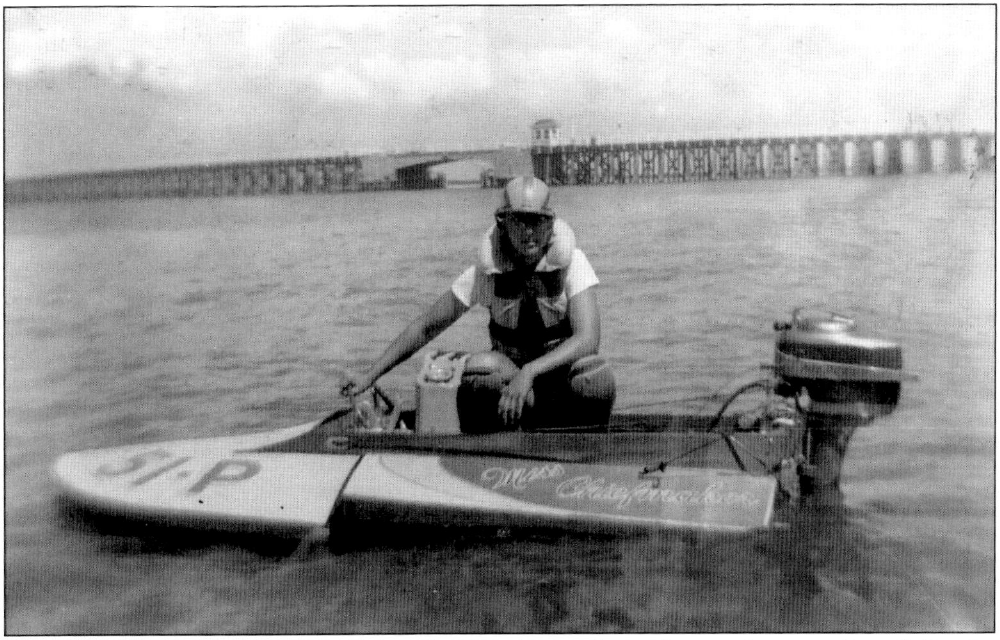

The race boat of the 1950s continues the Brooke family tradition of racing. Carroll Brooke replaced the older speedboat with an updated 1950s model in hopes of bigger trophies.

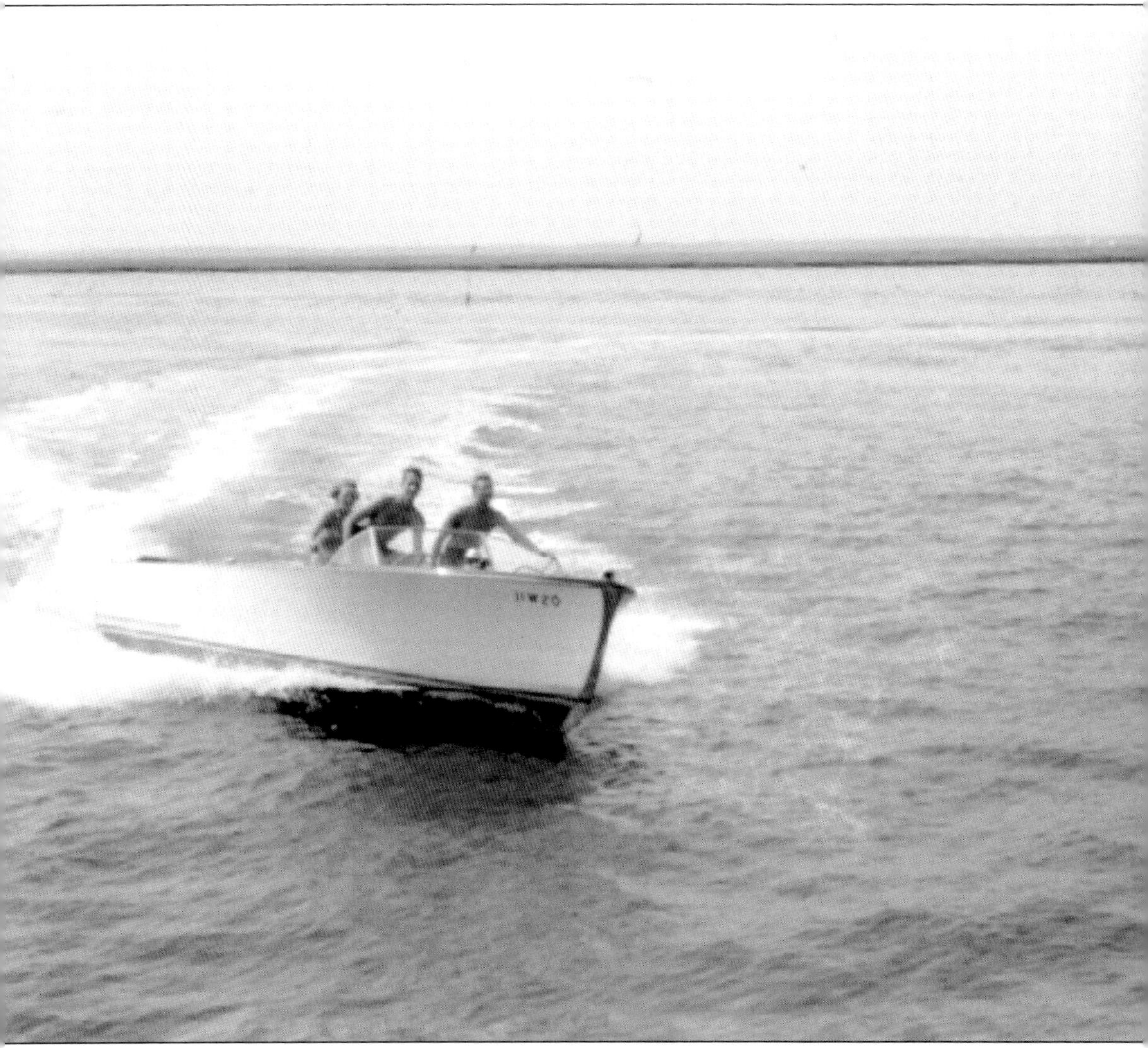

The thrill of these three young boaters in their newly purchased inboard speedboat is evident in this photograph. Owned by the Brooke family, the boat was used daily for water-skiing until the engine seized one day.

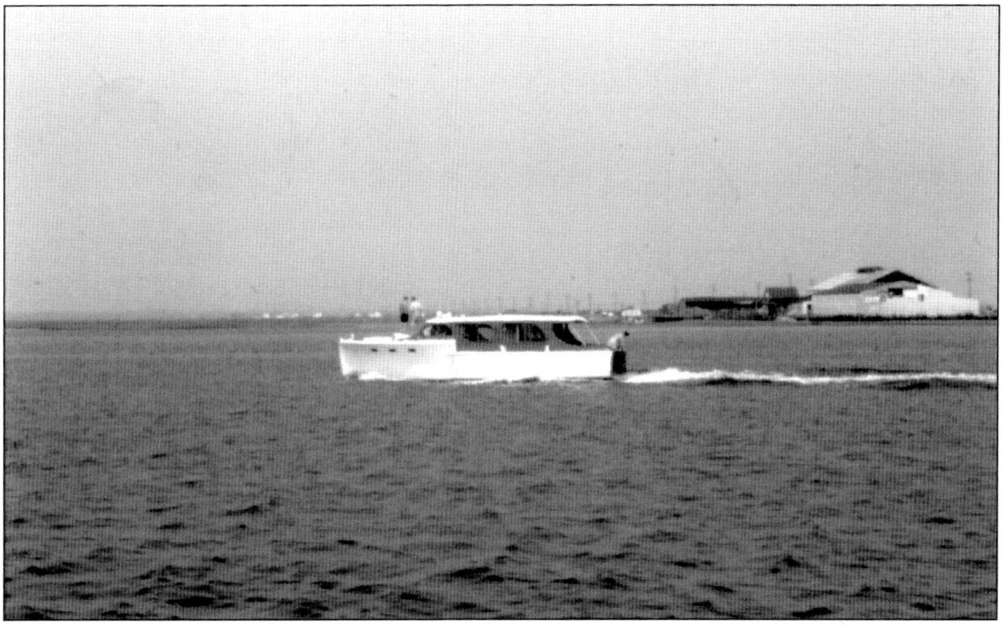

Typical of the many beautiful wooden cabin cruisers in Stone Harbor during the 1950s, this Wheeler 36 heads toward Hereford's Inlet and past the lumberyard.

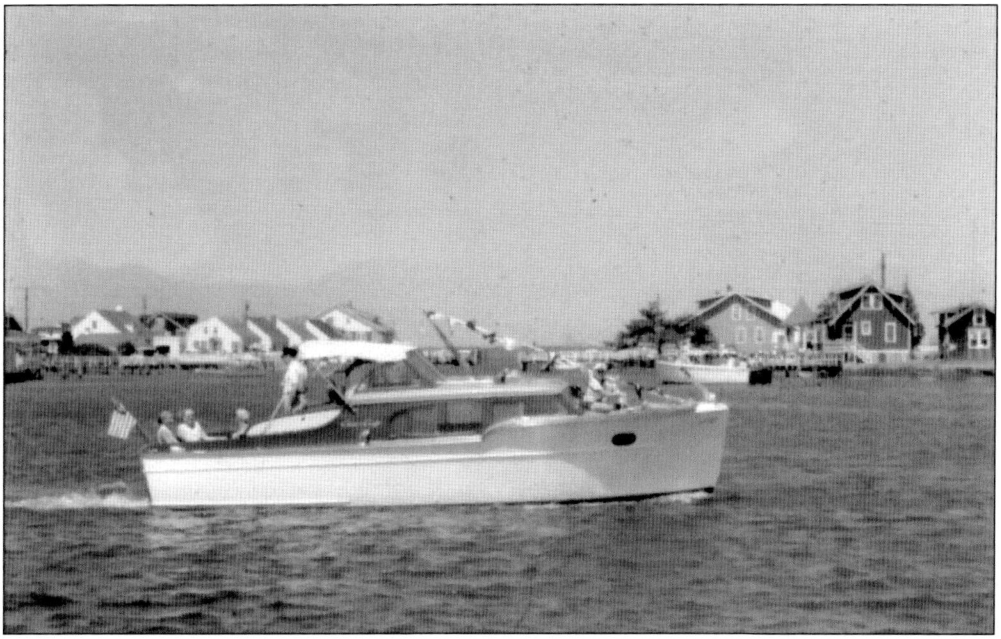

The Parade of the Fleet was held annually on the Fourth of July. Members of the Stone Harbor Yacht Club would bedeck their boats with flags and parade through all the basins. The parade began early in Stone Harbor's history and continued into the early 1970s. Seen here in the Stone Harbor Basin is a Chris Craft cabin cruiser.

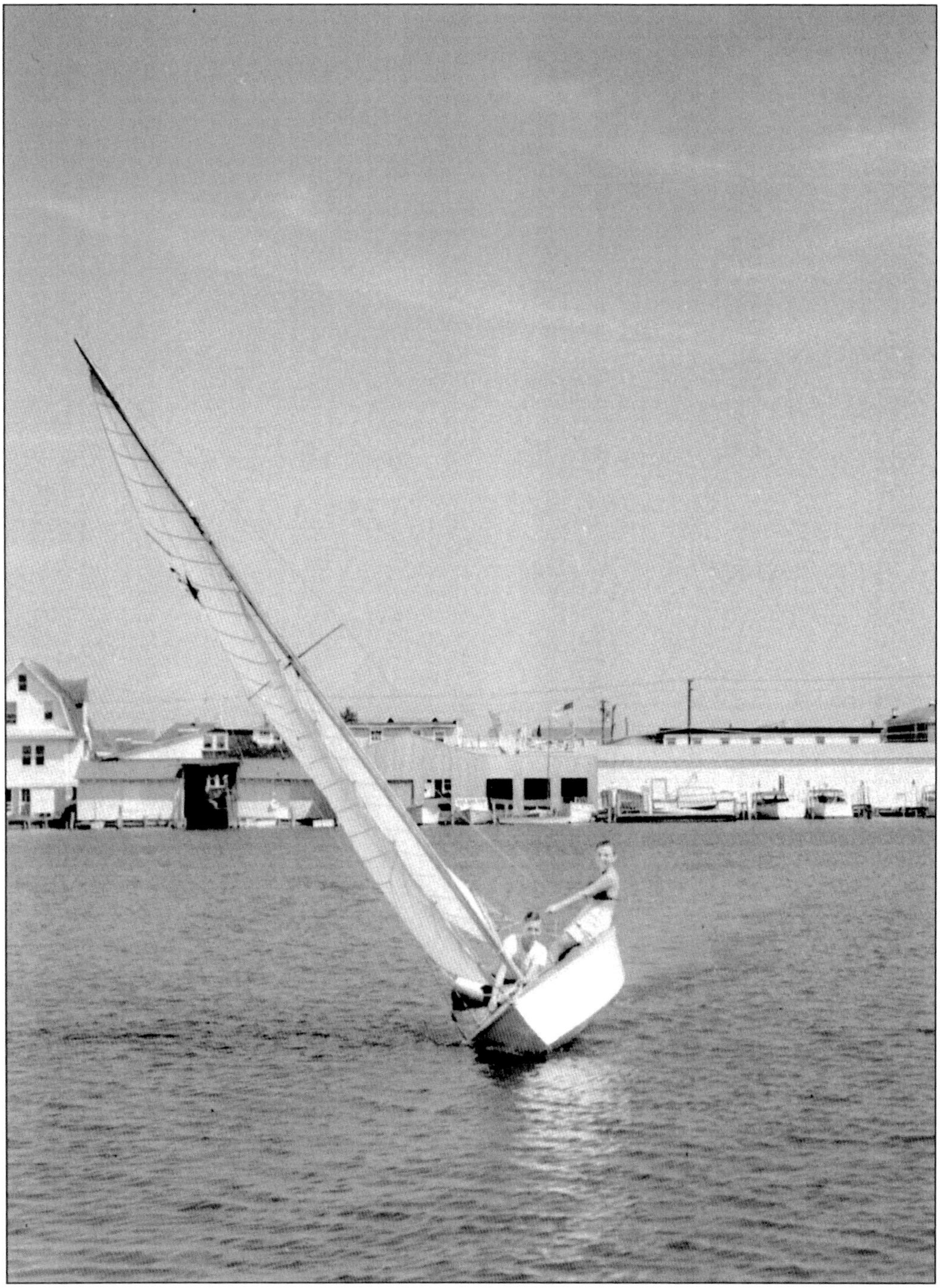

In the 1950s, our Penguin was replaced by this Comet. Stone Harbor was home to the Comet-class boat. It was designed by the famous Owen Stevens, who was part of Sparkman and Stevens of New England. Stevens designed many of the America's Cup sailboats. During the Great Depression, specifications of the boat required it to be available in kit form. Comet No. 1 and the original fleet made its debut in Stone Harbor. This boat was important enough to be included in Stone Harbor's emblem.

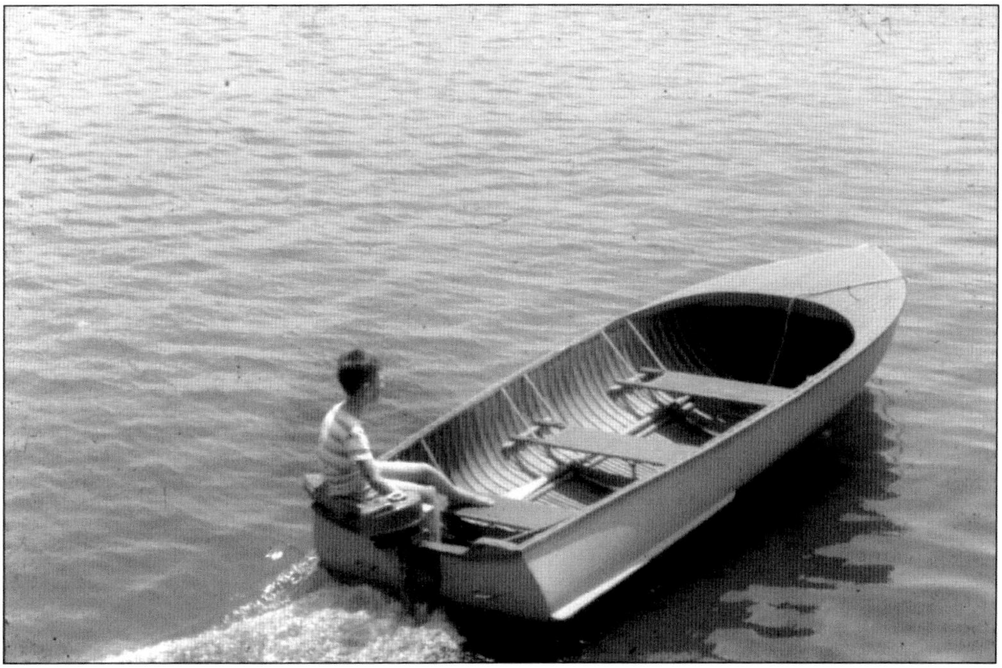

John Noone was nine years old when he set out on a solitary adventure, taking the helm of his first boat, a 16 foot Pennyan, which was framed in mahogany and covered with a green heavy canvas. This type of little outboard was commonly seen around Stone Harbor for fishing and short excursions.

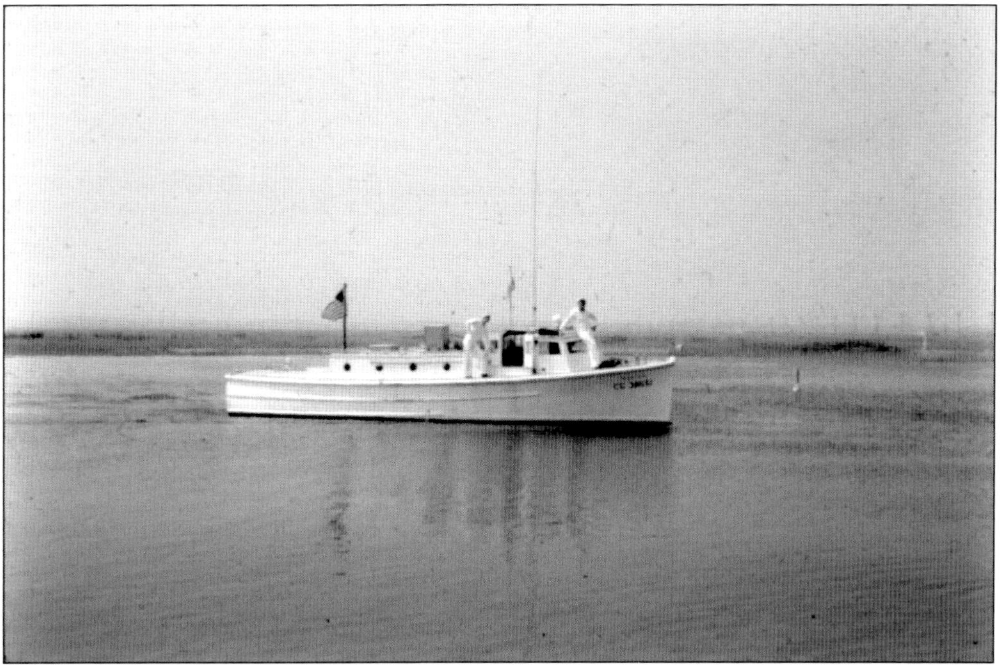

The Coast Guard regularly patrolled the inland waterway from its headquarters in Cape May. This 1950s photograph shows the typical Coast Guard boat of the day.

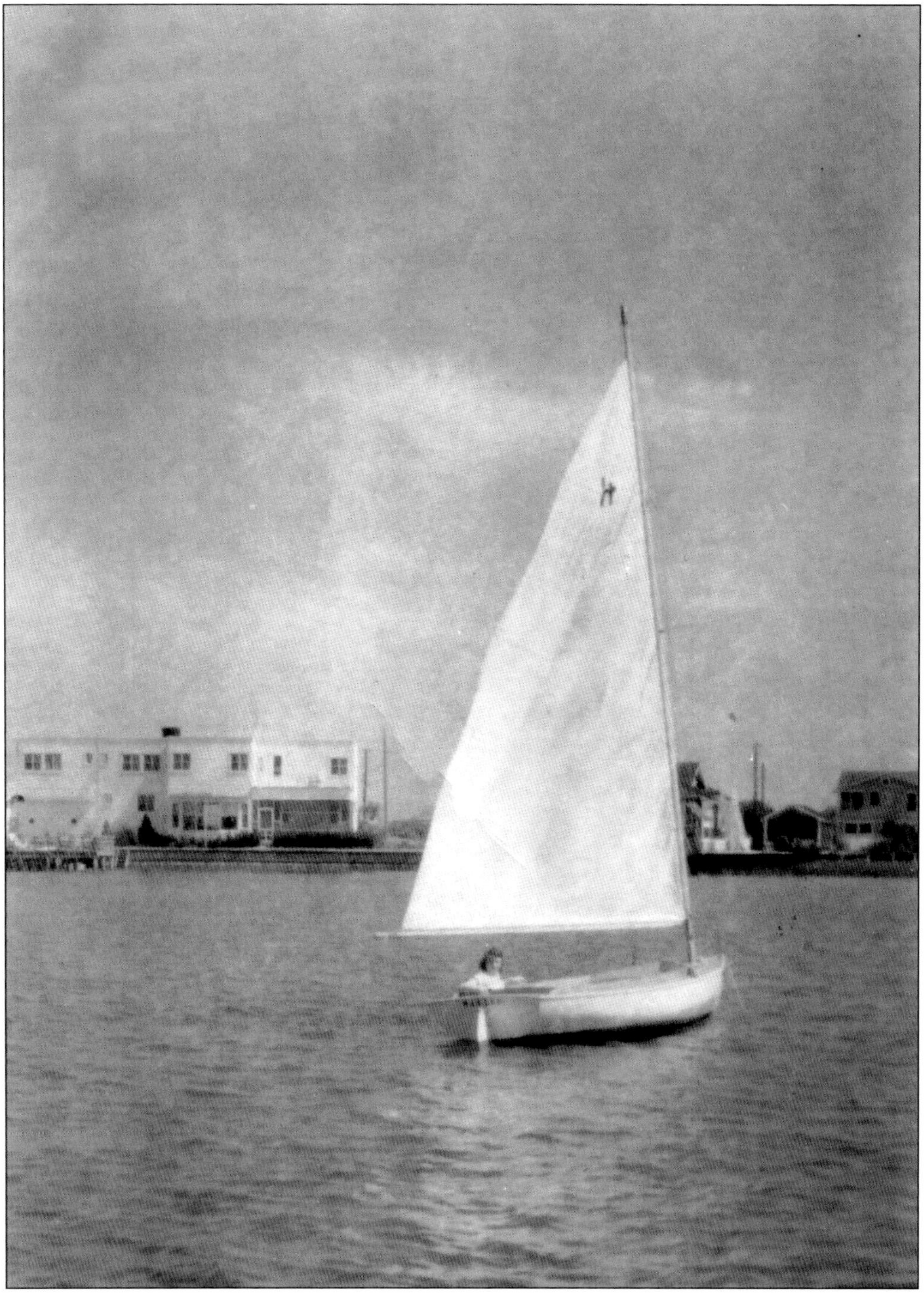

My mother poses in her new catboat in Pleasure Bay. This type of boat was built in New Bedford, Massachusetts, and was more prevalent in New England than in New Jersey. This catboat was bought by my grandfather, as he felt the wide beam would be safer to sail than the more common Comets and Penguins. In the background is a very large and very good example of an Art Modern house, which was built in the late 1940s and still stands today.

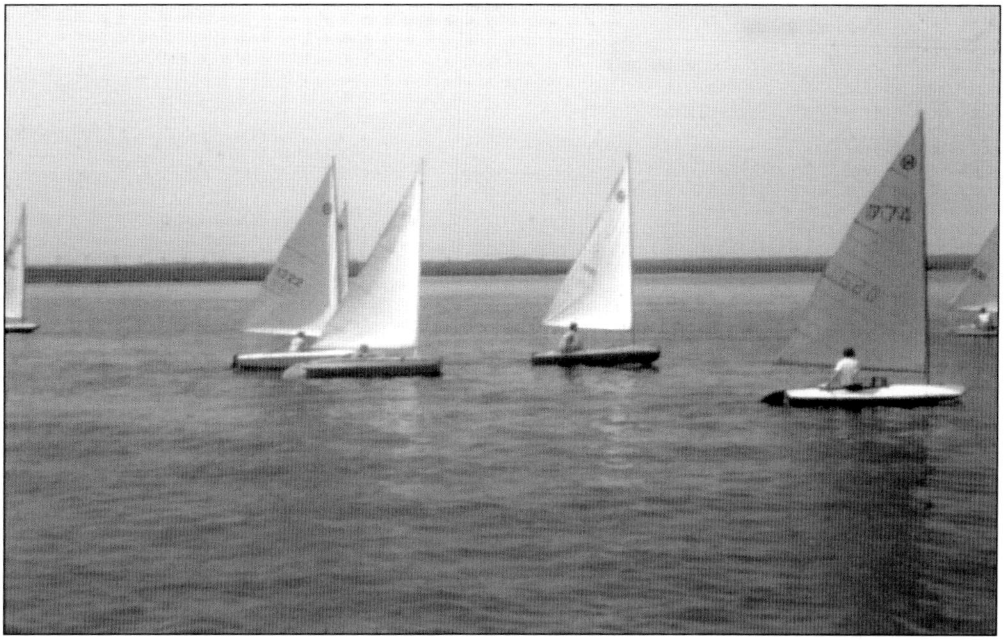

Moth boats are shown here during a race. Until the advent of the Sailfish and Sunfish of the 1960s, Moths were the smallest boats to be raced.

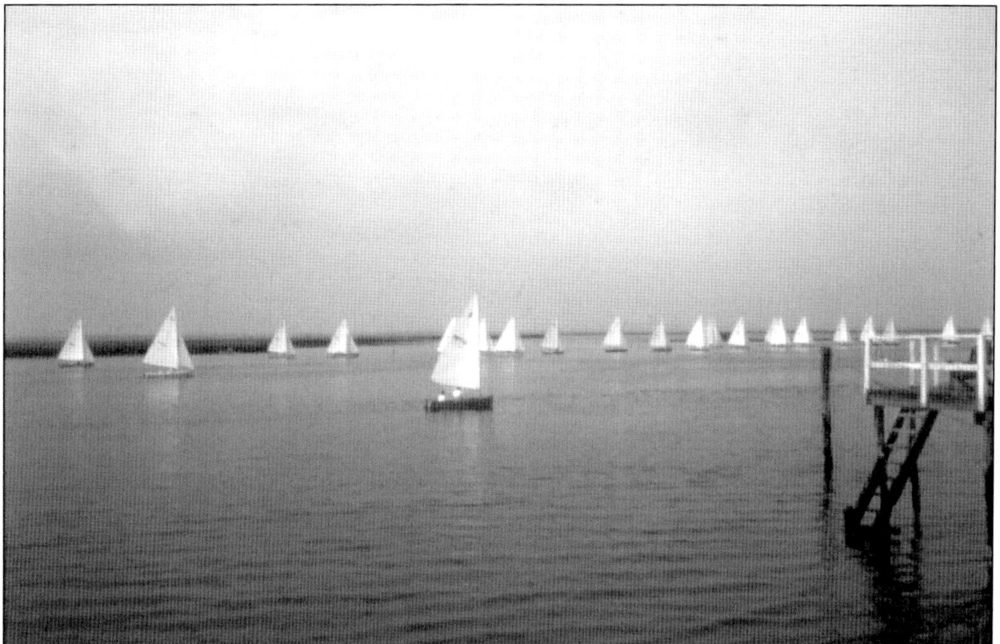

Like swans floating over a pond, these Comet-class sailboats are gliding in line across the channel. Out of line like the ugly duckling is a lone Penguin-class sailboat.

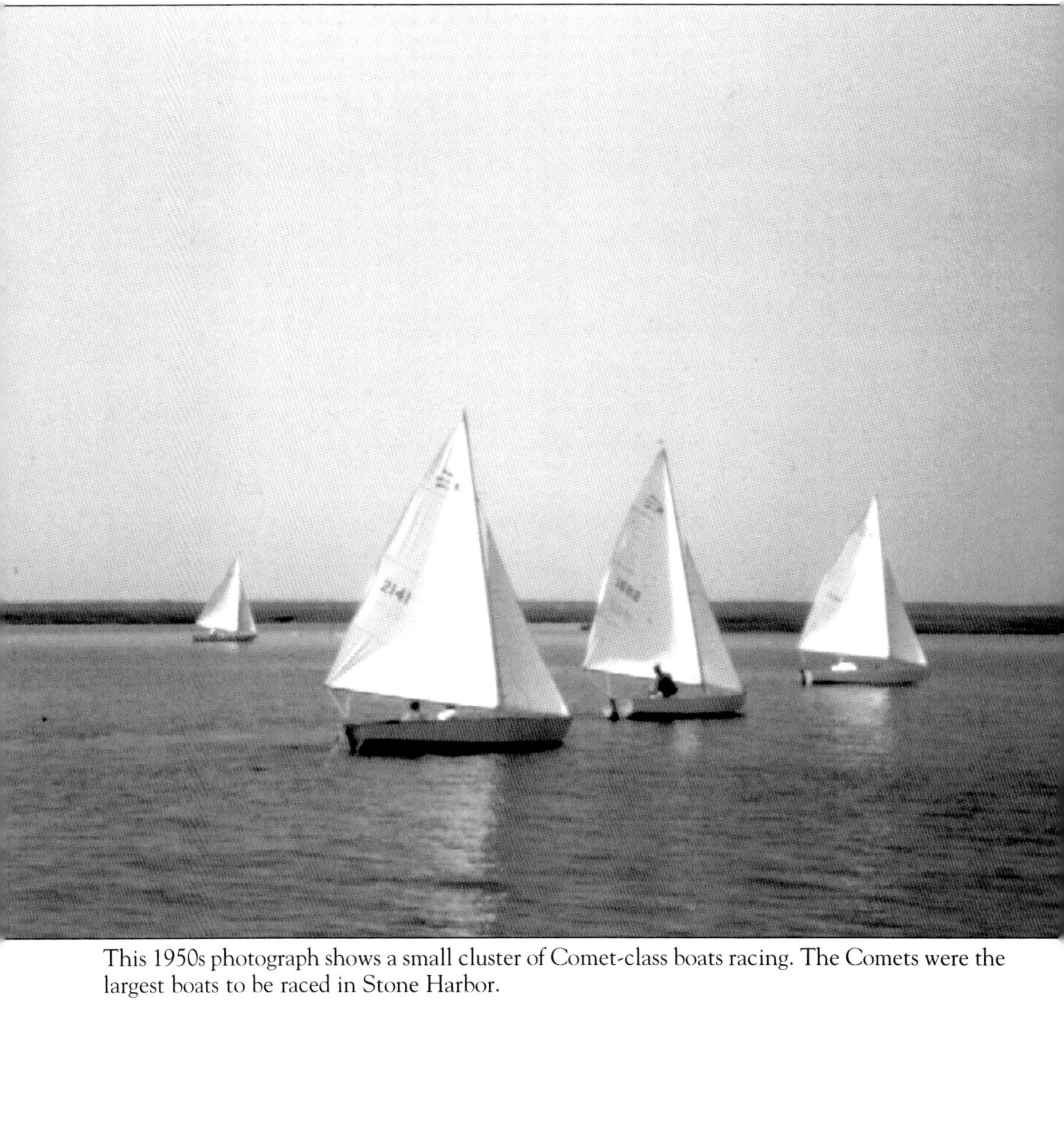

This 1950s photograph shows a small cluster of Comet-class boats racing. The Comets were the largest boats to be raced in Stone Harbor.

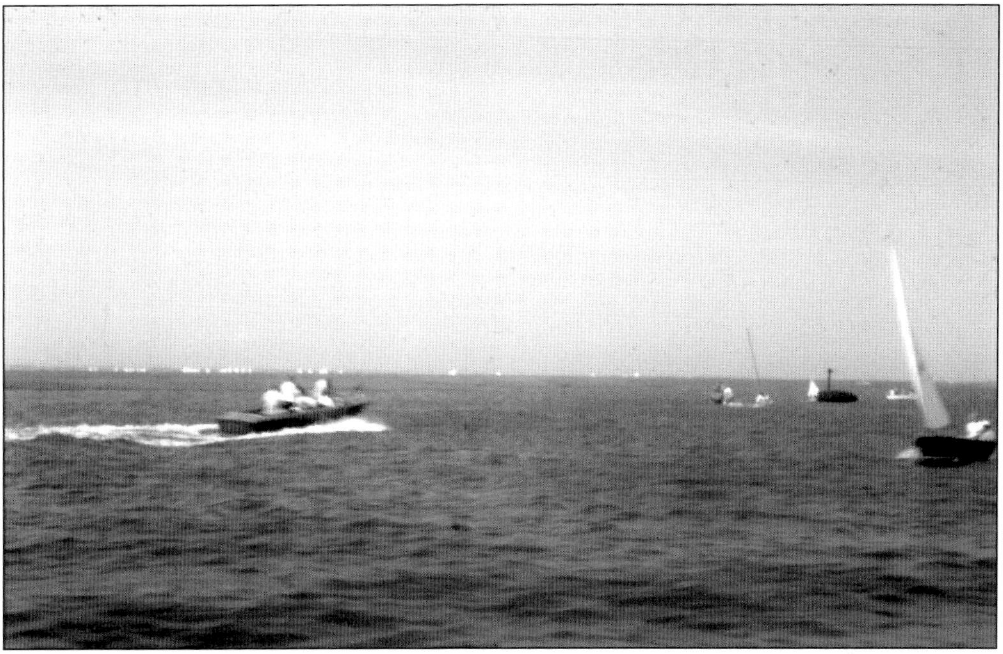

A committee boat, an old mahogany runabout, rushes to help a capsized sailor. The committee boat was there to supervise the race and to help those in distress.

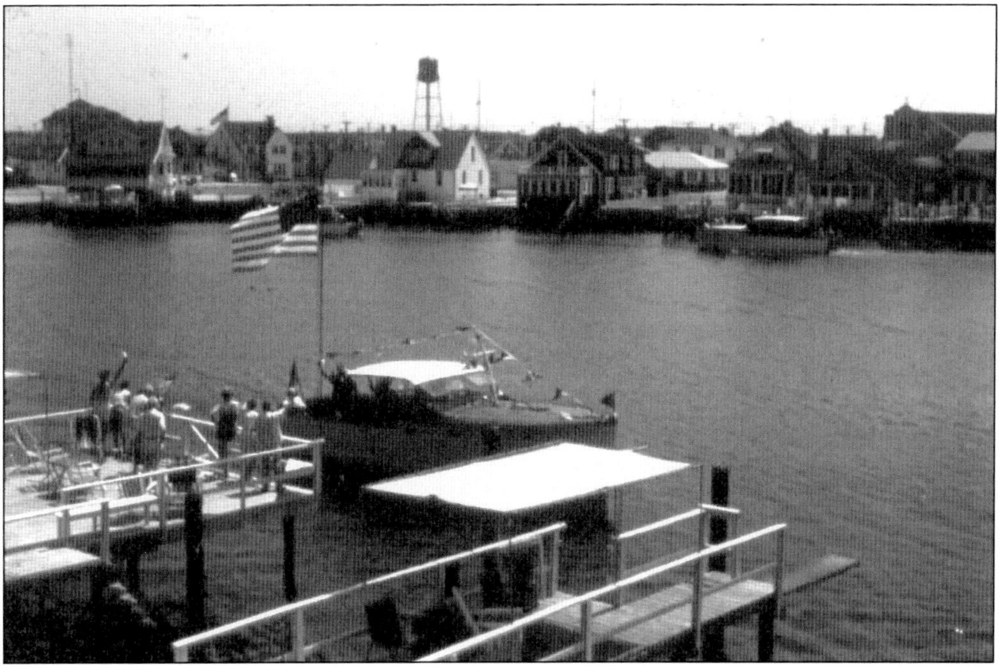

Taken from an upstairs deck, this view of the Stone Harbor Basin shows onlookers waving to a boat passing by during the Parade of the Fleet.

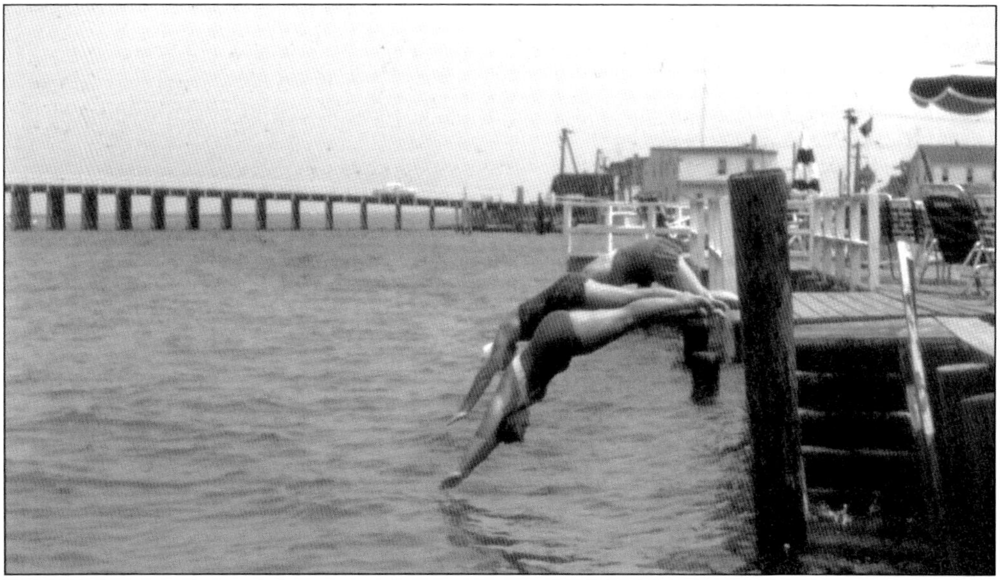

Last one in is a rotten egg. This challenge was usually accepted, as diving from the piers was a popular activity.

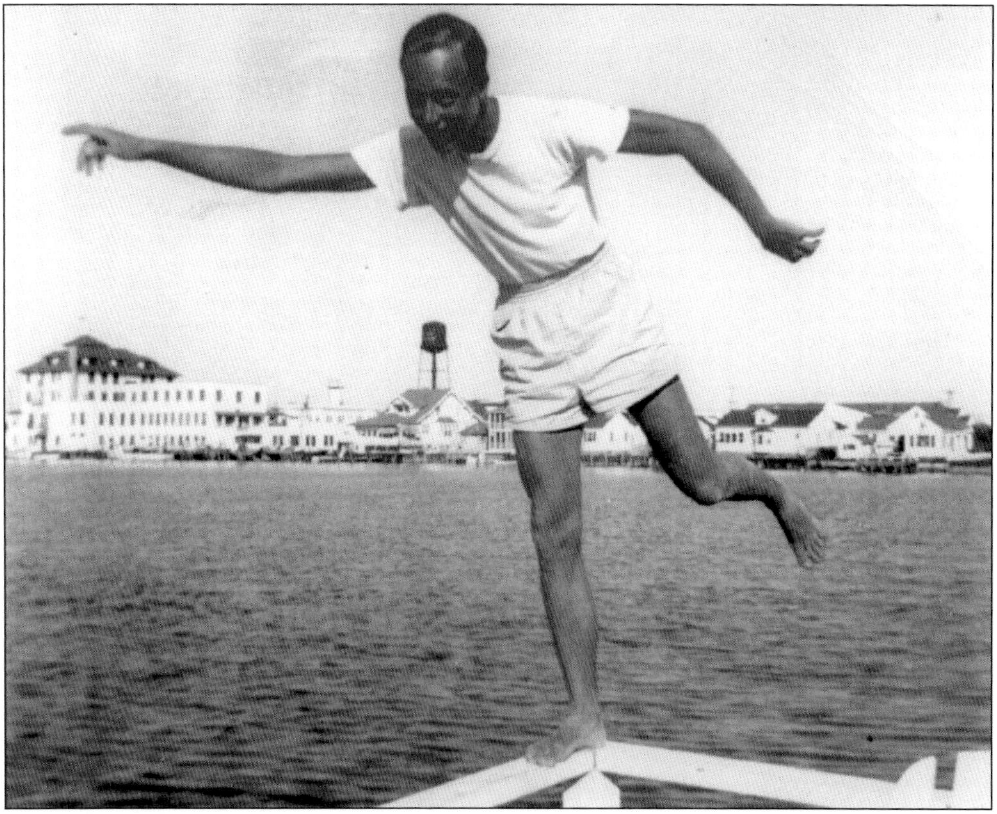

A pose on the dock was not necessarily *along* the railing but *on* it. The extended arm of this summer "Hermes" points out over the old Shelter Haven Hotel and the water tower in the background.

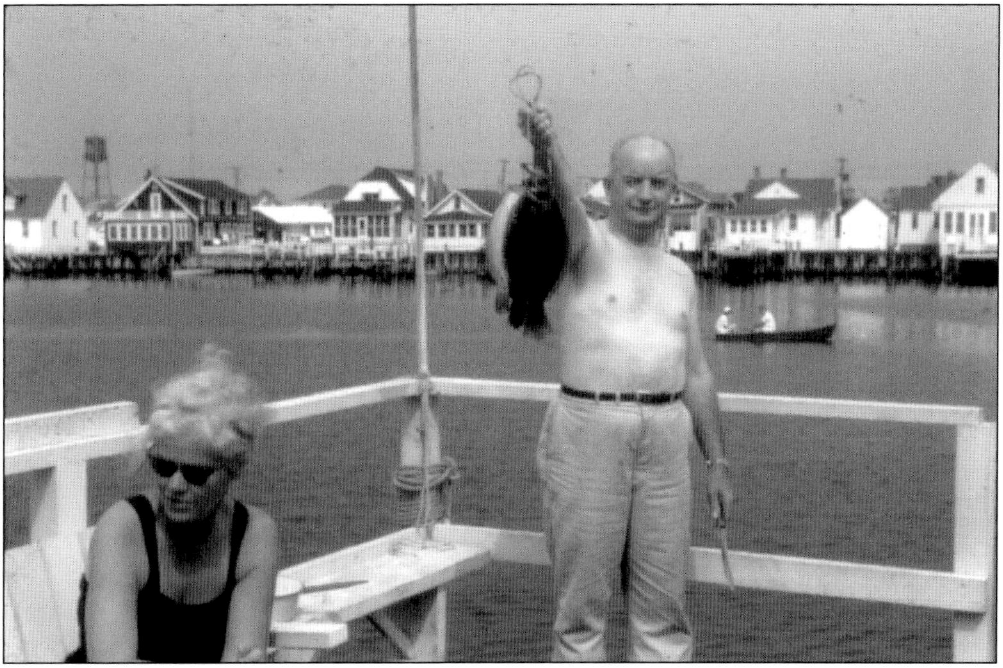

This proud fisherman gladly shows off the one that did not get away—a flounder he caught on a hot August day in 1957.

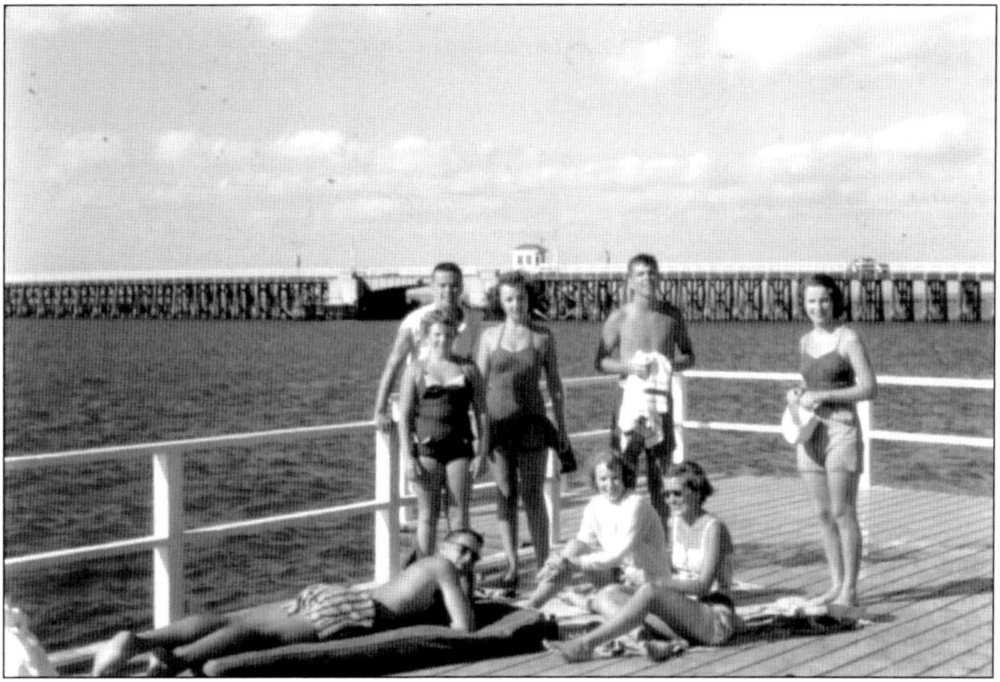

After a day of water-skiing, boating, and swimming, these sunbathers could view the drawbridge on the causeway into Stone Harbor from the Brooke family pier.

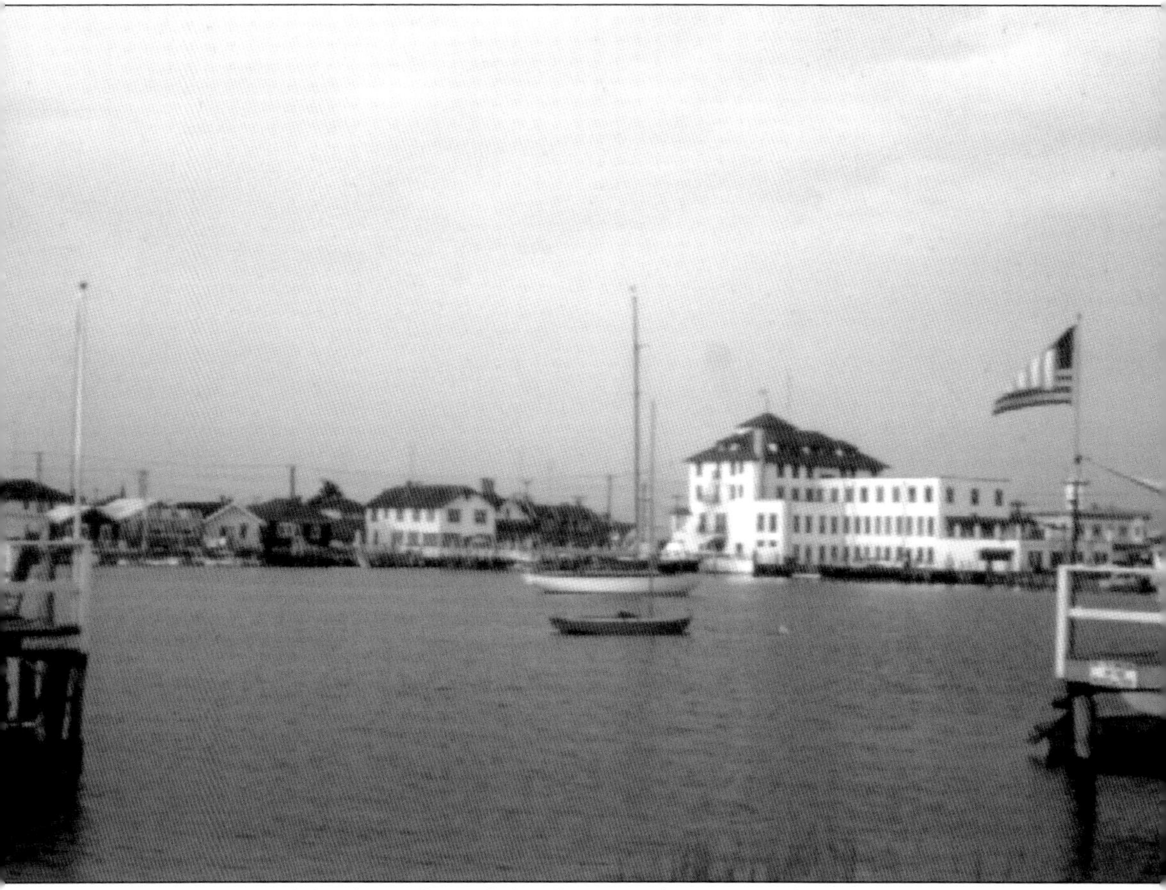

Boats are moored for the night and the flag is ready to come down as the last glimmers of sunlight fall on the old Shelter Haven Hotel.

The Jolly Green Giant would be pleased with these two peas in the baby parade of the 1950s. The baby parade, popular along the Jersey shore, began in the 1930s. Simple strollers were turned into fantasy settings for the length of the parade route.

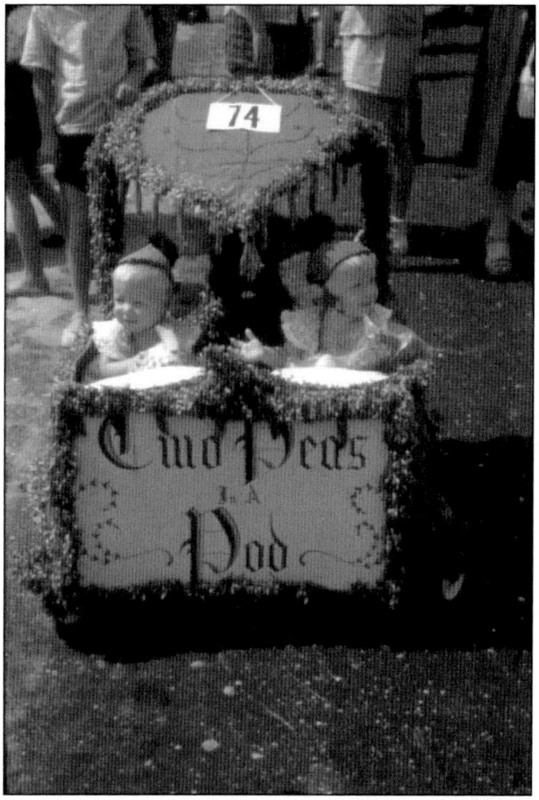

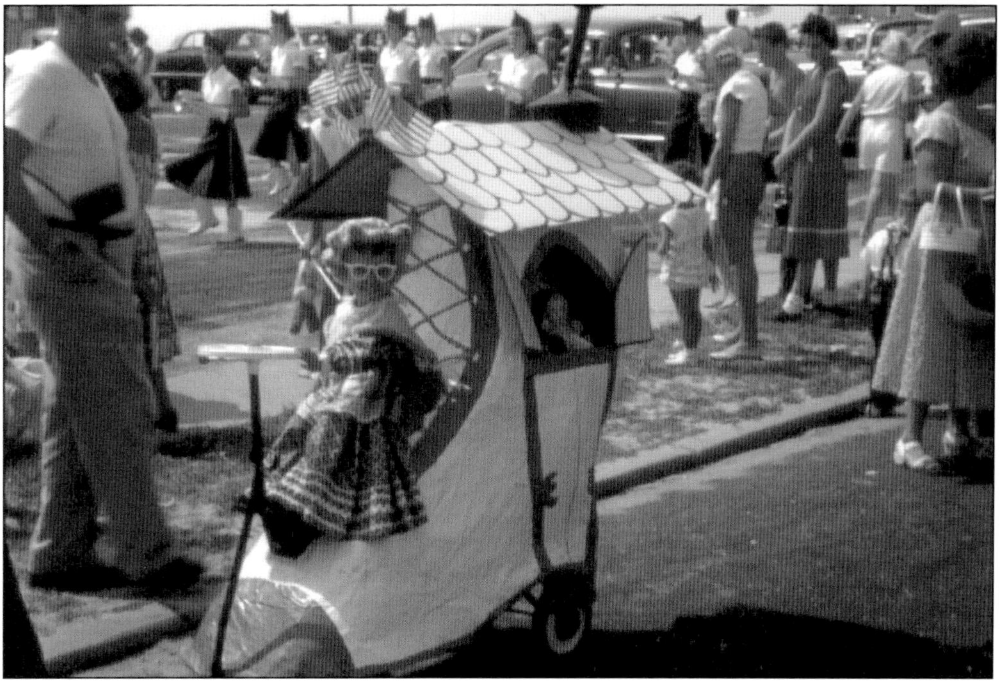

The old woman who lived in the shoe wears sunglasses while balancing on an unlikely home constructed over her wagon.

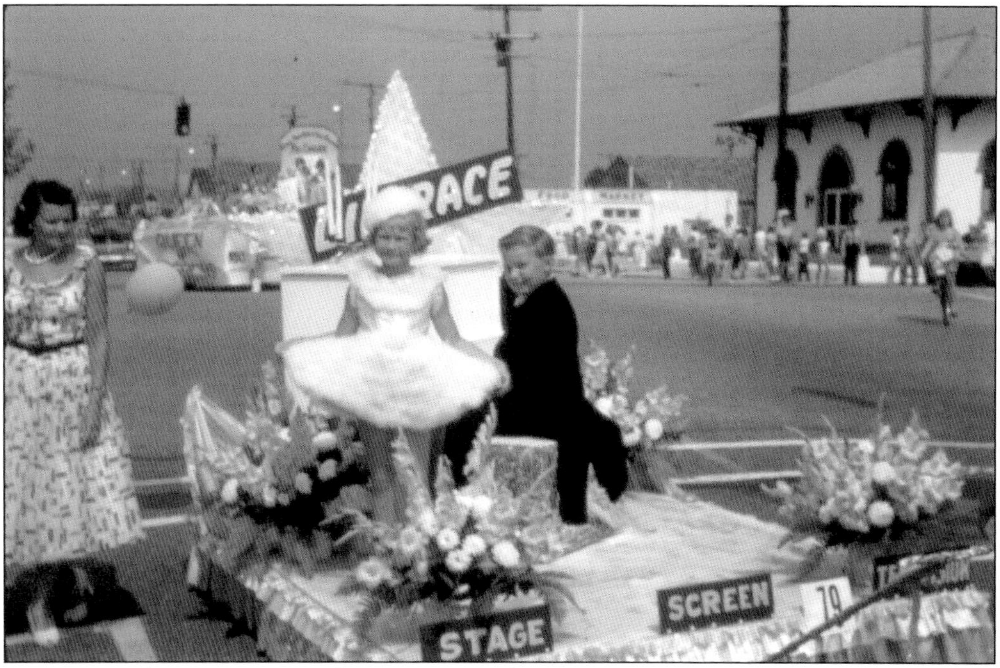

Move over Liberace! Stone Harbor was proud of its own stars of stage and screen—at least for the duration of the baby parade down 96th Street.

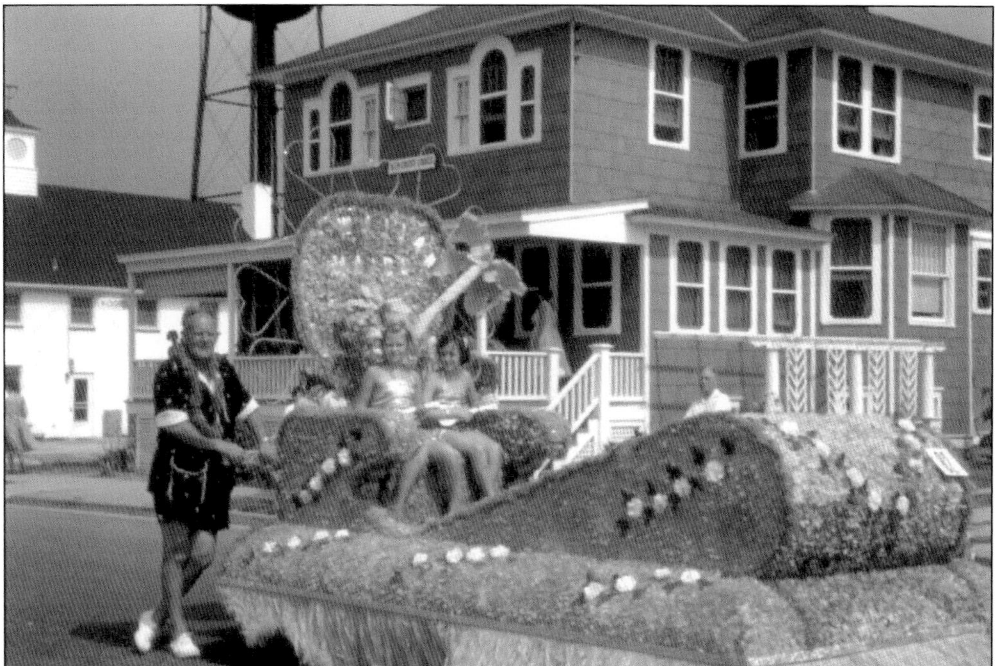

A father provides the power that pushes these preteens through the parade.

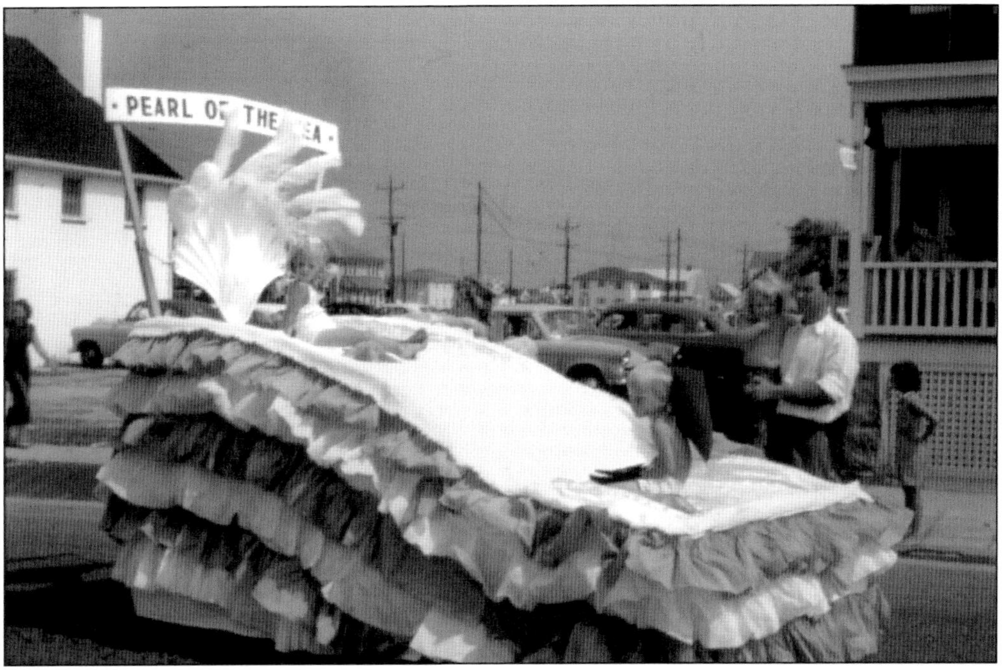

This "Pearl of the Sea" float reflects the feelings of Stone Harbor residents, who regard their town as just such a pearl.

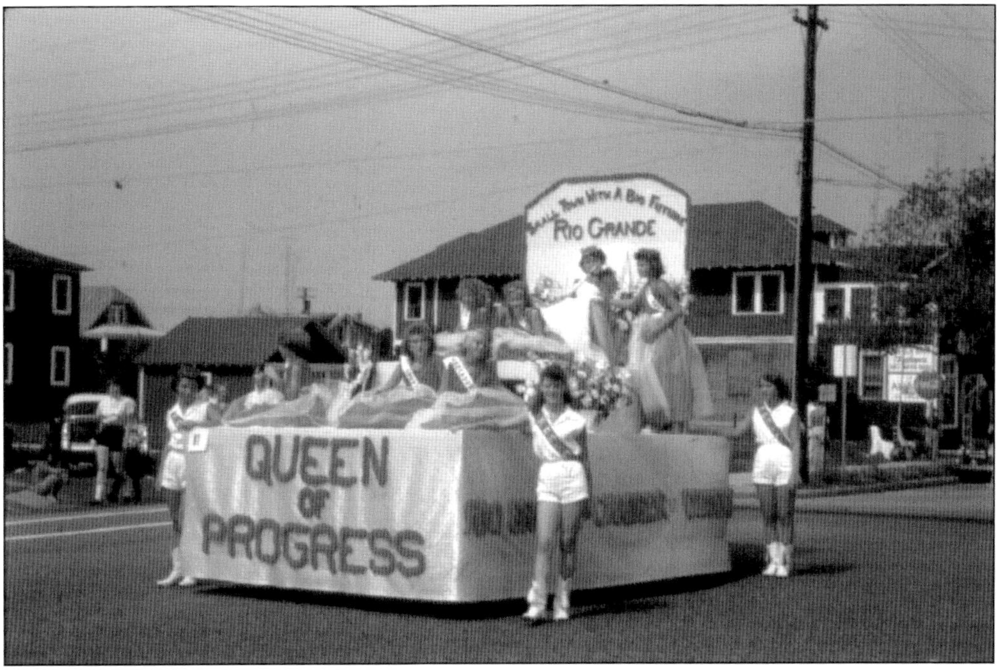

The queen and her court were always the main attraction in the Fourth of July parade.

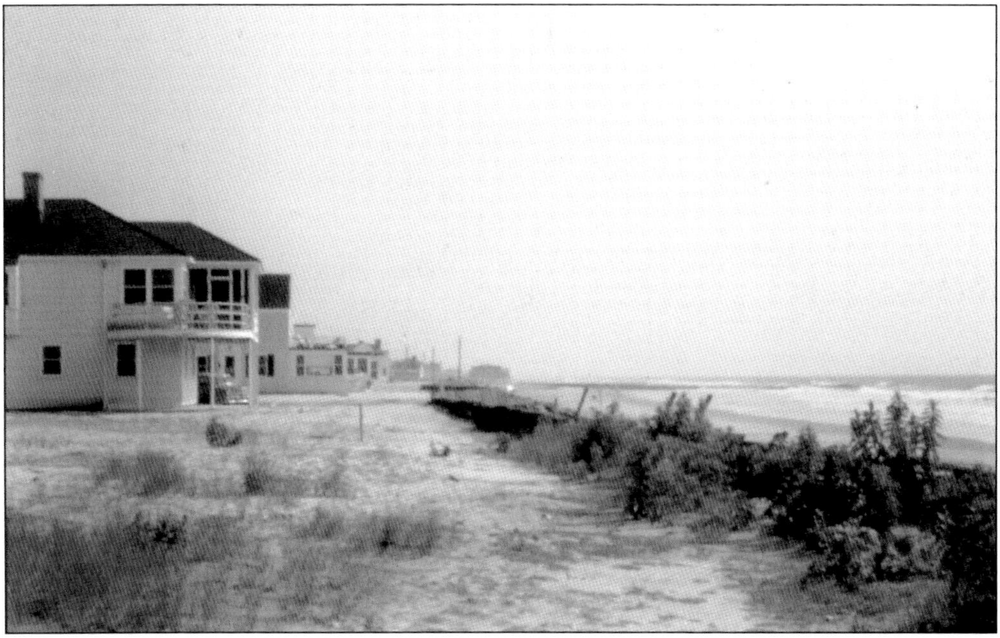

Looking from the convent to the north, this beach scene shows how vulnerable beachfront properties were with a very small bulkhead as protection. This house did not avoid damage in the storm of 1962, as seen in the photograph on page 100.

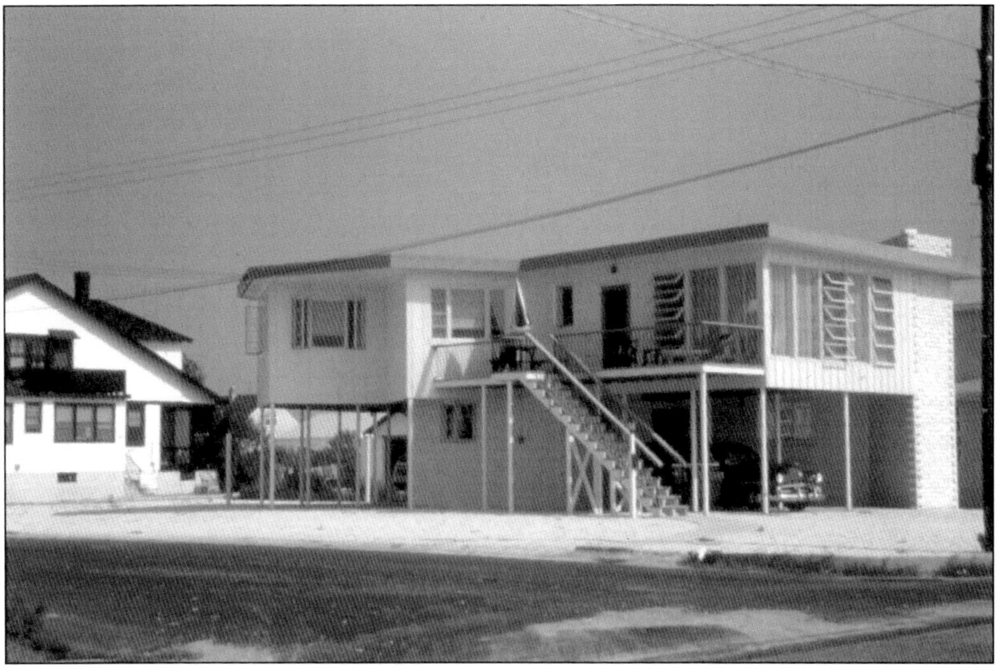

An austere 1950s-style beach house contrasts with the inviting 1920s bungalow to the left.

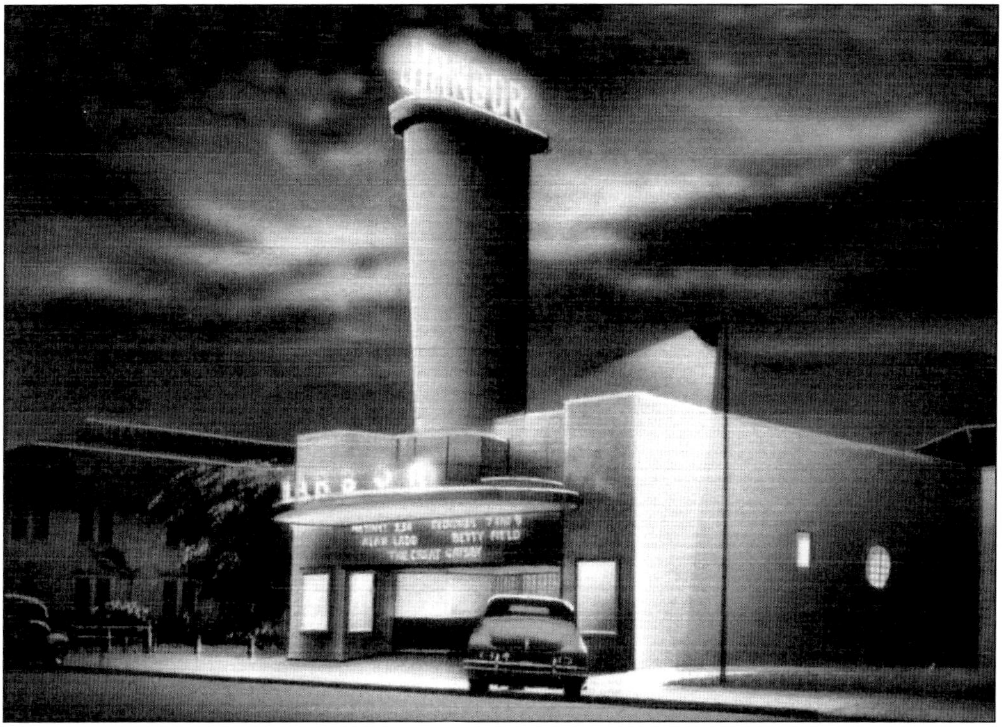

The Harbor Theater opened grandly in 1950 with a showing of *Royal Wedding,* starring Fred Astaire, Eleanor Powell, and Peter Lawford. In addition to the Harbor Theater, Stone Harbor also offered the older Park Theater.

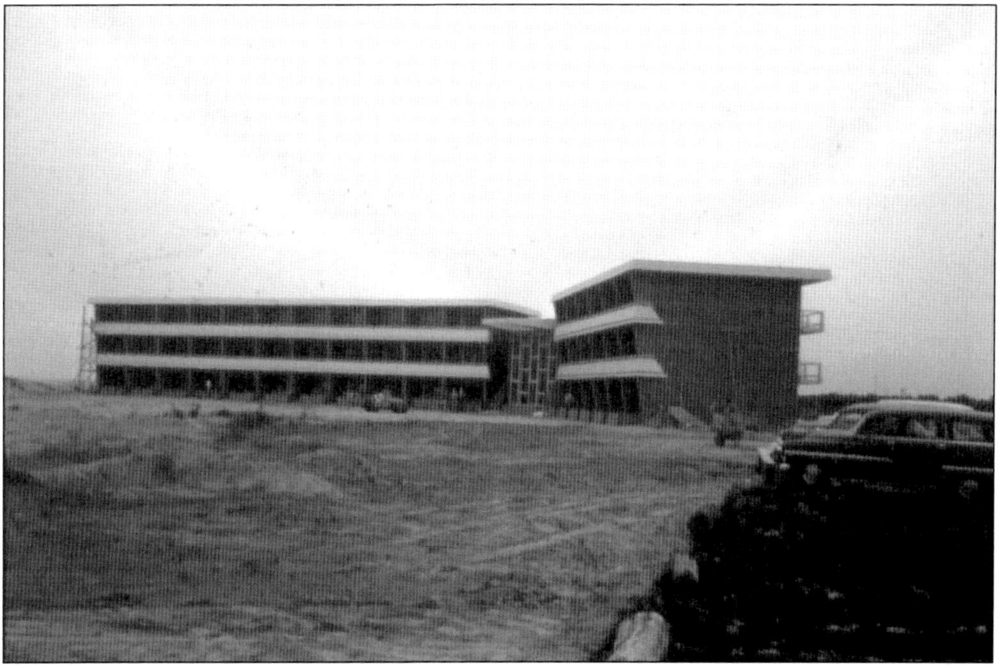

One of the first motels, the Golden Inn, was built on the Stone Harbor and Avalon border. Shown here nearing completion, the motel is typical of 1950s architecture.

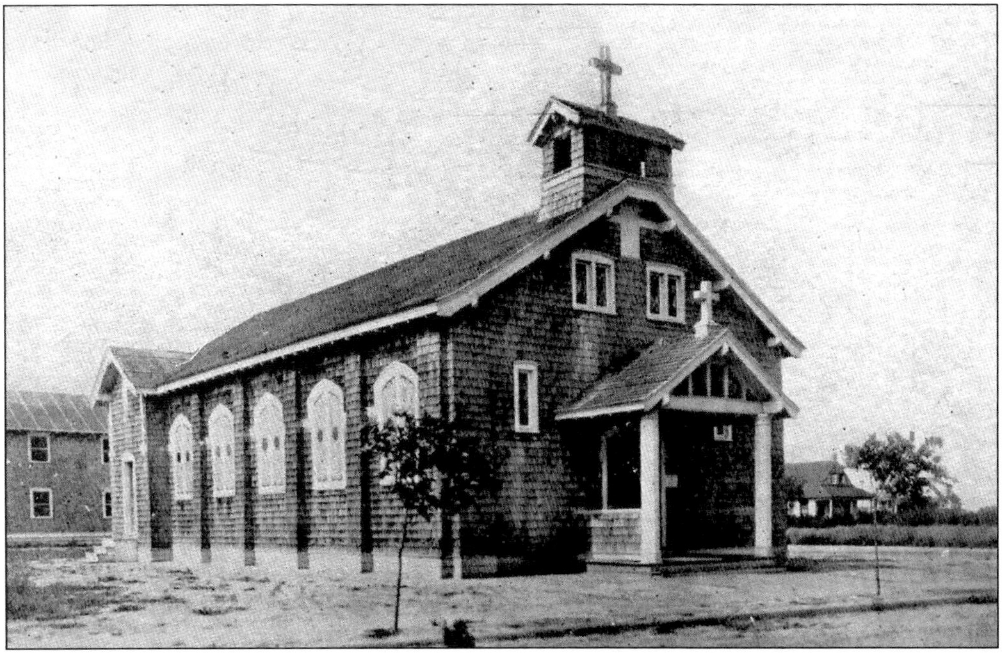

The first St. Paul's Roman Catholic Church was a simple shingled structure with Gothic, stained-glass windows. It was erected in 1911 on the southeast corner of 99th Street and Third Avenue. It was later moved to 100th Street to make space for the new church.

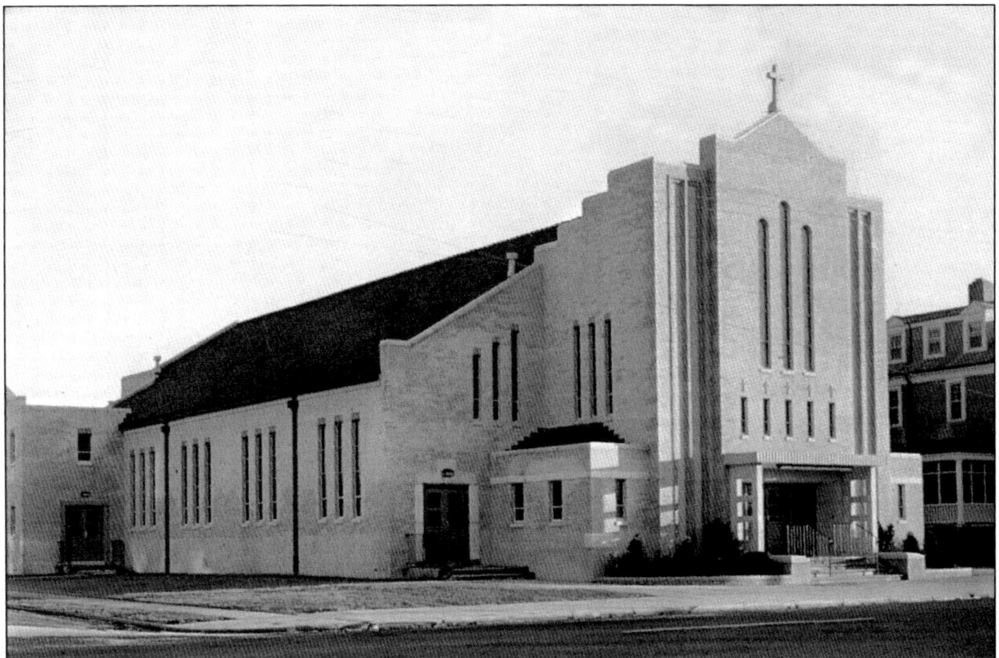

In 1953, the new St. Paul's was constructed, increasing seating capacity from 180 to 900 people. The church is typical of the ecclesiastical architecture of the 1940s and 1950s, reflecting traditional Gothic ideas with a modernist touch. It is constructed of concrete and brick to weather any storm.

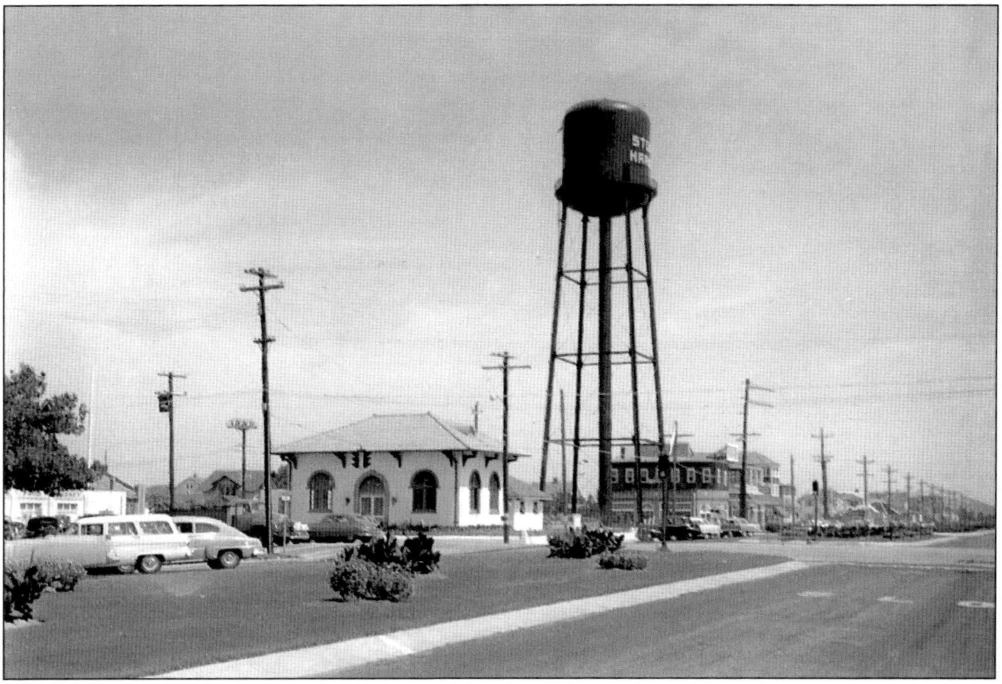

This 1950s view of 96th Street and the flowered islands of Second Avenue shows Diller's store and the water tower, with the post office just out of frame to the left. The lovely Mediterranean-style pumping station was built in the 1920s, and the water tower was replaced by the present one in the 1980s.

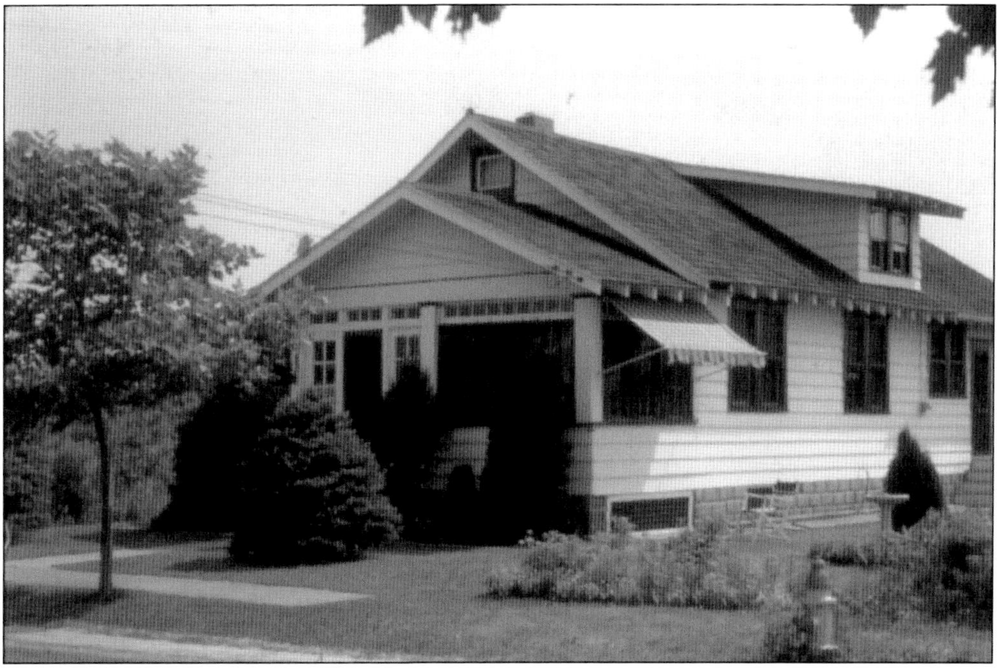

By the time this photograph was taken in the mid-1950s, the house and garden at the Colebin had matured into an idyllic setting, making it an ideal home to return to every year.

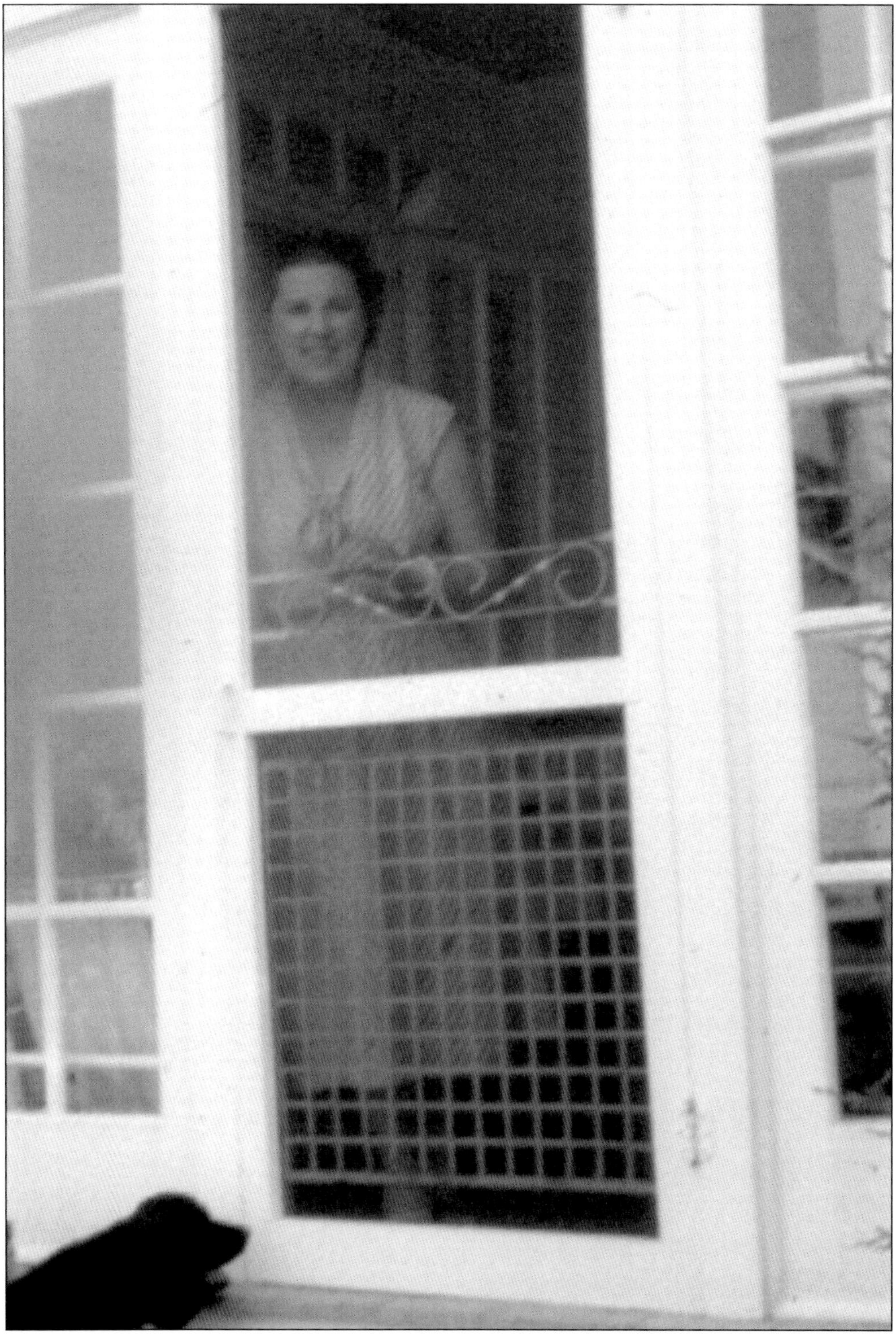

My grandmother maintained an open-door policy toward family, friends, and neighbors during the summer season.

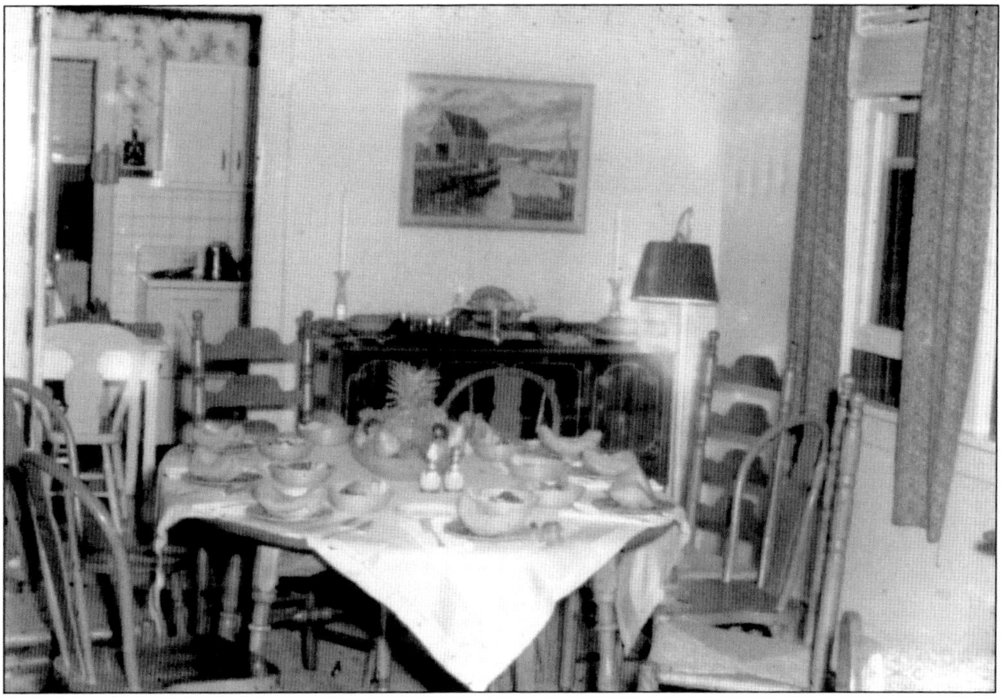
A cantaloupe appetizer awaits dinner guests in the dining room of the bungalow.

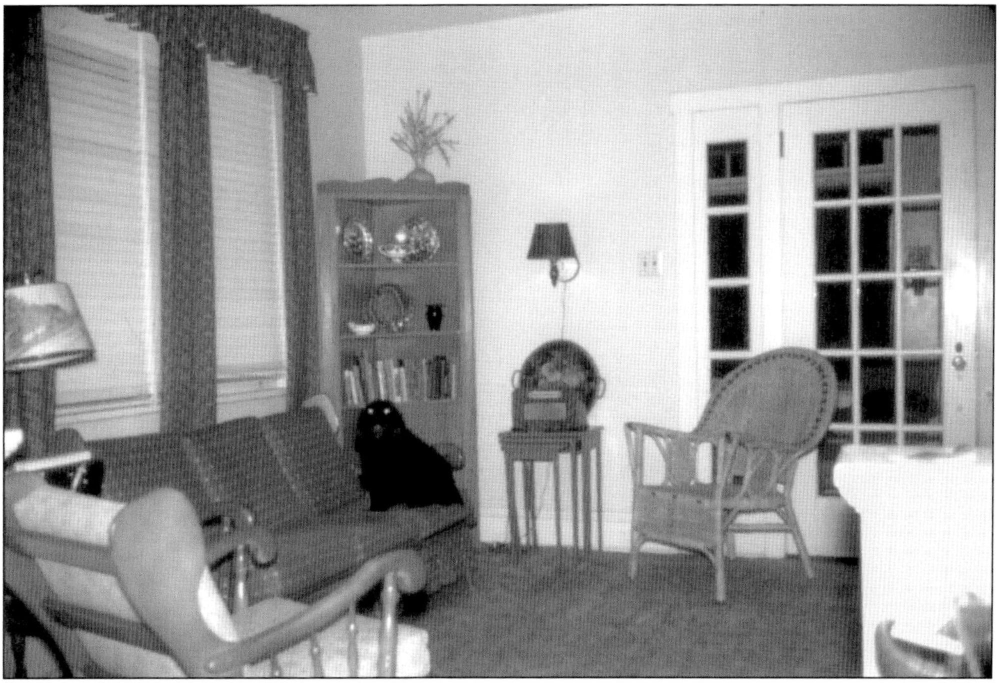
Shown is a typical living room of most summer cottages in the 1950s. Simple furnishings and decor were welcoming at the end of a summer day, and the absence of a television added to the sense of retreat.

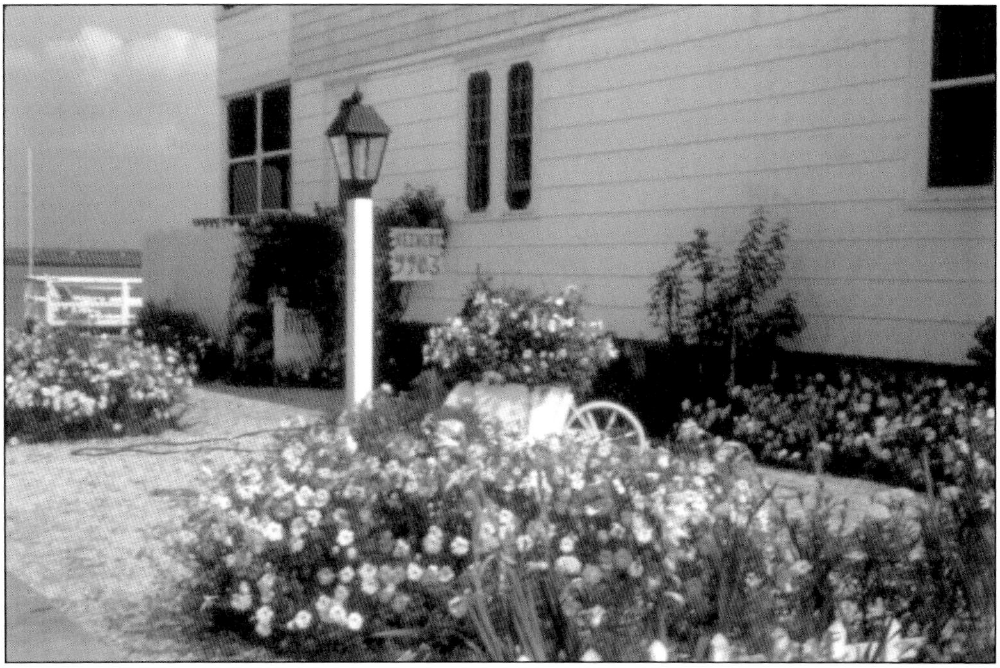

Gardening was a popular activity. This garden belonged to a Mrs. Rinehardt and is accented by colorful bursts of petunias. The photograph is a remembrance of both my grandfather's fascination with color and the pleasures of a small, well-kept yard.

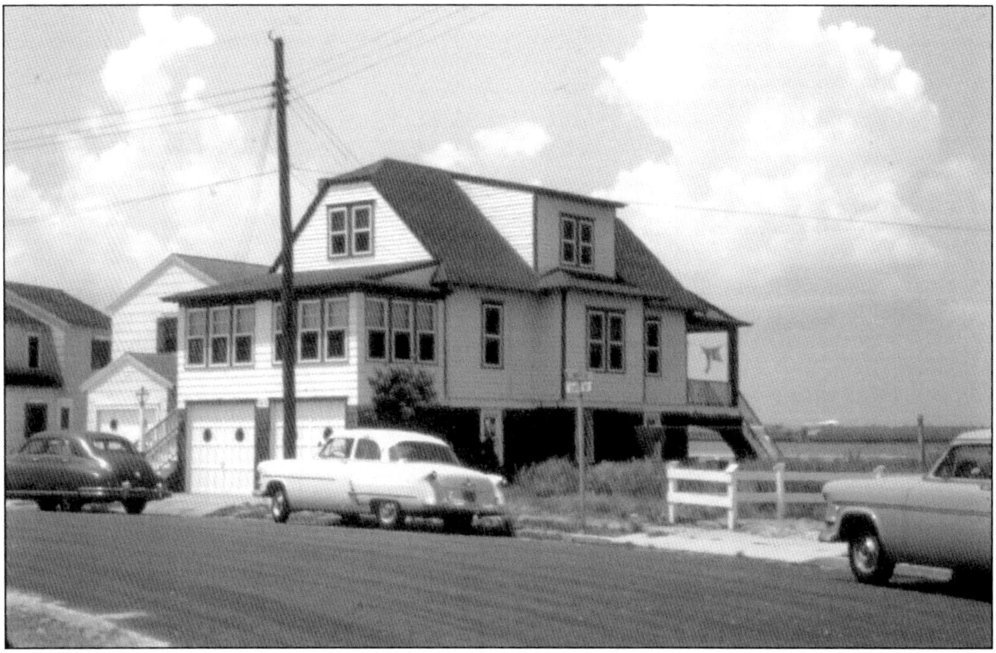

The street sign in the center of this photograph indicates that Sunset Lane curves into 98th Street. This home, which belonged to the Brooke family, stands on the channel and overlooks the bridge. It was the center of many boating activities.

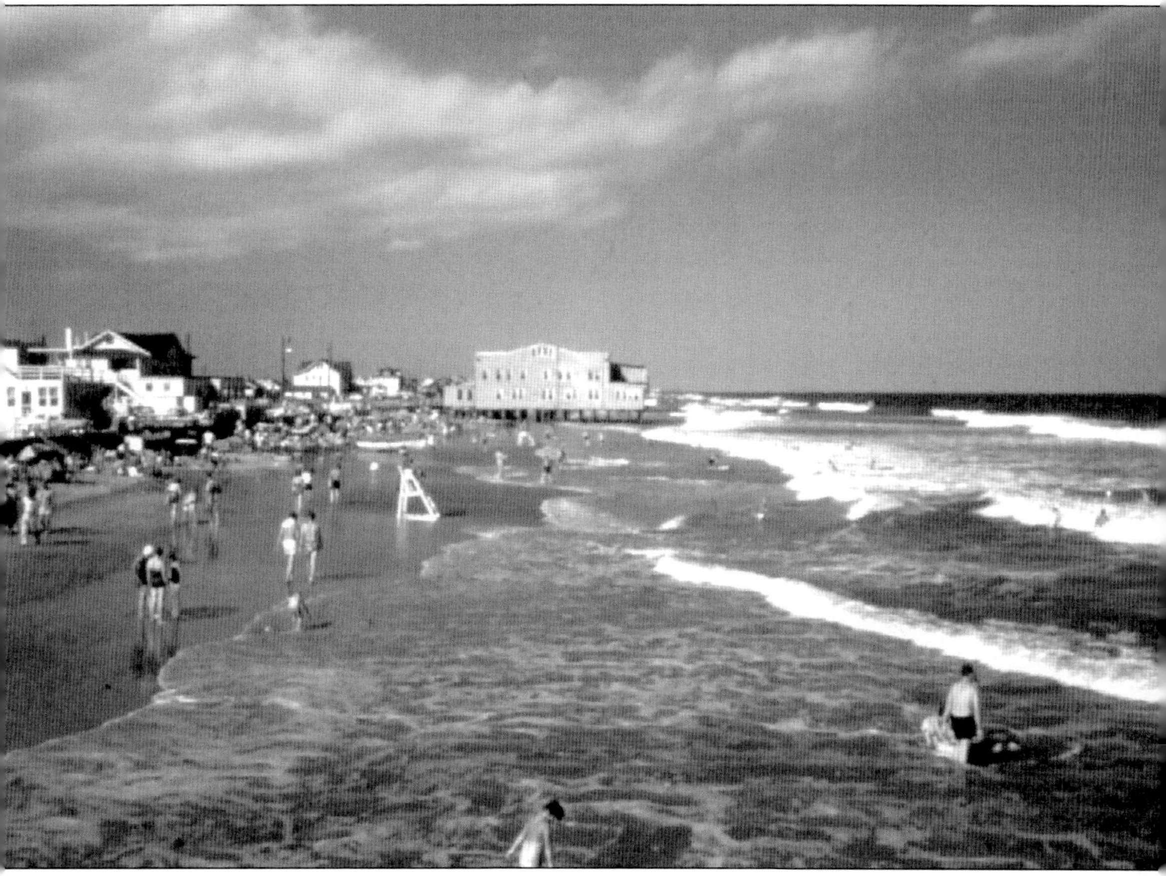

What is so rare as a day in June? This photograph was taken looking north from the 101st Street pier.

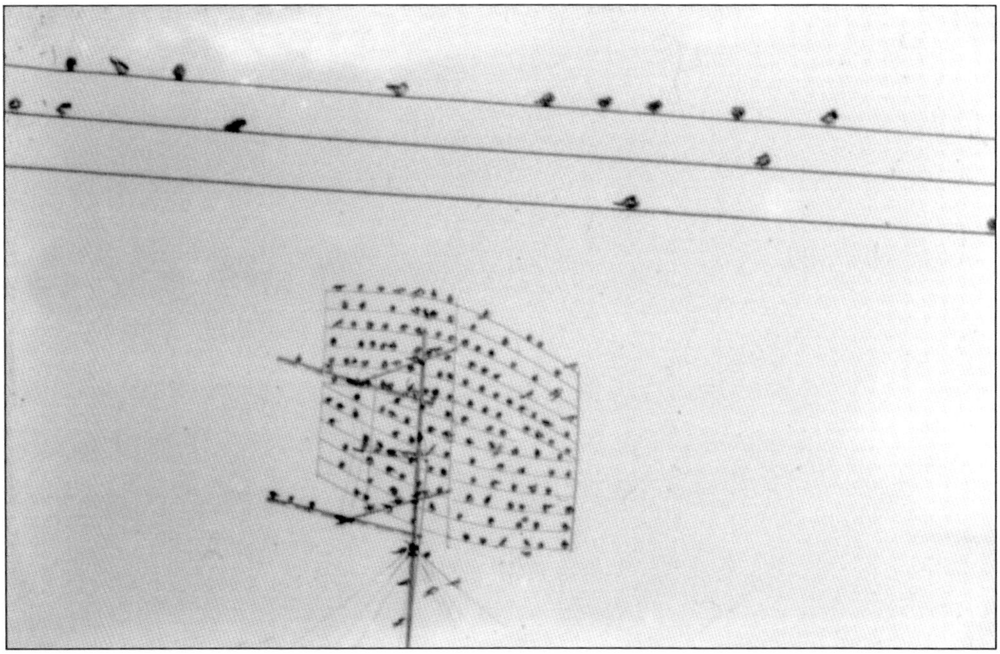

When television antennae dotted the skyline in Stone Harbor, they competed with telephone lines as bird perches.

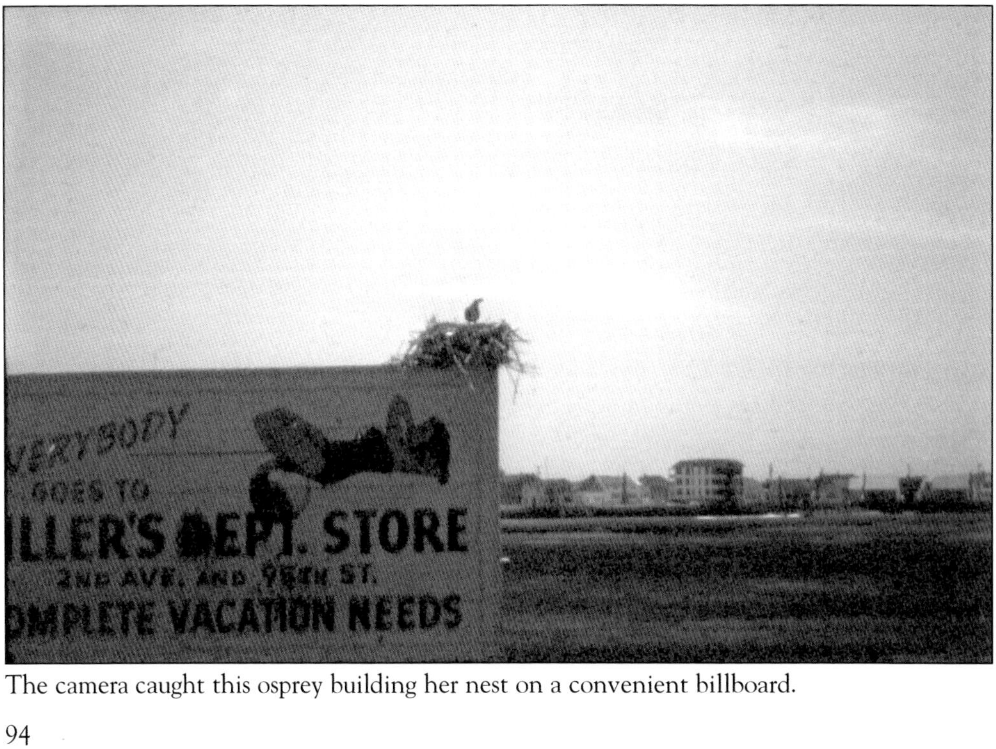

The camera caught this osprey building her nest on a convenient billboard.

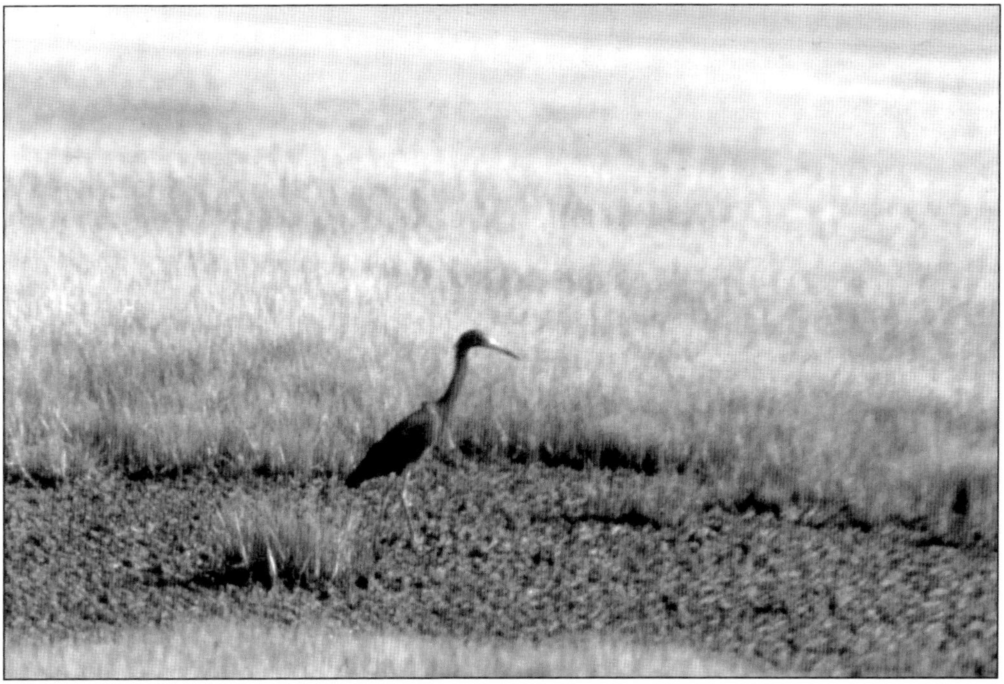

A lone egret in the marshlands foreshadows the decline of wildlife at the bird sanctuary in the coming years.

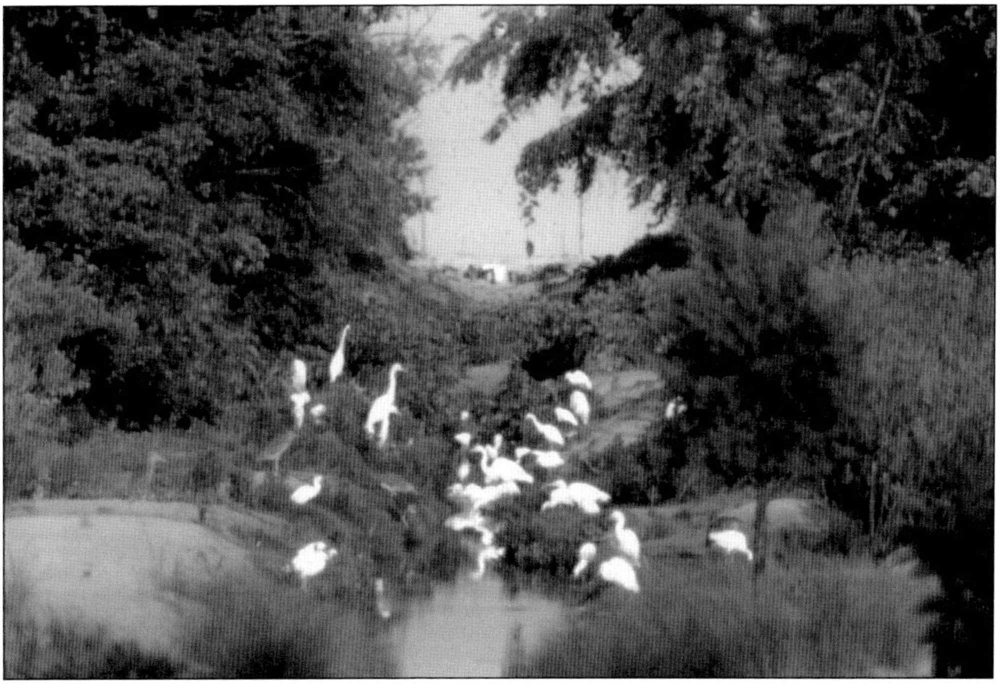

A flock of egrets rests within the bird sanctuary.

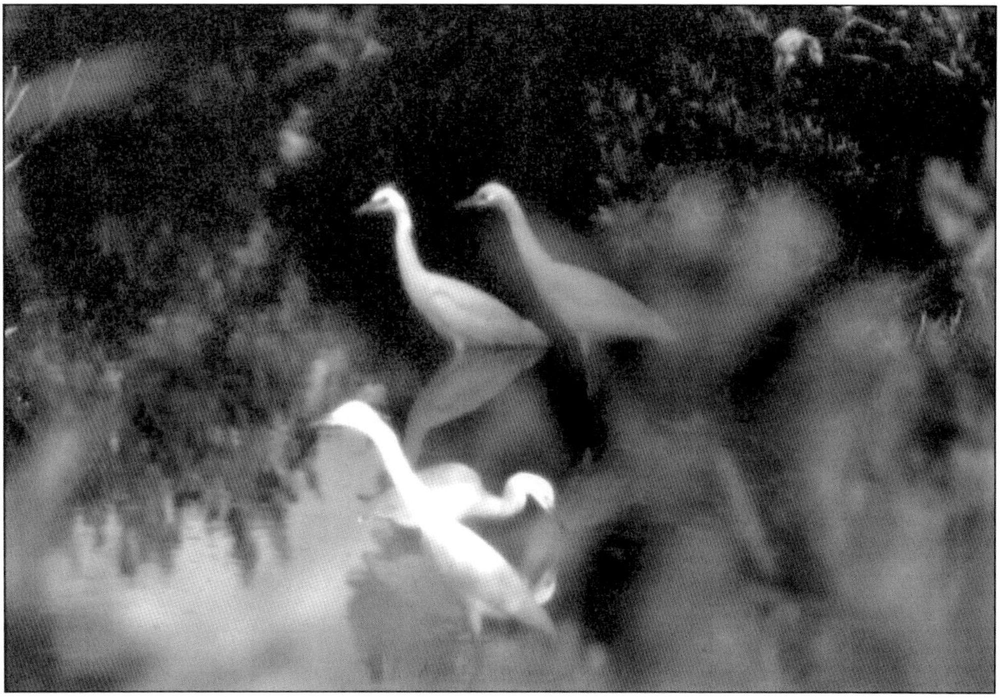

Egrets unknowingly pose for my grandfather's camera.

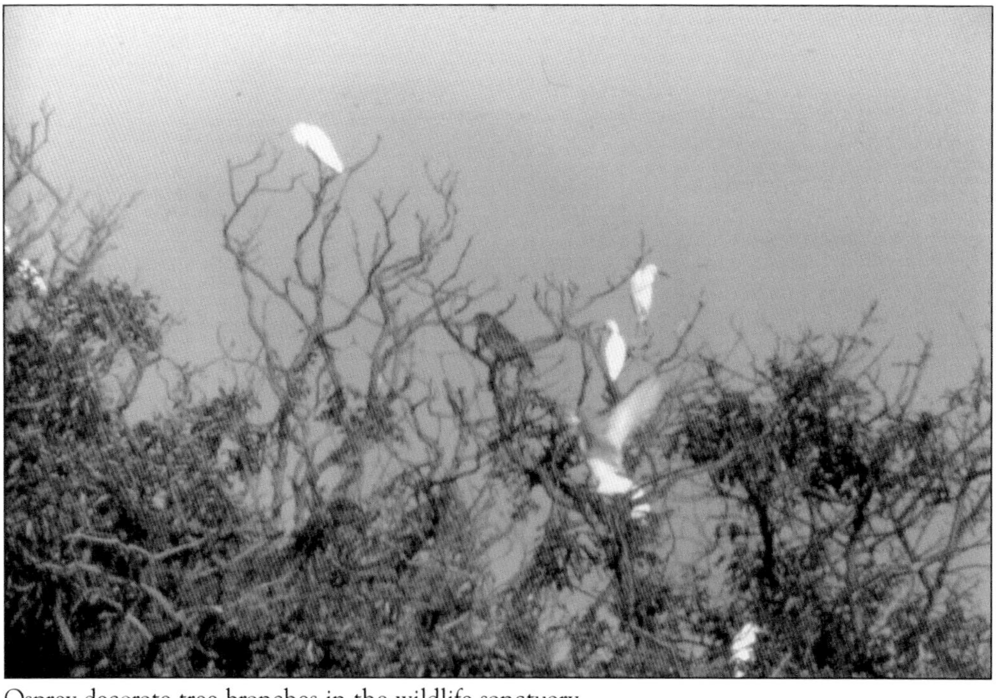

Osprey decorate tree branches in the wildlife sanctuary.

Four

A New Season: The 1960s and 1970s

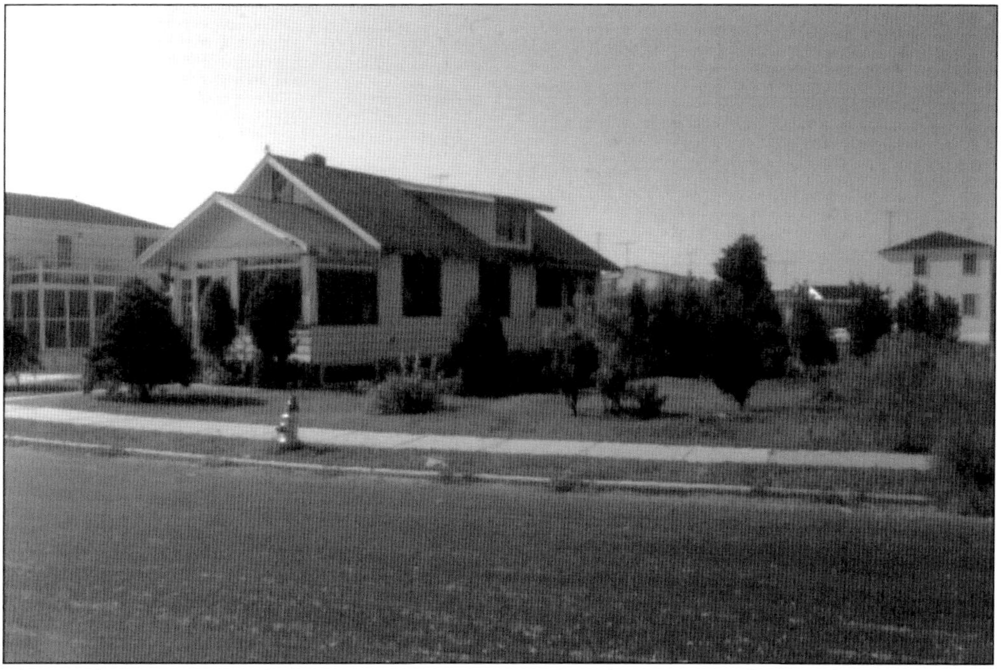

This early-1960s view shows a quiet morning with a house, a garden, and recently built apartment houses to the left and rear of the Colebin. The garden extended into the adjoining vacant lot. Lots such as these were still to be seen all around Stone Harbor, creating small wildlife refuges.

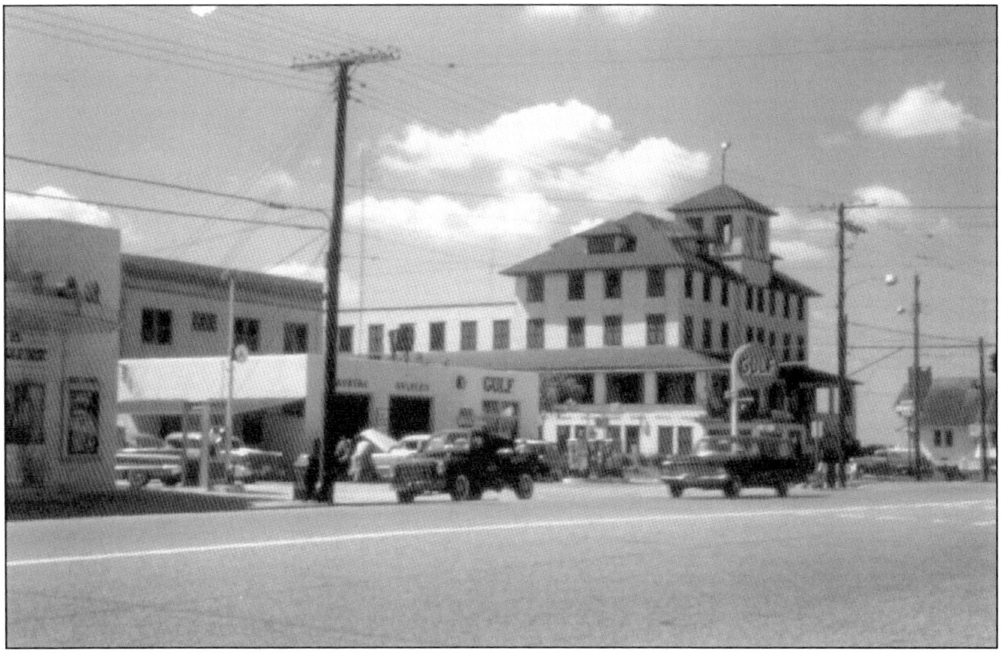

The old Shelter Haven Inn was photographed in the early 1960s prior to its demolition. Its replacement, the Shelter Haven Motel, and the Gulf station have recently been demolished. At the far left is the Harbor Movie Theater, which still exists.

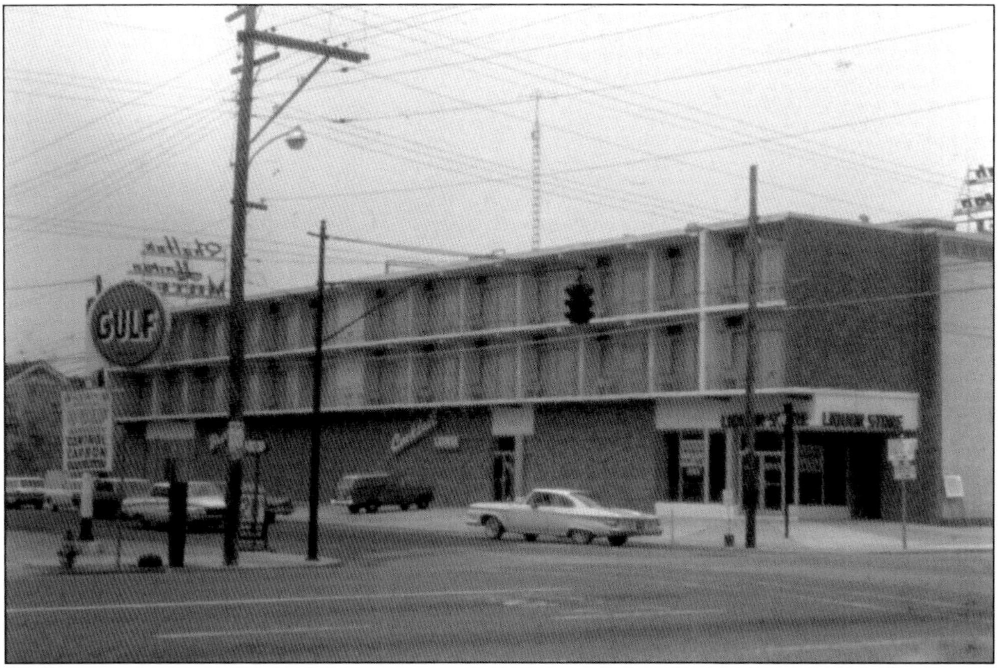

Shown are the new Shelter Haven Motel and the Gulf station, located at Third Avenue and 96th Street.

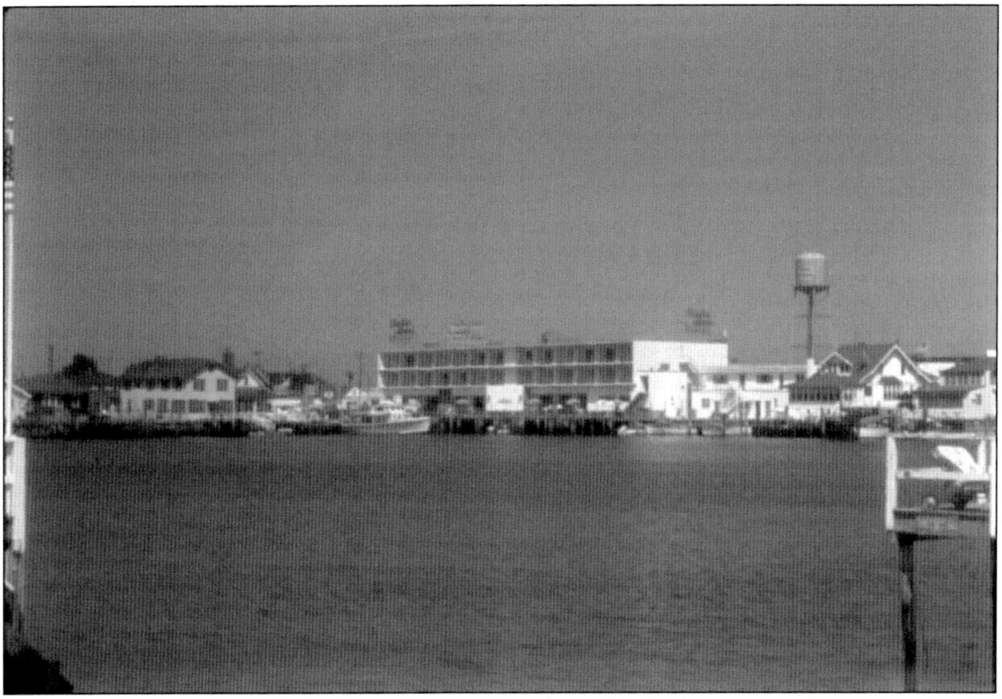

The old bay is seen here in new times, focusing on the modern Shelter Haven Motel. Compare this view with a similar shot on page 82.

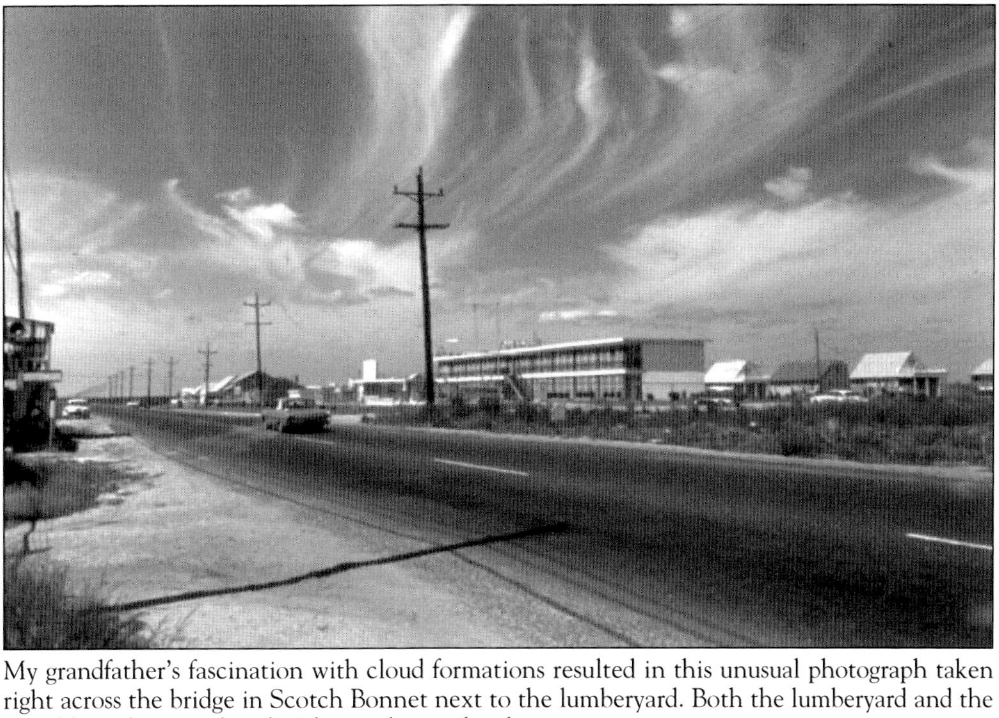

My grandfather's fascination with cloud formations resulted in this unusual photograph taken right across the bridge in Scotch Bonnet next to the lumberyard. Both the lumberyard and the motel have been replaced with townhouse developments.

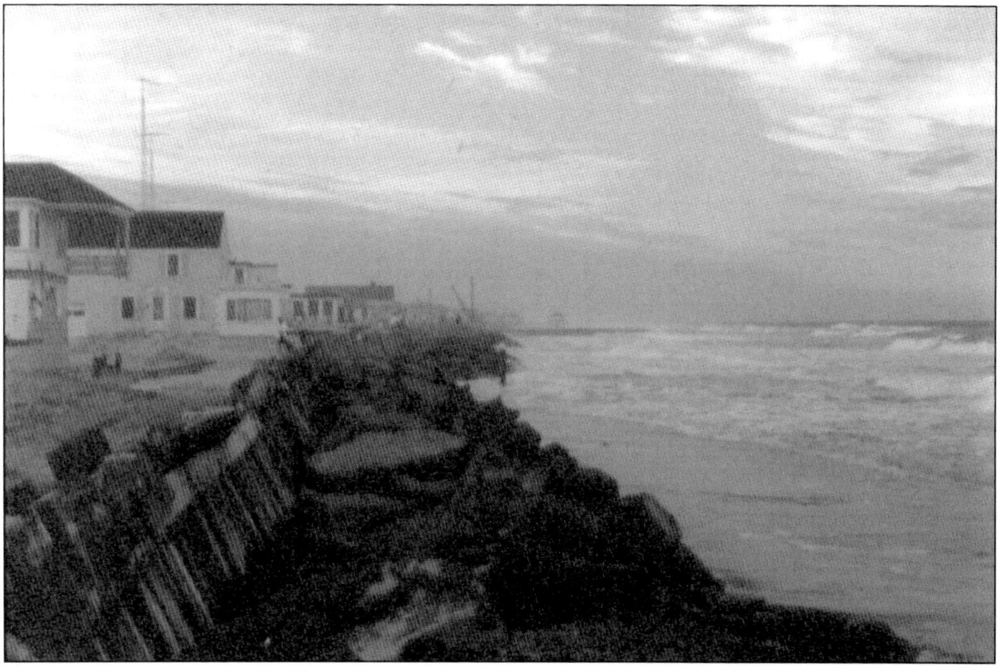

The storm of 1962 destroyed most of the bulkhead and many oceanfront properties. The rooming house would have been in the center of this photograph, but it was washed away. Note the damage to the first beach house, which is shown in happier times on page 86.

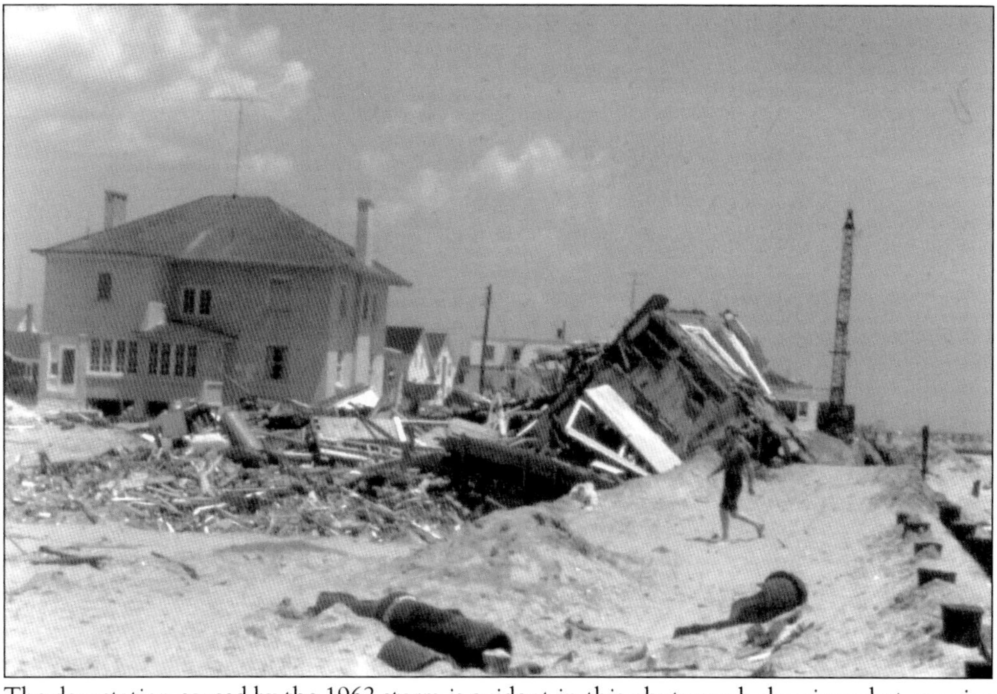

The devastation caused by the 1962 storm is evident in this photograph showing what remains of a beachfront home. The hip-roofed house to the left, the Horace Campbell house on 100th Street, still survives.

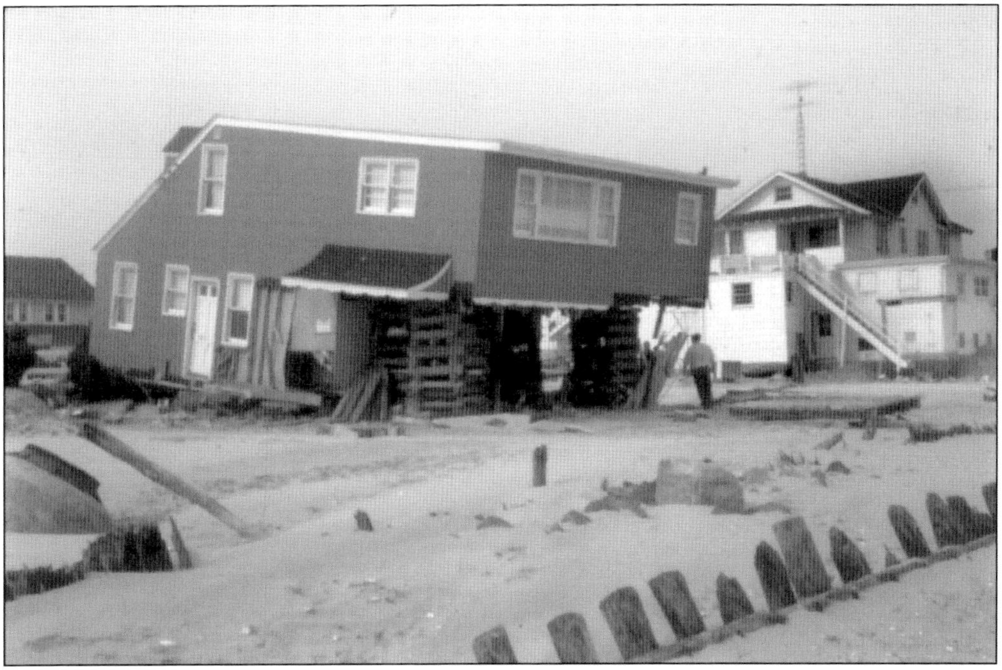

This house lost part of its first floor during the 1962 hurricane. In the foreground are broken pilings of the old seawall.

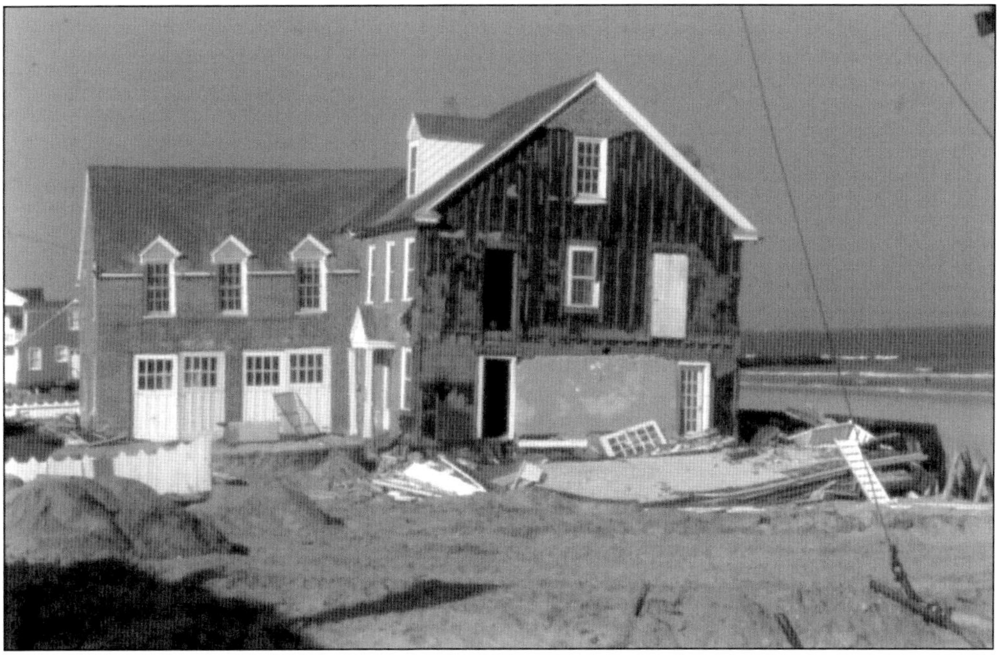

This lovely brick Colonial lost not only this side of the house but the whole oceanfront side as well.

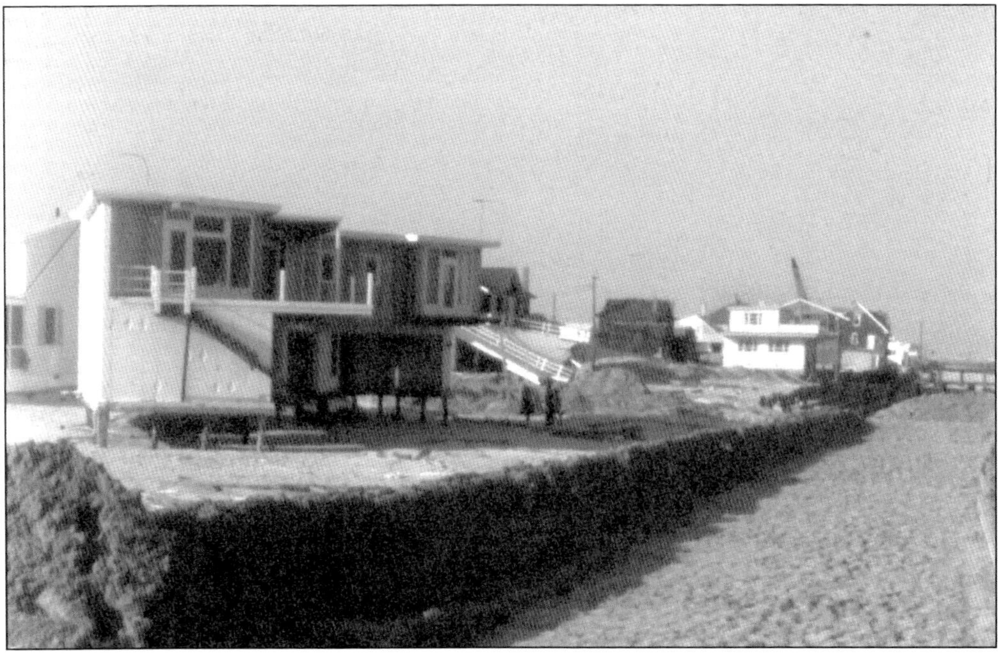

This view shows both the destruction of a modern house and the construction of the new seawall.

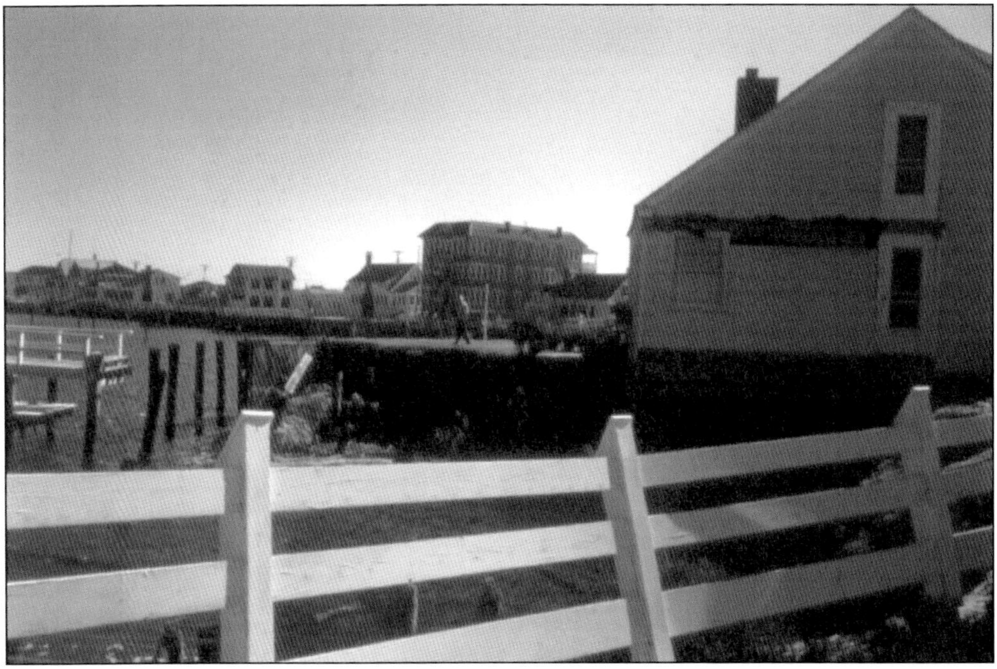

The 1962 hurricane also did considerable damage to homes on the channel. This picture shows a home without its yard.

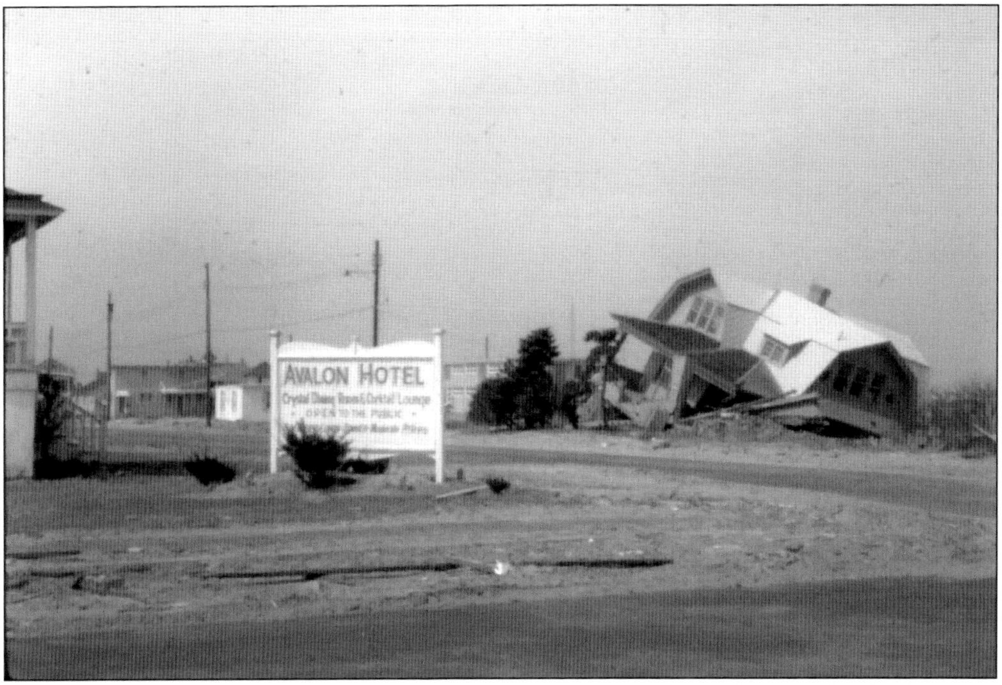

My grandfather photographed damage from the storm throughout the island. This home in Avalon had completely collapsed. It was totally rebuilt and still stands today.

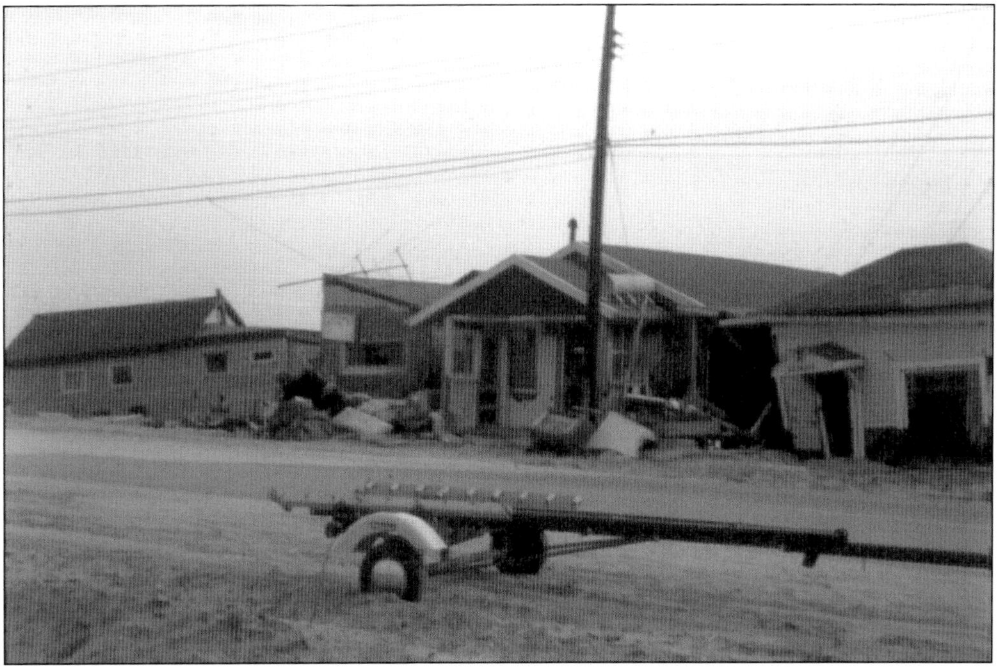

Not even Scotch Bonnet escaped damage during the hurricane of 1962.

Sunday morning in a quiet neighborhood is reflected in this early view of homes along the Stone Harbor Basin.

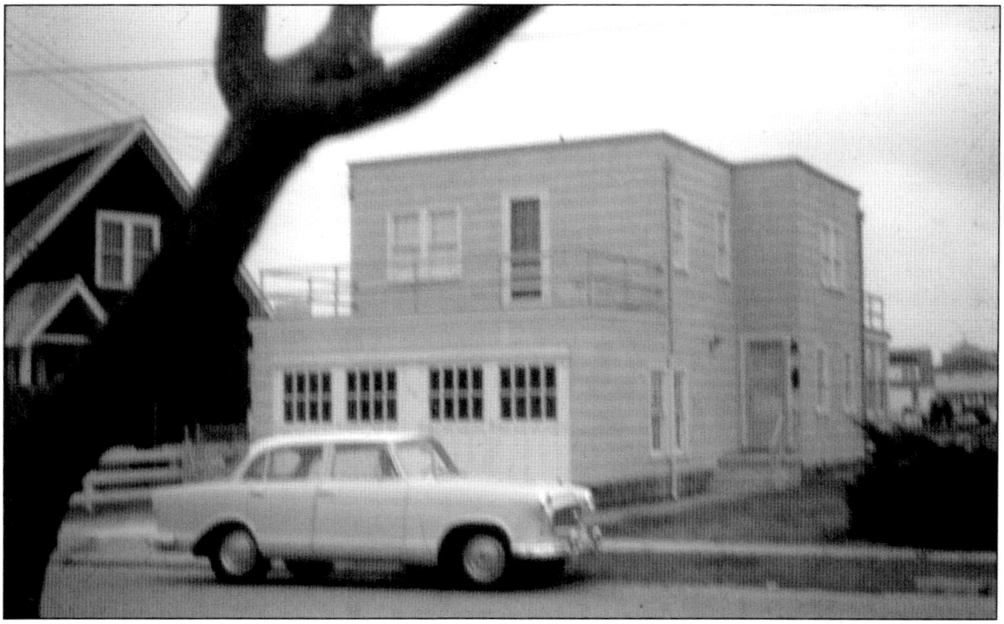

In 1963, my maternal grandparents finally bought a home on the Stone Harbor Basin along Corinthian Drive, just a few blocks from my other grandparents' home. The house, built in the Art Modern style of the late 1940s and early 1950s, still stands, although considerably altered. The Rambler American in front was my grandmother's first car and was the same color green as the house. The home to the left is that of William Lange, who owned a dress shop and served as mayor of Stone Harbor.

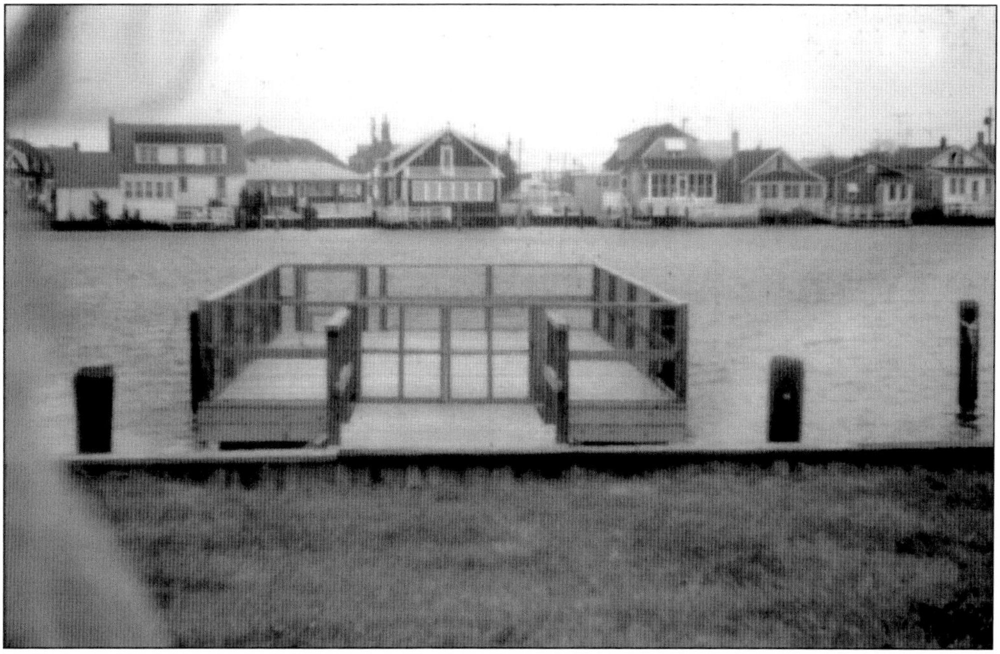

Soon after buying the house, John J. Noone designed and built a pier larger than most piers. With wire fencing on the railing and gates, it doubled as a safe play area for my sisters and me. Centered on the property, the pier had lower platforms for two boat slips.

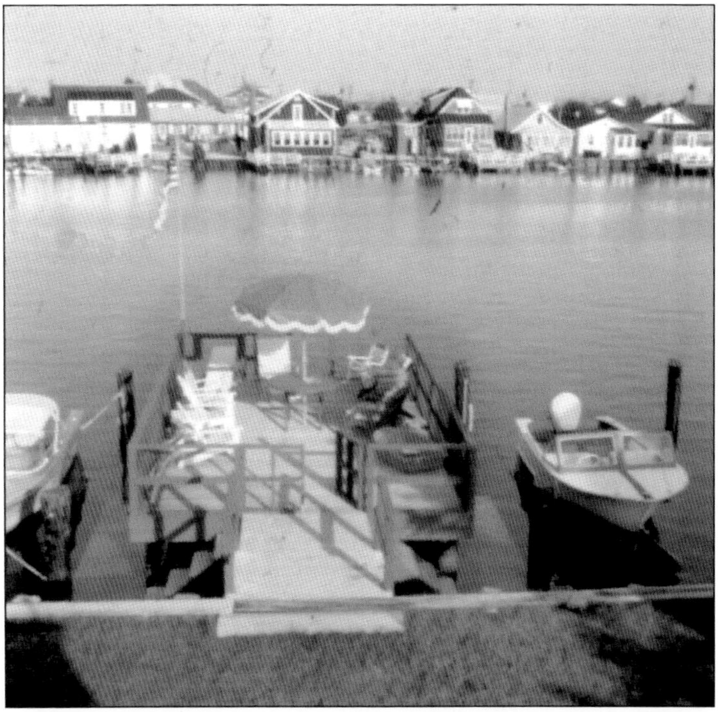

In this afternoon view, we can see the fully furnished dock. This house had a luxury that few bayside homes could boast. As it was directly across the bay from 100th Street, you could wake up to see the morning sun glistening on the ocean. The view has since been altered by the demolition of several smaller homes for one large house.

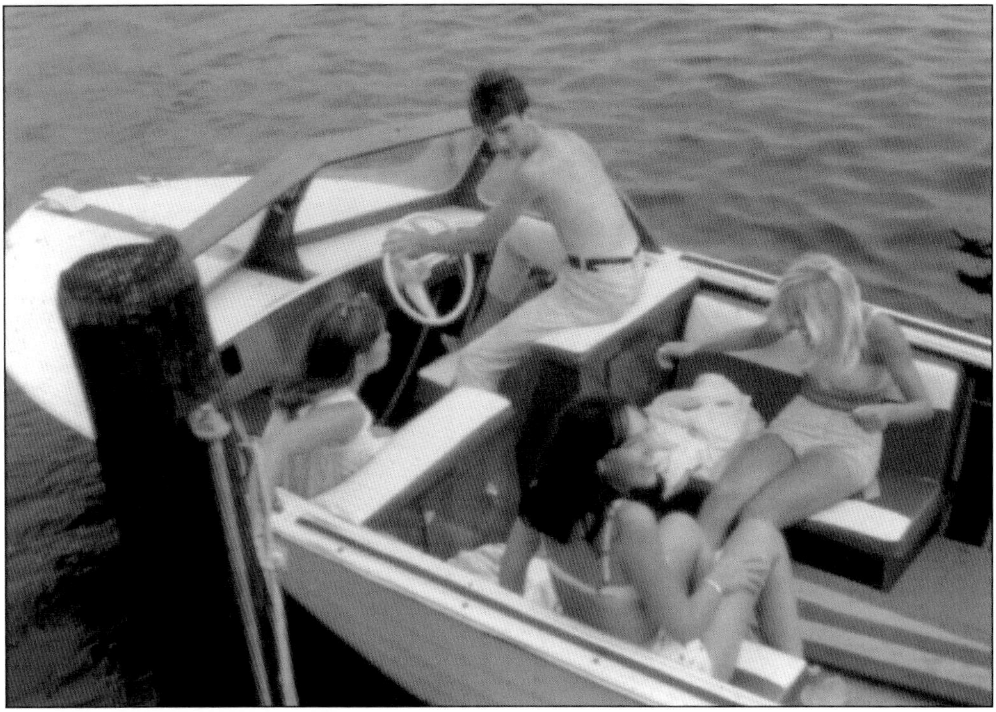

My uncle enjoys the swinging sixties with his second boat, a 16-foot Mason with a 60-horsepower Johnson outboard. He practically lived in the boat while water-skiing and buzzing around the bay. The Mason, built in the Canadian Maritimes, was a very popular wooden boat of the time.

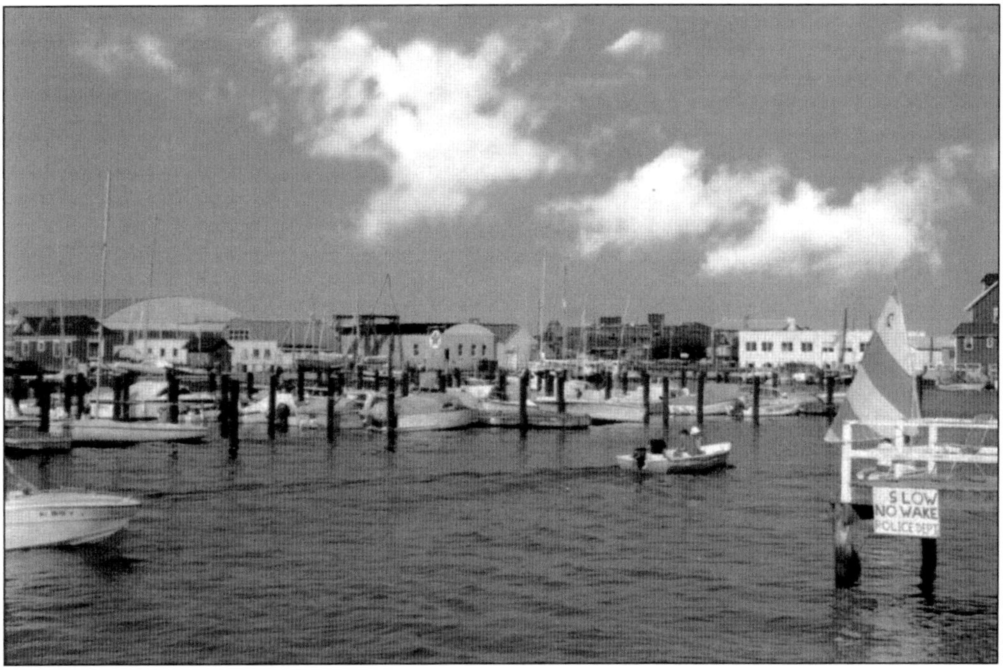

The Stone Harbor waterways had become congested with many powerboats by the 1960s. Compare this shot with an earlier view of the marina on page 57.

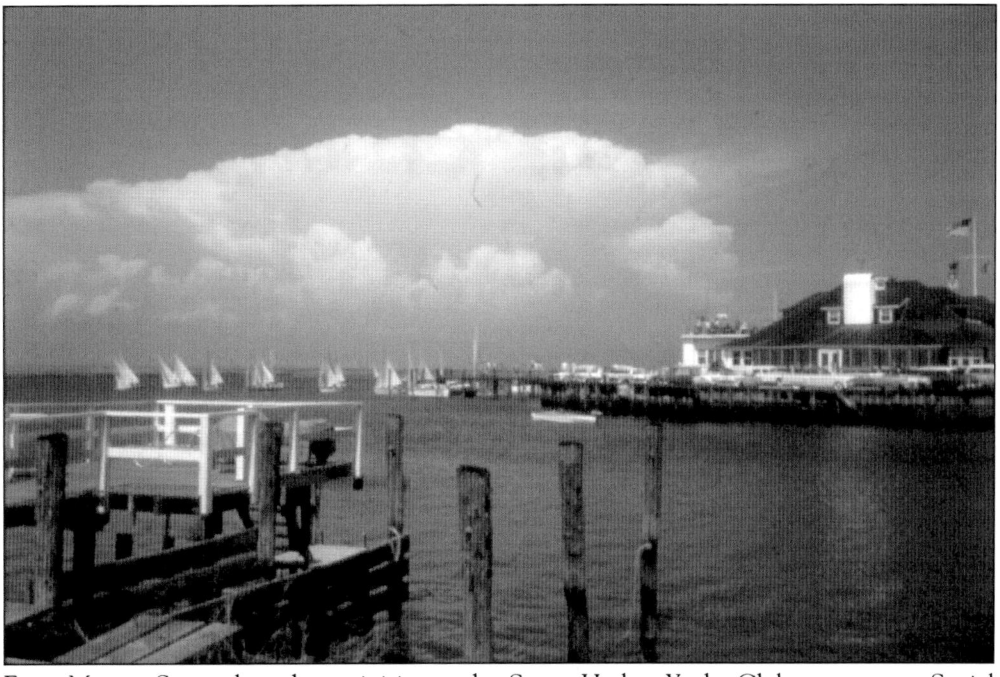

From May to September, the activities at the Stone Harbor Yacht Club were many. Social and sailing events filled the summer months. This shot of a typical Saturday race shows more fascination with clouds than what is going on in the water.

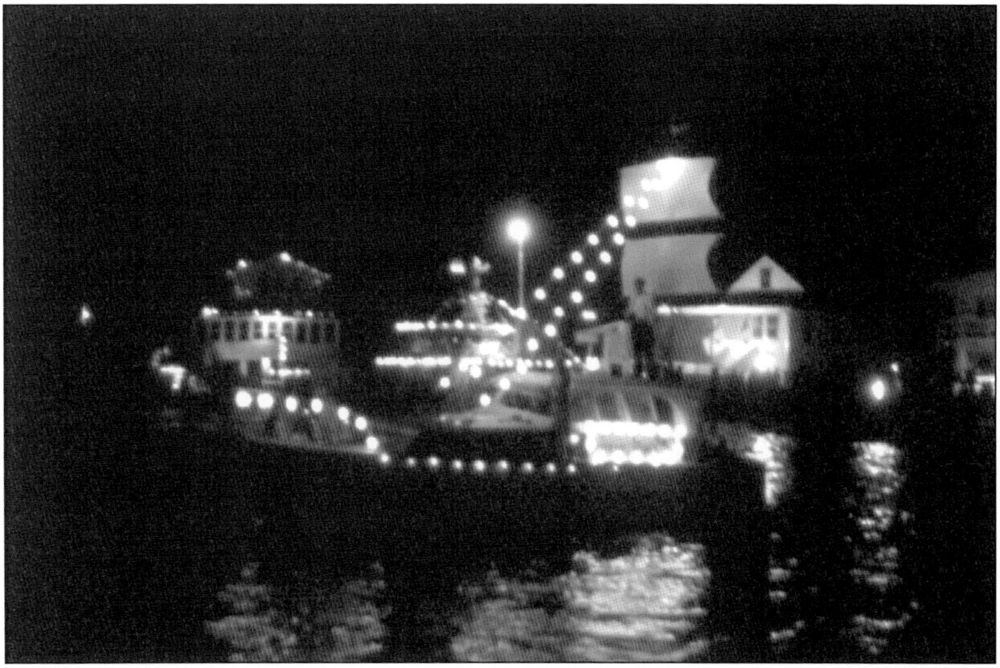

The Festival of Lights was an annual event held in August. It was first held in the mid-1960s. Both boats and private piers were decorated with lights in a theme and were judged for trophies. The Festival of Lights was originally sponsored by the Stone Harbor Yacht Club. Later, the town and the chamber of commerce organized it.

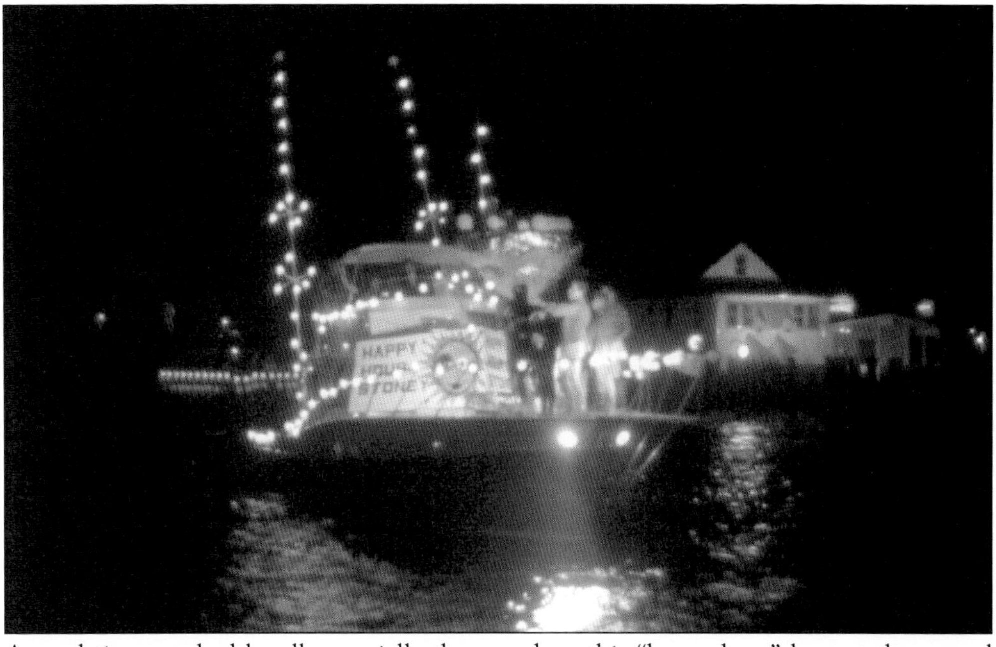

A good time was had by all, especially the crowd on this "happy hour" boat at the annual Festival of Lights. This boat's theme epitomizes the reason the event was dropped by the Stone Harbor Yacht Club, as they were coming under scrutiny for heavy drinking by members. The event was permanently canceled after a large boat burned at its dock, causing a fatality.

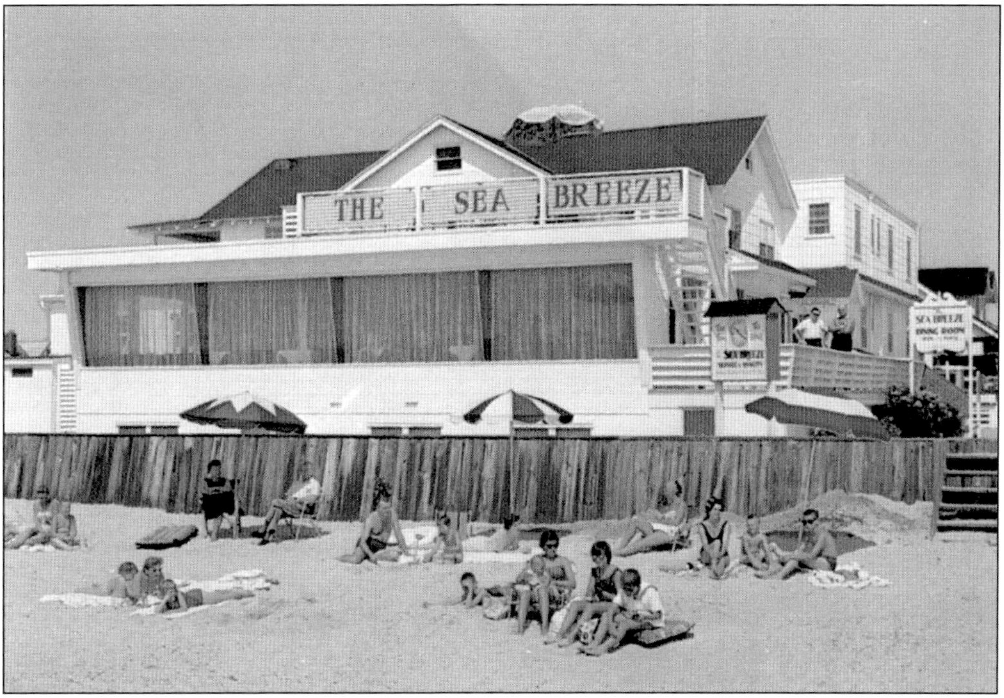

The Sea Breeze was altered and enlarged over the years. It provided accommodations and good food with an excellent ocean view. Located on 99th Street at the beach, the building now houses condominiums. This shot shows the new seawall after the 1962 storm.

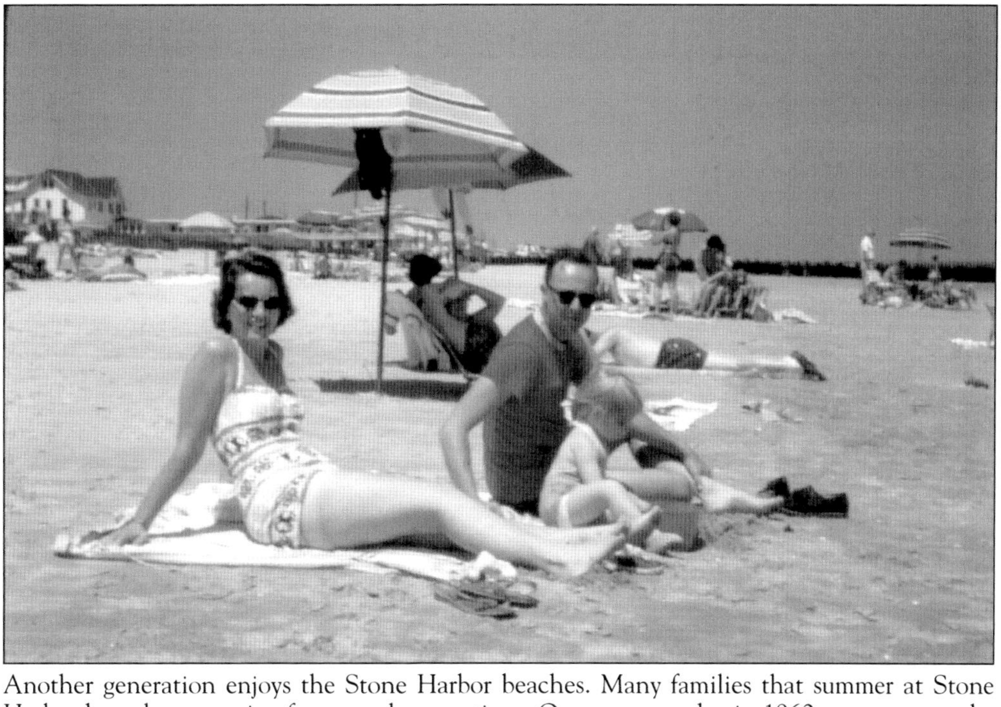

Another generation enjoys the Stone Harbor beaches. Many families that summer at Stone Harbor have been coming for several generations. On a summer day in 1960, my parents take my sister Elizabeth to discover the joys of a sand pail and shovel.

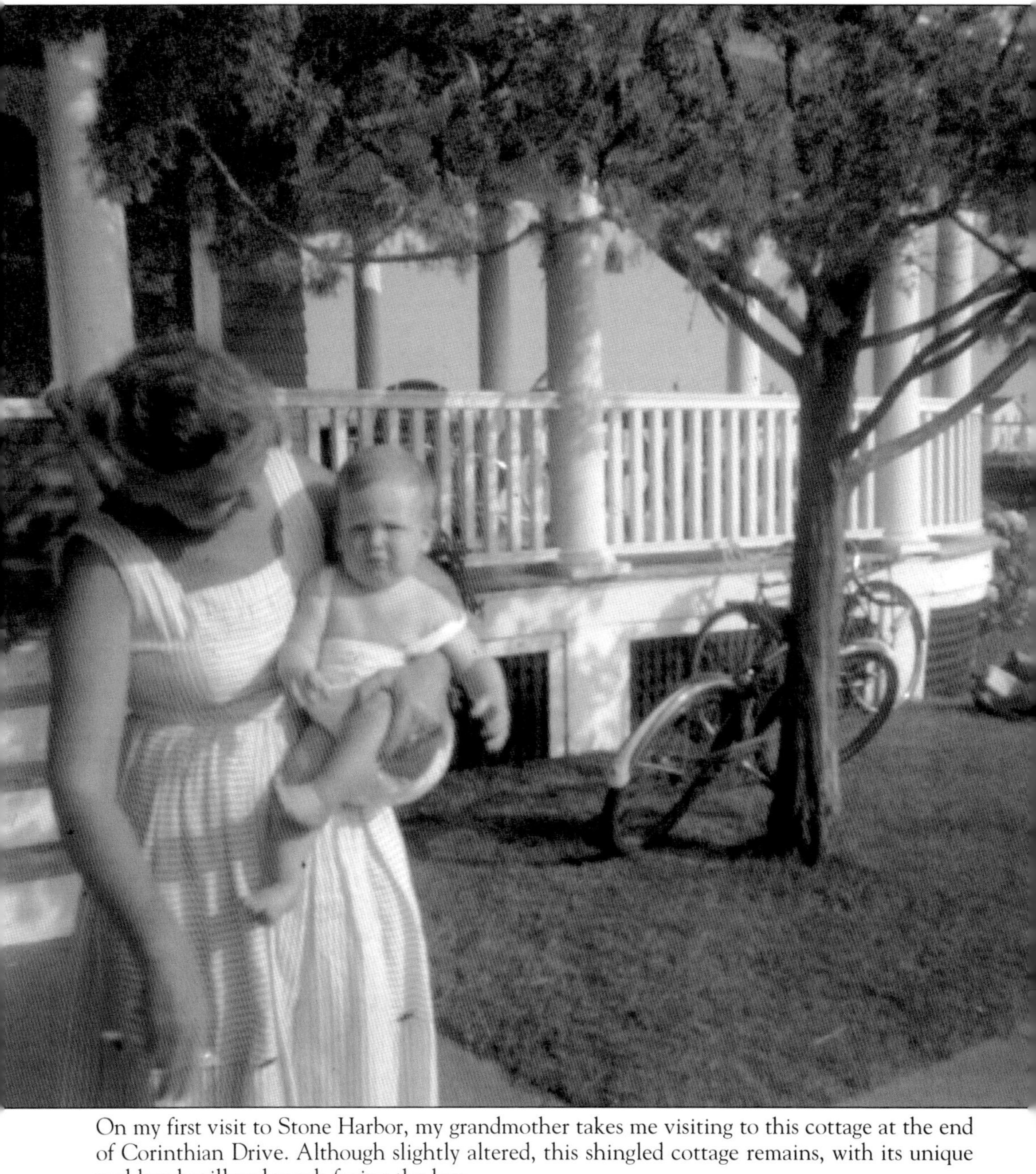

On my first visit to Stone Harbor, my grandmother takes me visiting to this cottage at the end of Corinthian Drive. Although slightly altered, this shingled cottage remains, with its unique and lovely pillared porch facing the bay.

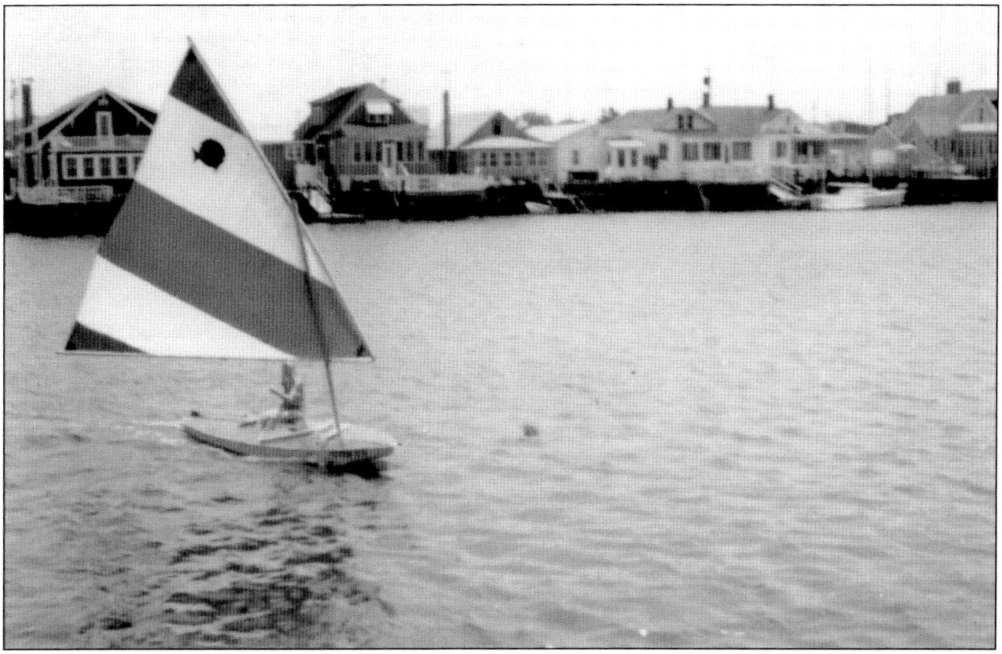

Fiberglass was replacing wood as the material of choice in boat construction. The Sailfish and Sunfish were quite popular in Stone Harbor and could be found all over the Jersey shore as beginning sailing boats.

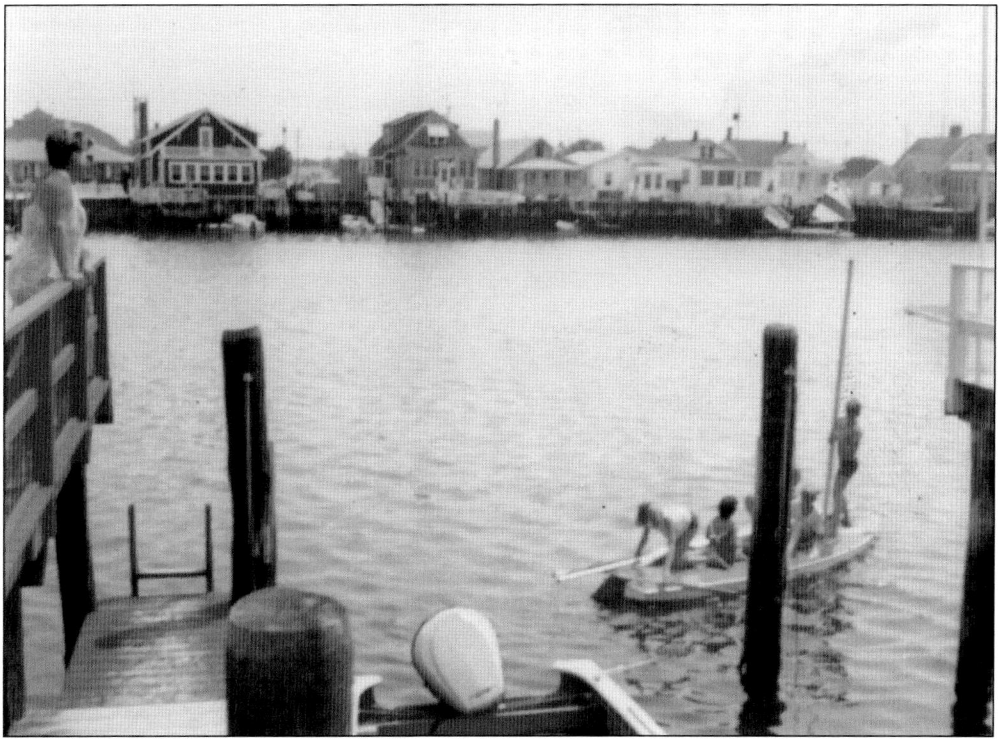

With this little sailboat, many new adventures were found to fill the day as children set off to unexplored waters.

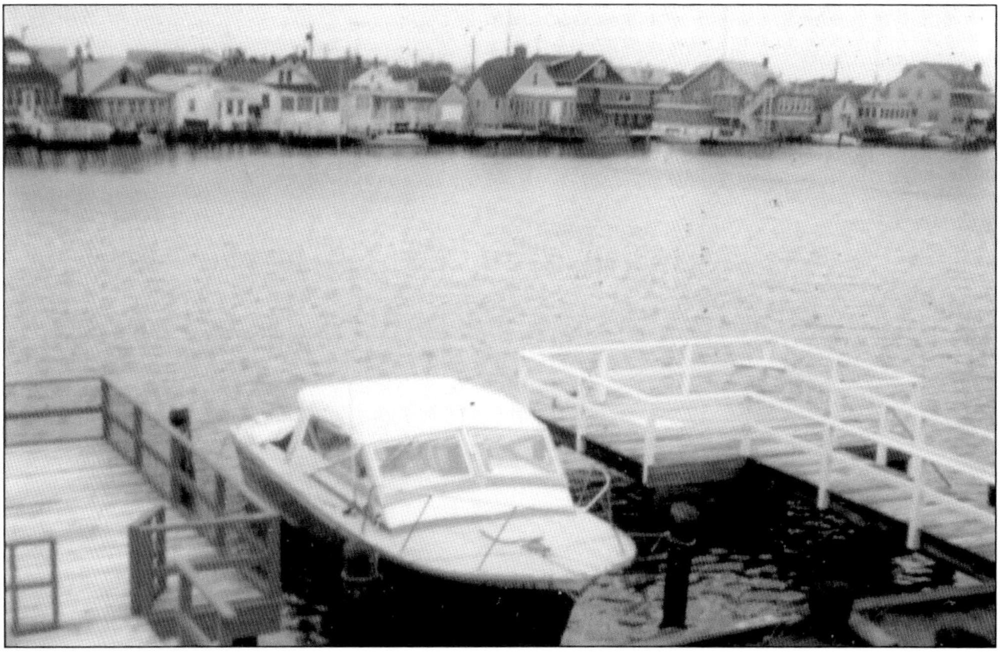

By the 1970s, John Noone replaced his Mason with this 26-foot Lyman as his need for fishing in comfort replaced water-skiing. This Lyman—built in Sandusky, Ohio—was one of the last wooden ones before the company switched to fiberglass and eventually folded. This boat was hugely popular in Stone Harbor.

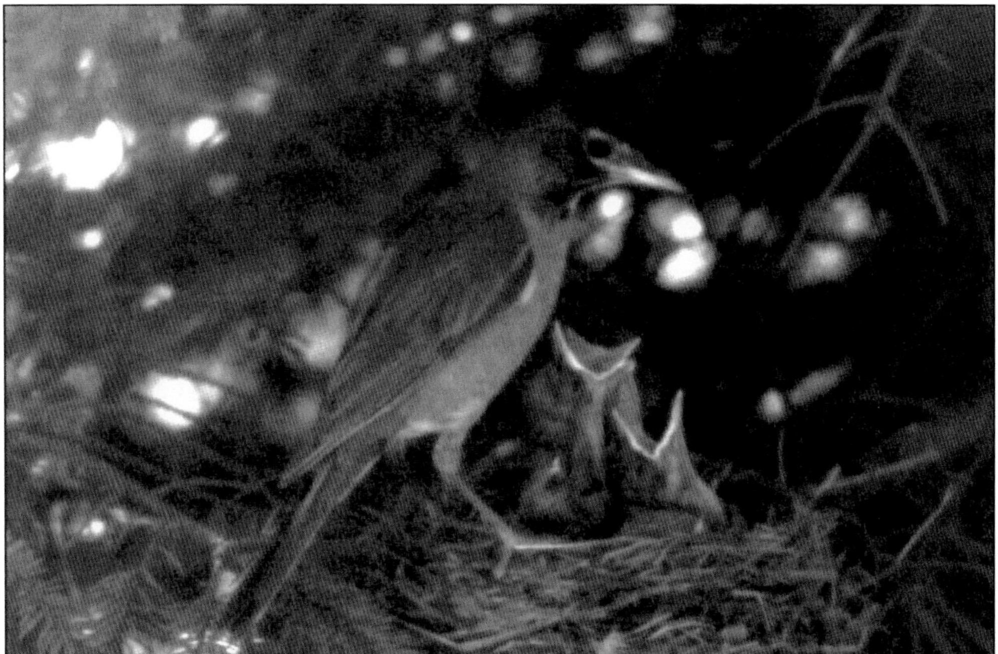

Baby birds anxiously await the worm their mother carries to them. This view was caught with a telephoto lens. In 1941, the Stone Harbor Bird Club was organized. As early as 1911, Stone Harbor residents had formed an active Nature Study Club.

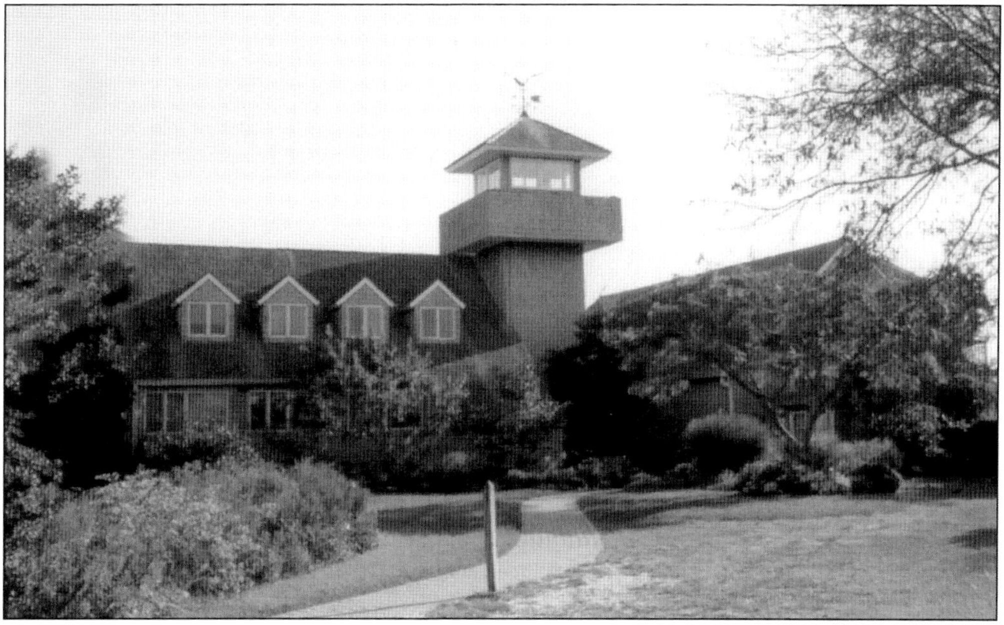

In addition to a nationally famous bird sanctuary, Stone Harbor is also home to the Wetlands Institute, established in the marshlands along Stone Harbor Boulevard. The building, dedicated by Prince Bernhard of the Netherlands in 1972, was donated by the World Wildlife Fund International. A visit to the institute was always educational.

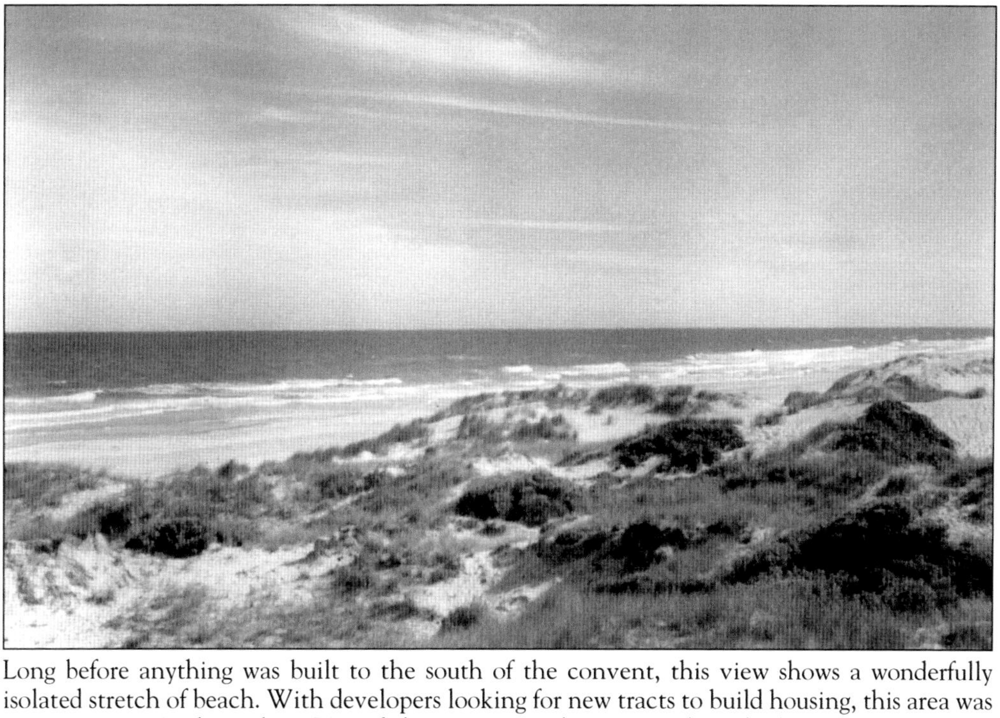

Long before anything was built to the south of the convent, this view shows a wonderfully isolated stretch of beach. With developers looking for new tracts to build housing, this area was a prime target. In the early 1970s, a fight to preserve the area was launched—a campaign called Save the Point. As a result of this effort, the southern end of Stone Harbor is now preserved in its natural state.

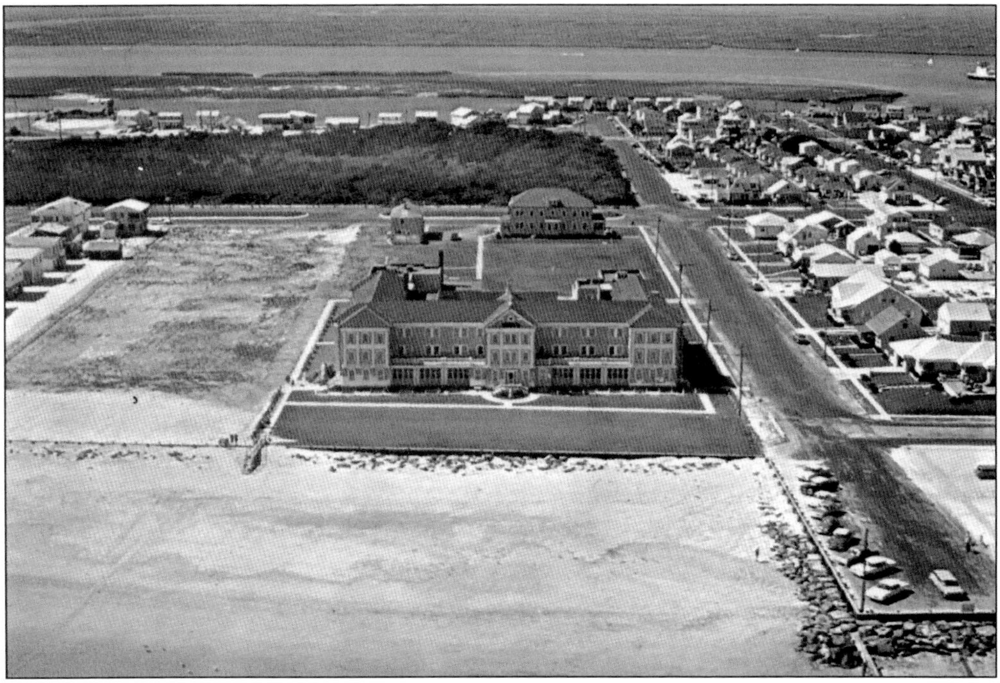

Villa Maria, a summer retreat house for the Sisters of the Immaculate Heart of Mary, was built in 1937. The convent's location between the beach and the bird sanctuary was compromised in the 1970s as new housing encroached on open land toward the south.

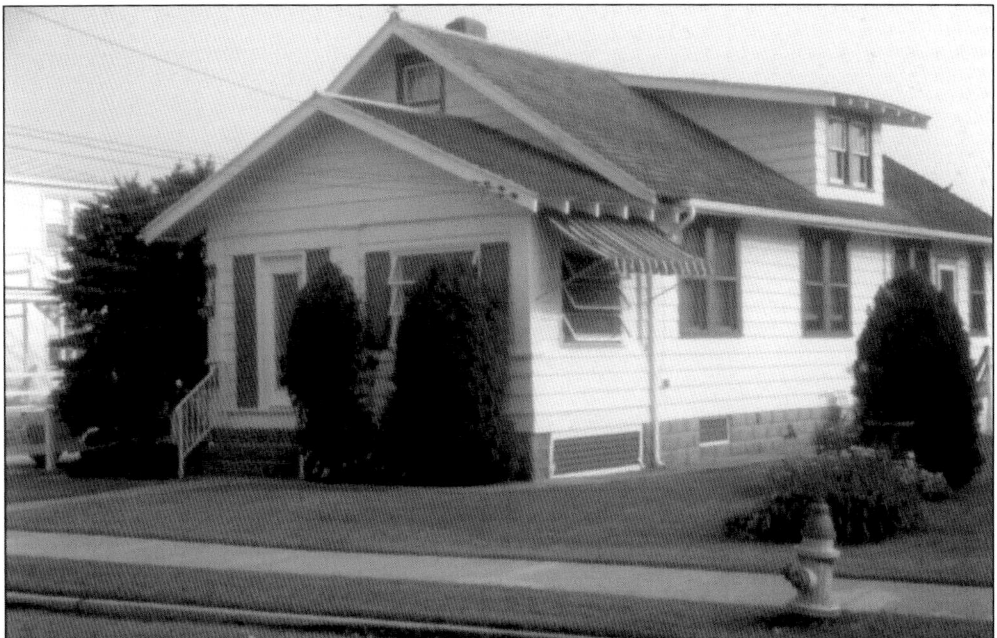

The replacement of the front windows of the Colebin led to the loss of the much beloved sun porch, which foreshadowed the eventual sale of the house. This type of remodeling has been done to a number of summer cottages as they have been converted for year-round use.

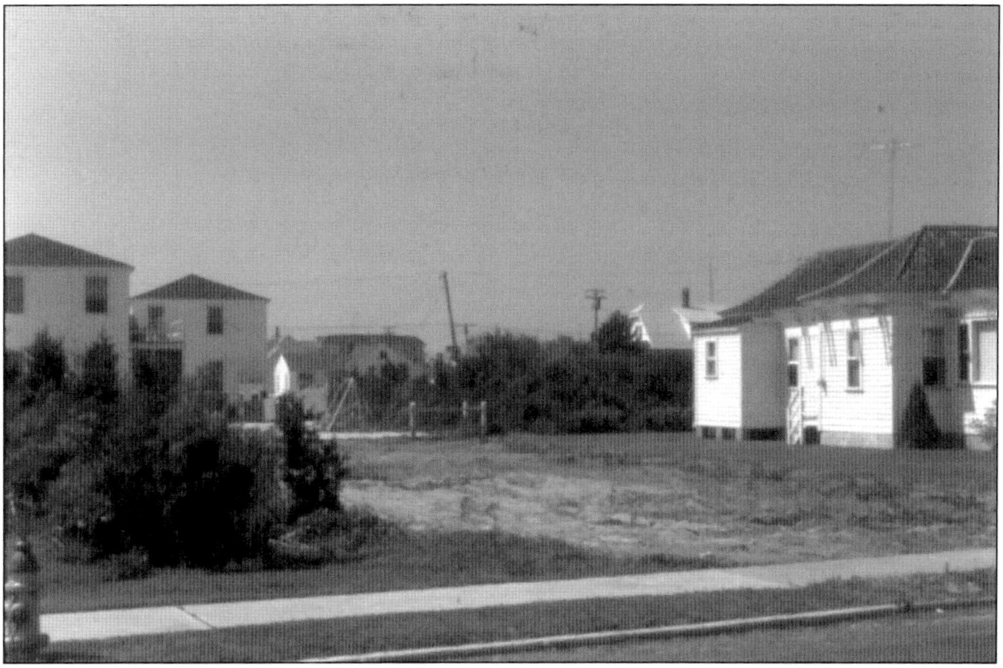

This photograph shows the lot between the two houses being prepared for construction in the 1970s. At this time, many more lots started to disappear.

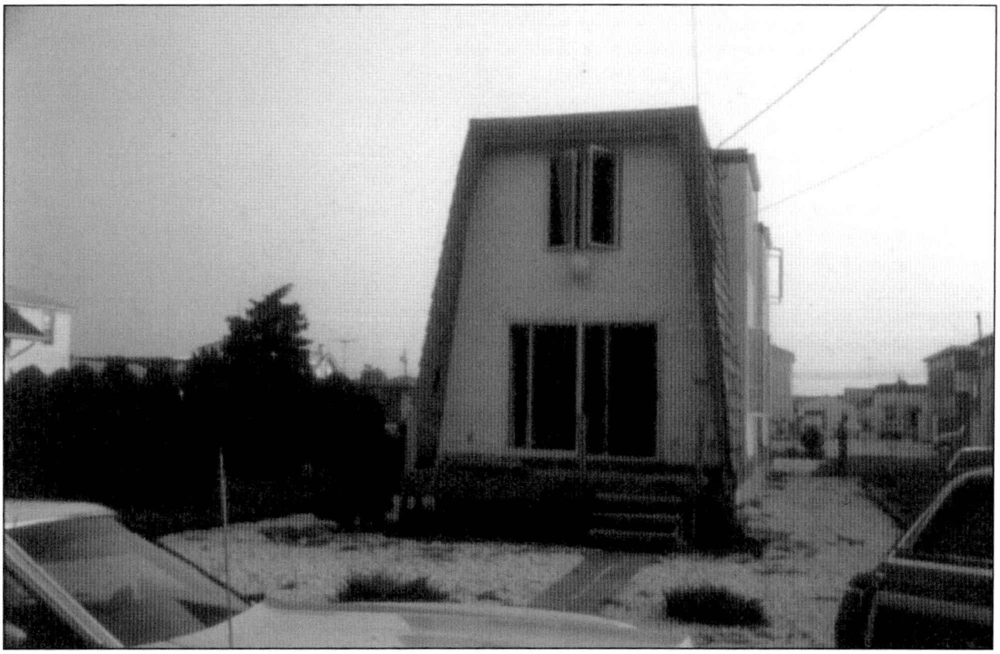

Symbolic of what began to happen all over Stone Harbor, developers were finding any building lots and filling them up. This signaled the end of the wildlife and the end of the view.

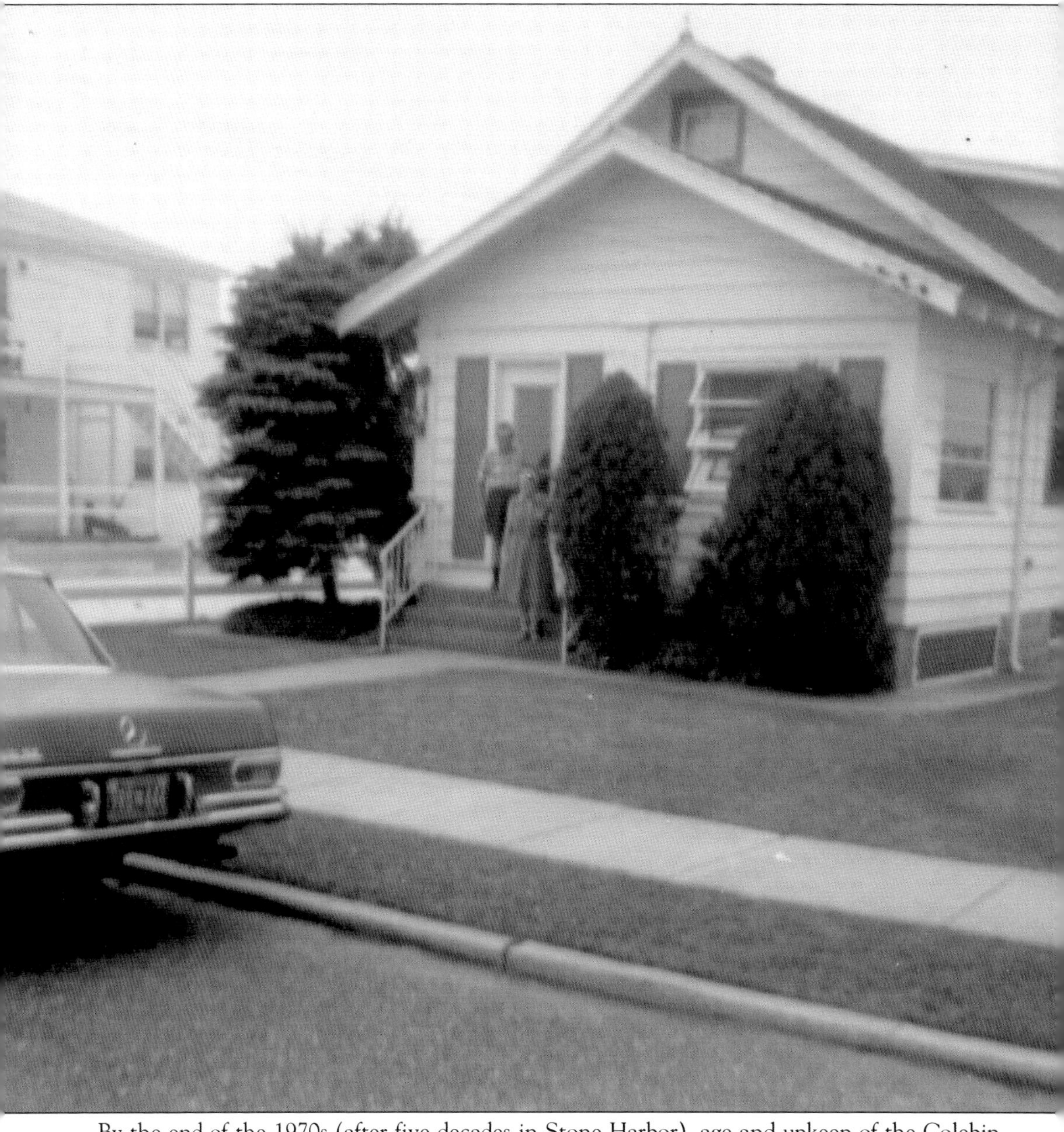

By the end of the 1970s (after five decades in Stone Harbor), age and upkeep of the Colebin led to my grandparents' decision to sell it. With the car packed and ready to go, they are shown locking up for the last season.

Five

TIMELESS

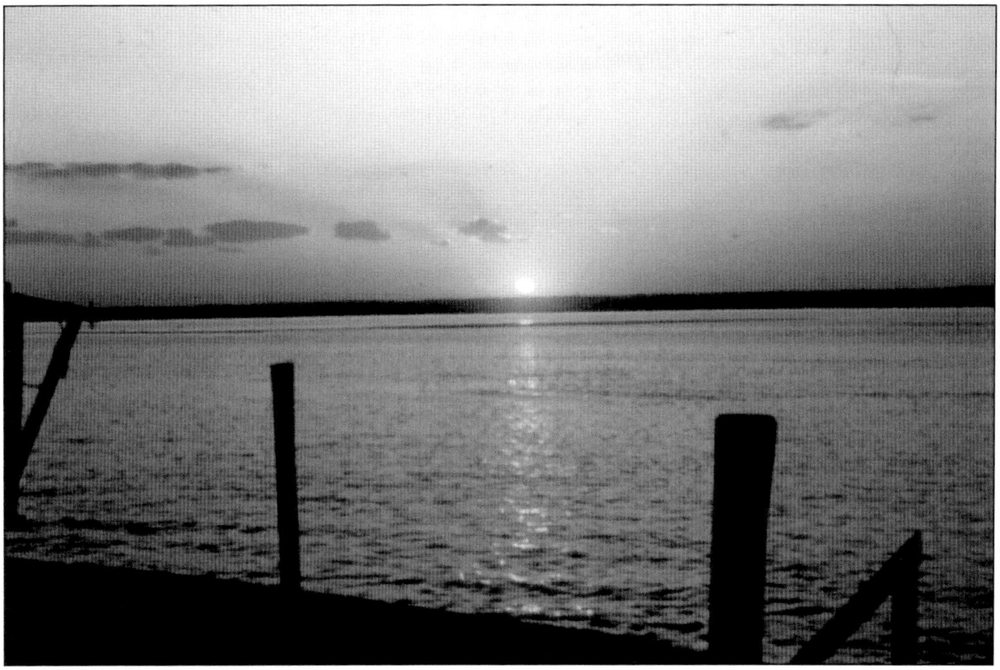

The photographs in this final chapter represent the ageless Stone Harbor. The settings and scenes have been captured often on canvas and in photographs over the years. It is this timeless quality that continues to draw us to the shore.

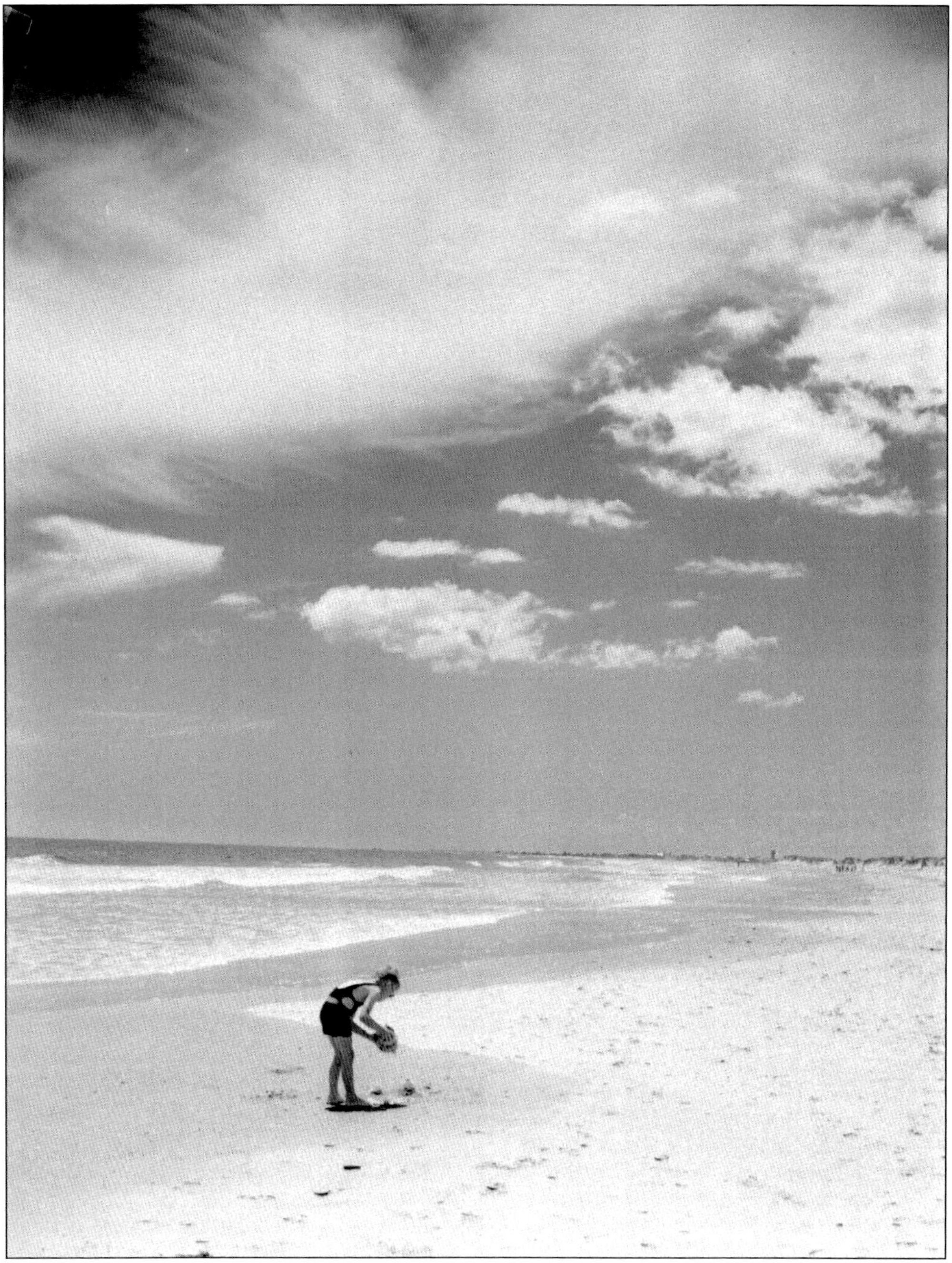

This image depicts endless sand and sky—the world as a child's oyster.

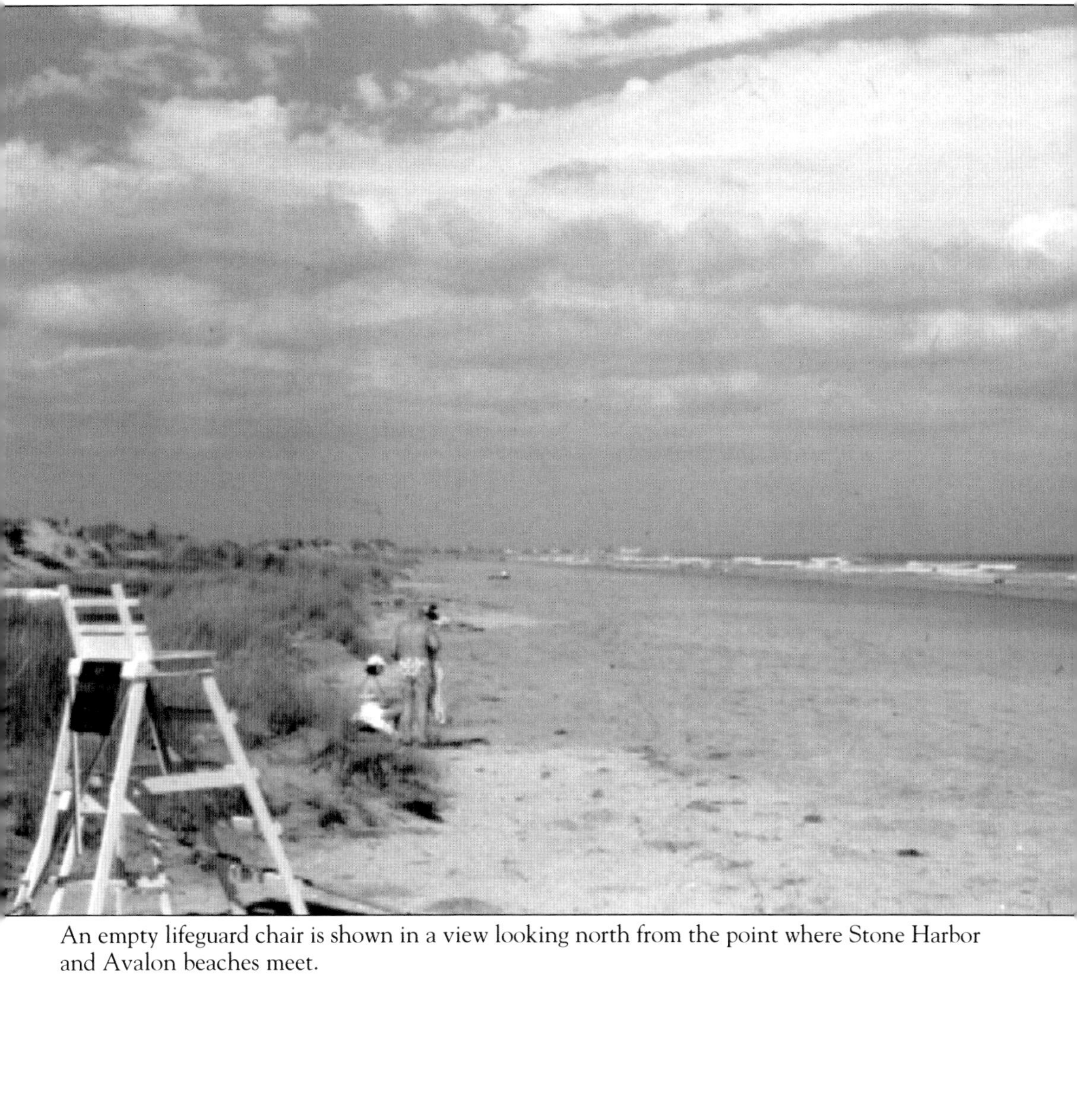

An empty lifeguard chair is shown in a view looking north from the point where Stone Harbor and Avalon beaches meet.

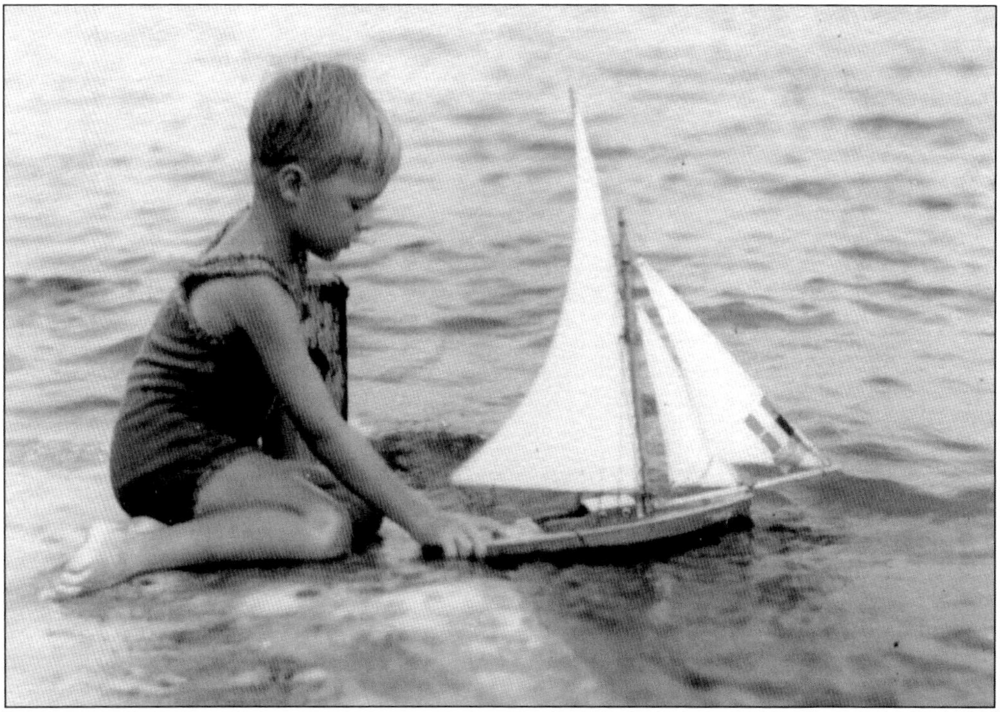

"Boats of mine a-boating—Where will all come home?"

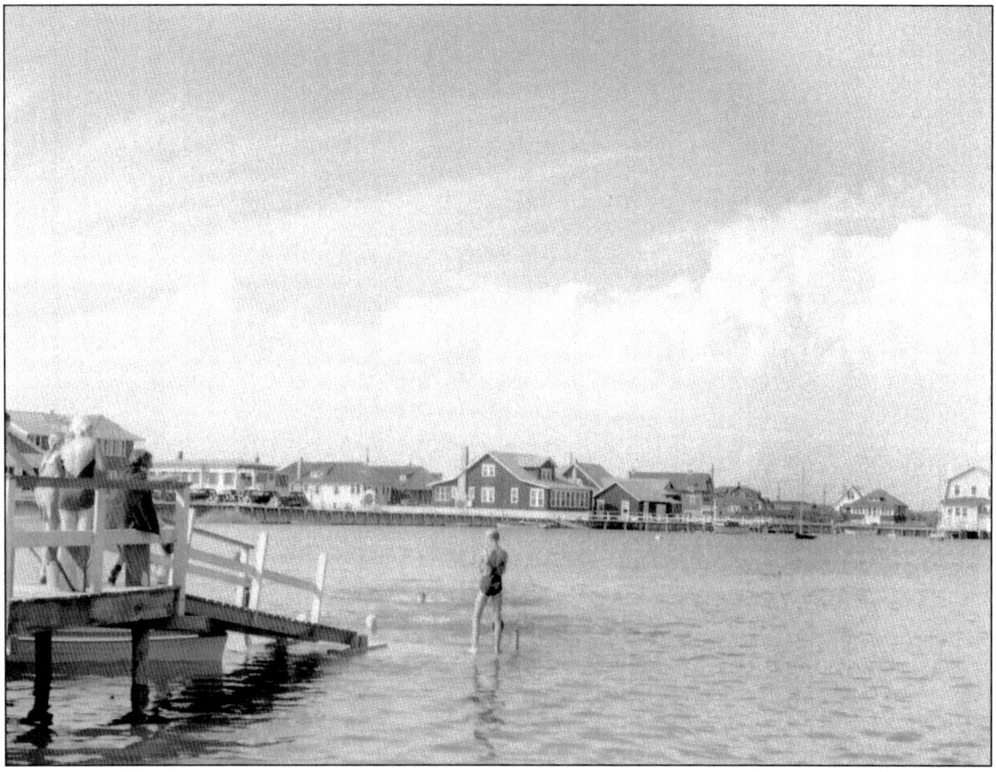

Swimmers enjoy the bay in the early 1930s.

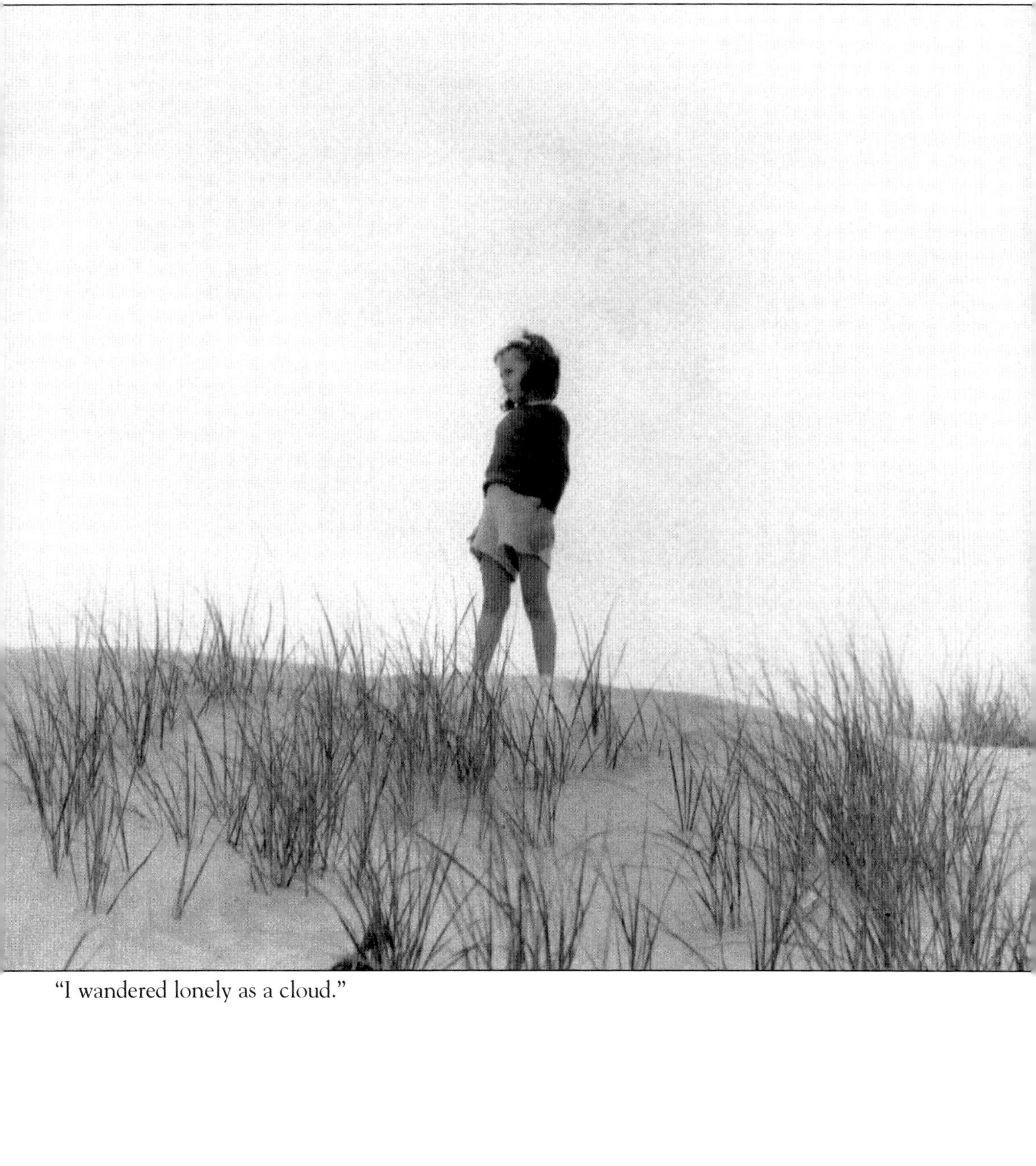

"I wandered lonely as a cloud."

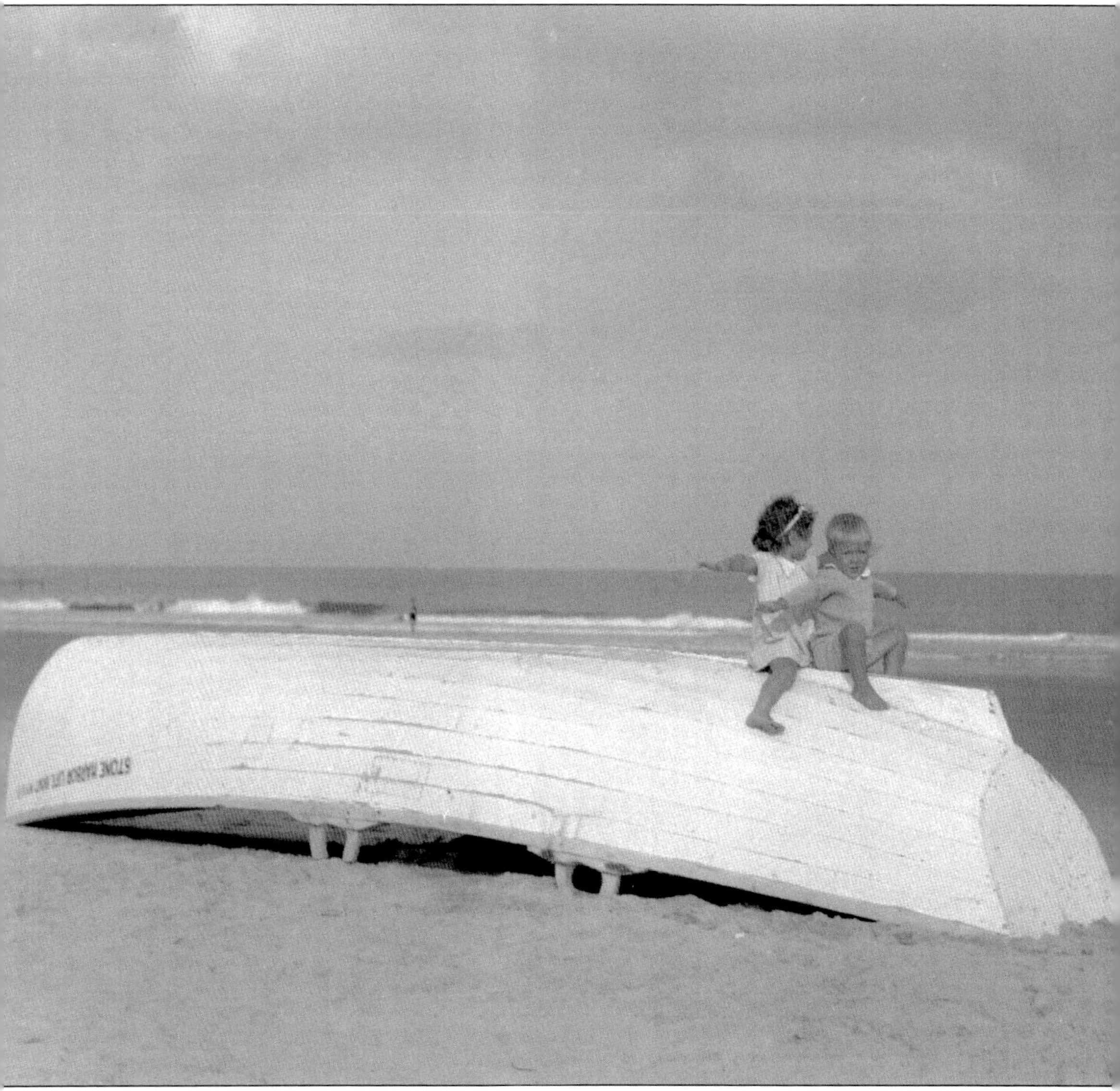

An upturned lifesaving boat is seen as an airship in the imagination of these children.

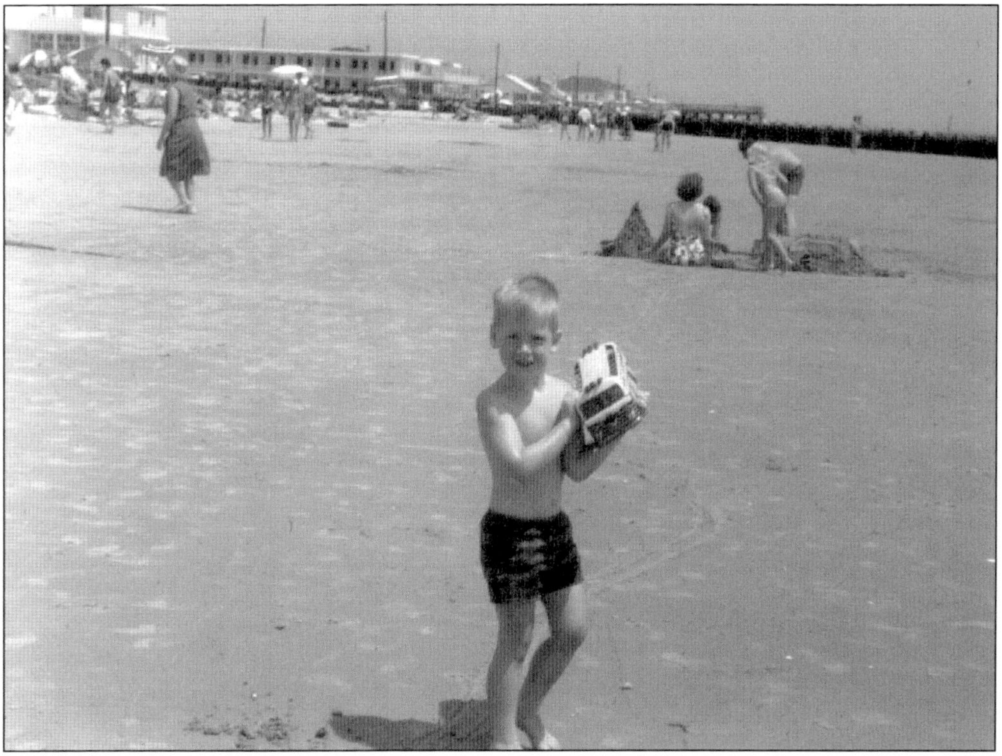

Gathering data for a future book, the author stands at the 99th Street beach in the early 1960s.

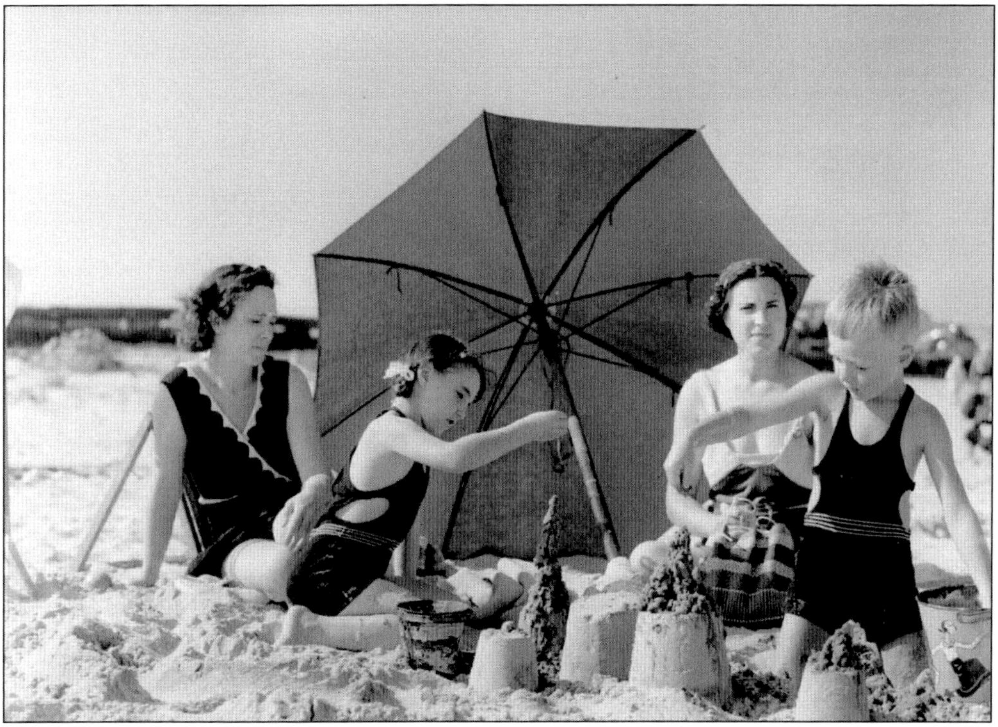

Time and patience build the ever popular drip sandcastle.

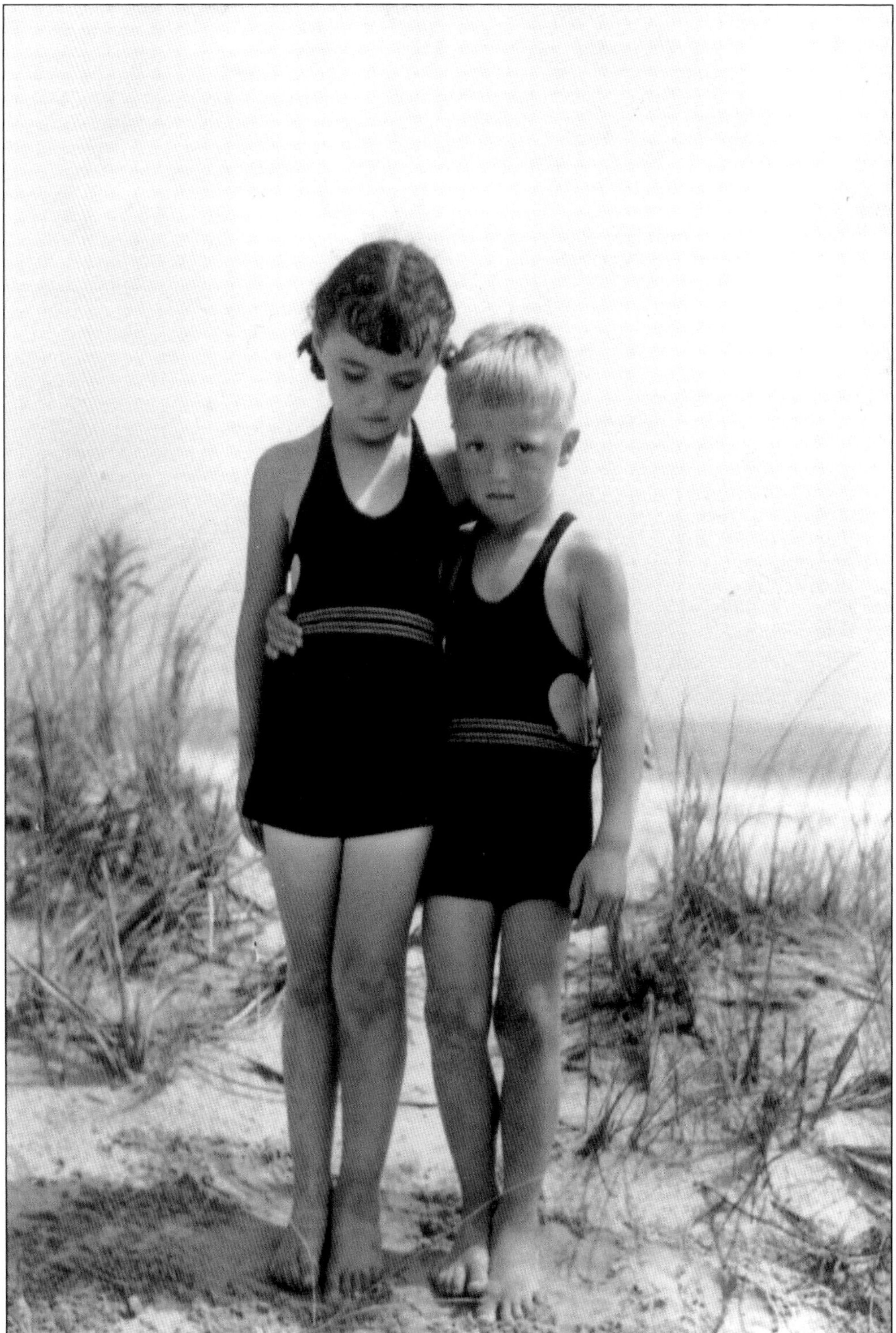

A long day at the beach led to burnt shoulders and wearied posing.

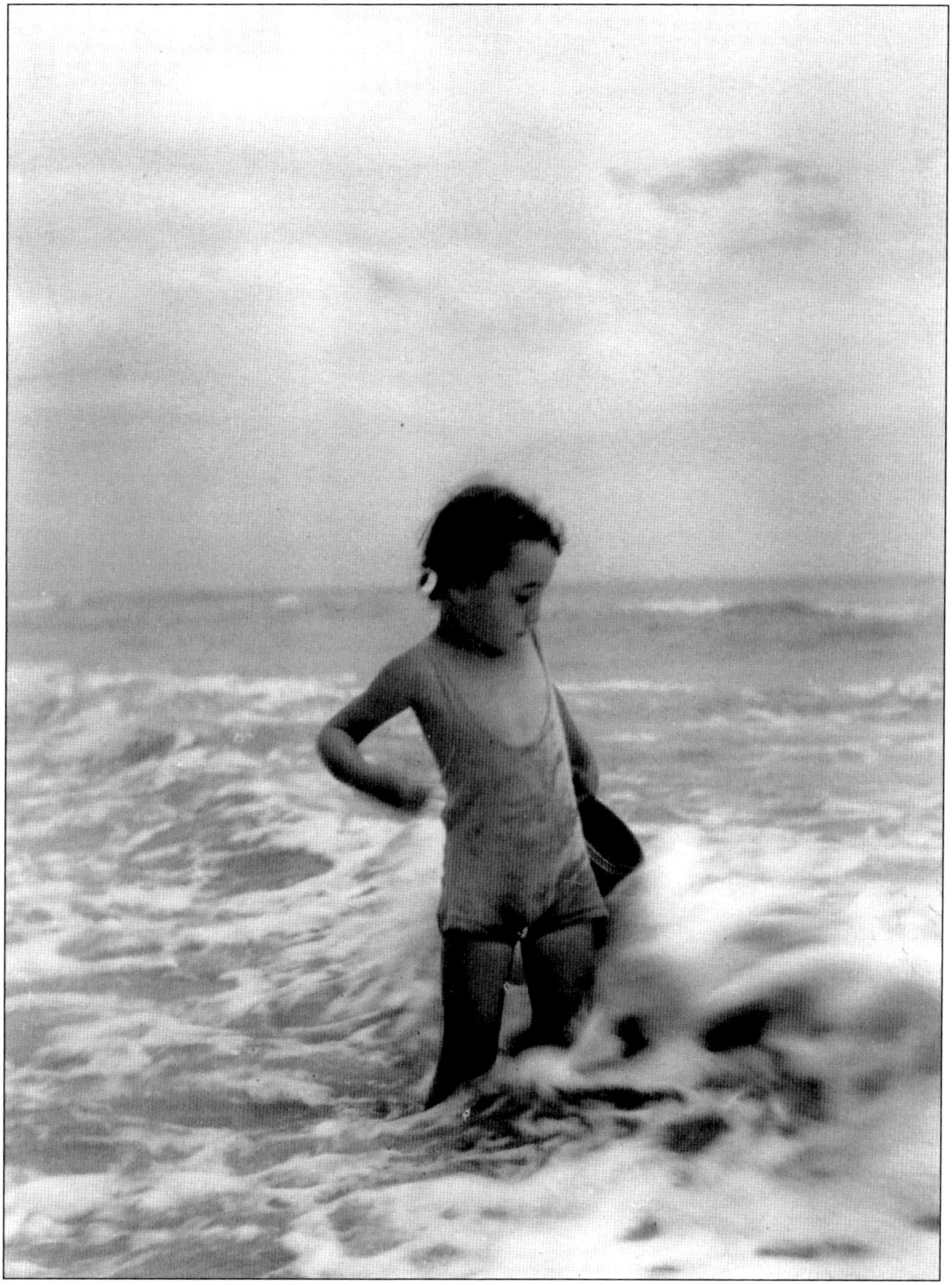

A defiant mermaid battles the oncoming tide.

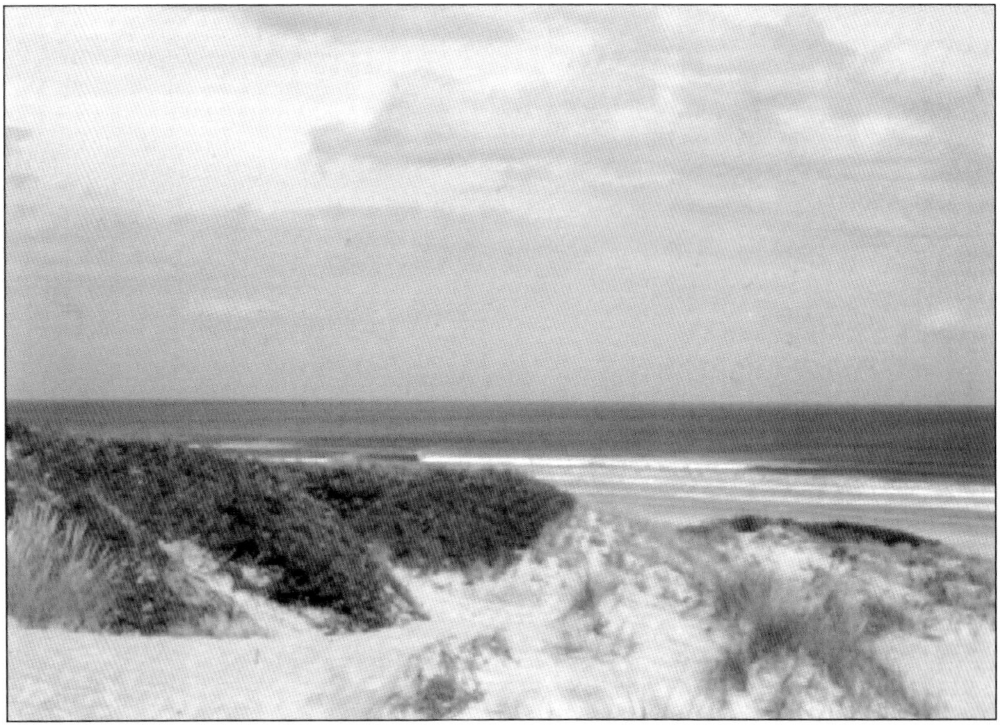

The sandy solitude with ocean spray lends an air of tranquility.

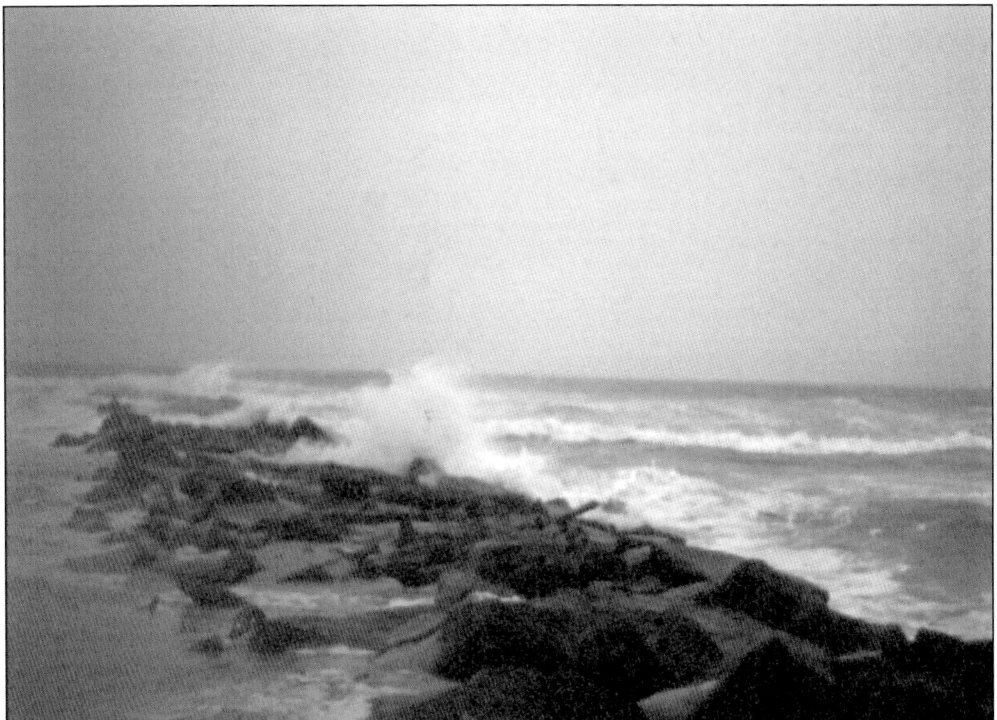

Stormy weather lies ahead as heavy seas break on the jetty.

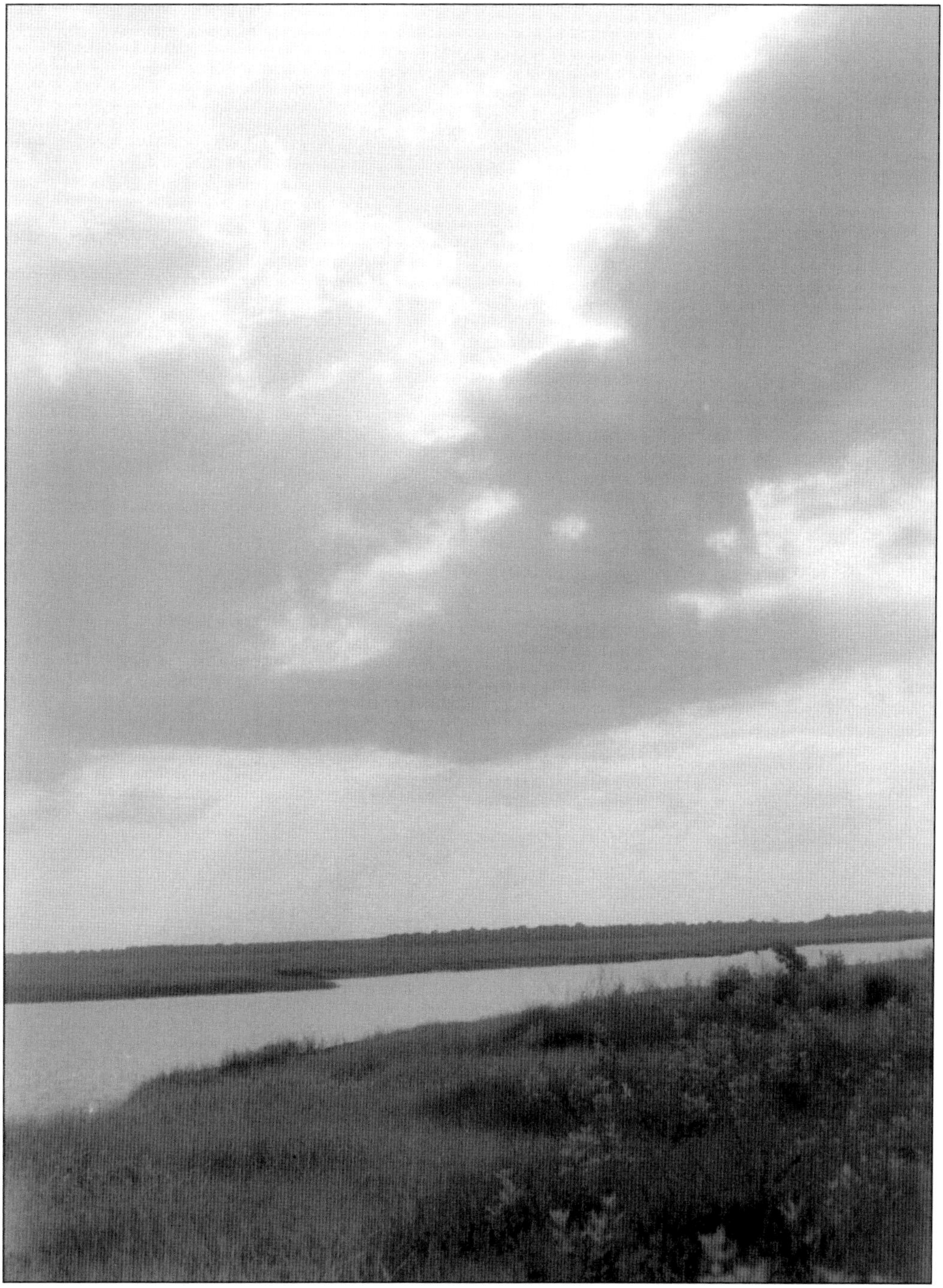

Clearing clouds and still waters reflect the passing storm.

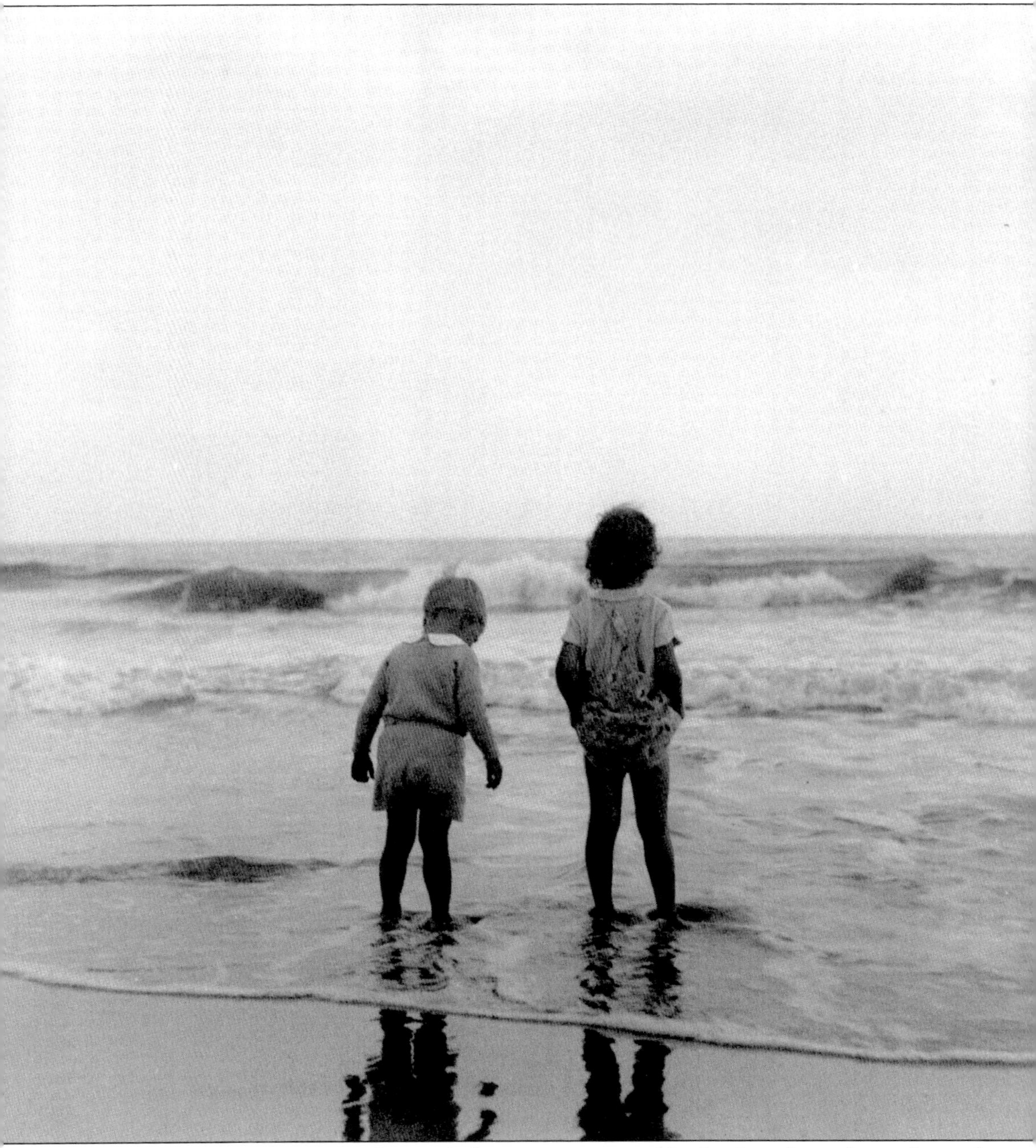

As August turns to September and the water turns cold, the last dip reflects the end of summer.